Praise for the A[illegible]

Thank you so much for organizing such a wonderful Angel party. I know it will change my life in ways I can't begin to imagine at present. I have been going round grinning like a Cheshire cat all day!
Liz, UK

A BIG thank you! Since the Angel Party weekend I welcome negative things. I won't ask, "WHY?" anymore. I will just get on with it positively. The weekend turned my whole attitude on life round. It now all makes sense! I now believe, thanks to you, that we will be taken down the right road. I can't wait, as we know where that road leads now! Thank you soooo much, again. Keep up the great work.
Inderjit, India

Thank you for spending so much time clarifying the platforms; it helped enormously. Now I'm more aware of where I am and what I need to build on for my soul path.
Stephanie, UK

It was a relief to hear my own story in many others, and fascinating to hear from those on a higher platform. I could have spent days just listening to their stories.
Graciella, Chile

On arriving home after the Angel Party I had a sudden realization that I actually felt more at home at the Angel Party than I have in my own home, which I love dearly.
Suzanne, Sweden

It enabled me to look at where I am and what I am doing in a new light and know I am happy with where I am. Everything

made sense. I looked at my childhood and post-university years in a new light, and had lots of tears in the part about LOve. I saw steps I need to take to move forwards. Felt deep pain was being released and great to understand other people go through the same issues. It touches me somewhere deeply and the body knowing is deeper than my conscious knowing. The part on relationships helped me understand more about my marriage relationship, along with LOve. I need support to practice.
Kitty, UK

Secrets of Angels on Earth

Life-Changing Clues to Liberate and Inspire

Secrets of Angels on Earth

Life-Changing Clues to Liberate and Inspire

Allan J. Sweeney

BOOKS

Winchester, UK
Washington, USA

JOHN HUNT PUBLISHING

First published by O-Books, 2021
O-Books is an imprint of John Hunt Publishing Ltd., 3 East St., Alresford,
Hampshire SO24 9EE, UK
office@jhpbooks.com
www.johnhuntpublishing.com
www.o-books.com

For distributor details and how to order please visit the 'Ordering' section on our website.

ISBN: 978 1 78904 135 4
978 1 78904 136 1 (ebook)
Library of Congress Control Number: 2020933435

A CIP catalogue record for this book is available from the British Library.

Design: Stuart Davies

Printed and bound by CPI Group (UK) Ltd, Croydon, CR0 4YY
Printed in North America by CPI GPS partners

Contents

It is with great joy that I dedicate this book to every angel, both those above and on earth, that have ever existed, do exist now, and will exist in the future.

This is a grateful dedication to how angels above embody so much time and energy from within their Godly souls, to help those in need.

It is a special dedication to angels-on-earth who currently search without finding, and who secretly and selflessly endure and overcome the trials of living, to leave behind trails of LOving.

And it is a global dedication that the tasks of all angels to alleviate suffering and bring happiness can one day be respected and honored by everyone, everywhere, under every circumstance.

This book might not be relevant to everyone.
It is just how it is.
Being an angel-on-earth does not make you a better or worse person than others.
Others may be going through different lifetimes or lessons.
Then they can get to where an angel-on-earth is now.
It is just how it is.

A flower in bloom is not better than a seed.
It is just how it is.
A butterfly is not better than a caterpillar.
It is just how it is.
What a caterpillar calls the end of the world,
Others call it, a butterfly in transition.
It is.

Allan J. Sweeney

Preface

Parts of the story of how my First Angel Party came about are in the main text. But the full story is included here to show how this all started during a personal search for whatever God could possibly be, then a personal soul growth and teaching, and then eventually discovering and uncovering many angels-on-earth on my courses.

Over many years I studied and taught regular intensive classes under three umbrella headings: "Reiki and Therapies", "Psychic and Mystical", and "Spiritual and Soul". There were few subjects under these three headings that I did not lecture on, teach, and practice. For example:

Reiki and therapies targeted determined conditions with interventions specific for those conditions, to gain quicker, easier, safer, cheaper, more permanent results. This pathway culminated with a prestigious Harley Street, London, UK clinic, a 22-bed residential clinic by a beach, being therapy trainer for UK prisons, attending House of Commons committee meetings with the Doctor Healer Network, being invited to be the Honorary President of Japanese Reiki Masters, developing an anticancer program supported by top oncologists, and conducting academic research with universities.

Psychic and mystical teachings included 63 subjects such as how to see angelic people, past and future life therapies, and 11 types of psychic surgery. This path culminated in a brief, daily, SKY TV show. Viewers related their psychic and mystical experiences that no one had previously been able to explain. The brief was to explain, live on air, all experiences in detail. Spiritual and soul teachings included ones about soul evolution toward God, and a range of meditations chosen to support mind, body, emotions, spirit, or soul. Techniques included how to bring the class to LOving ecstasy and absolute peace in hearts, thoughts, and souls.

The point of explaining all that is one thing became clear. Regardless of what the class subject was, some students seemed different. The students' motivation for taking the class was different. Their energies were different. Their outlook on life was different. And very often they believed they were different.

I began to see that some of these students indeed were different. They were subtly aware of goals for their lives emanating from their unconscious minds. Occasionally their goals had conscious clarity of an agreement they had made to share beauty to help our world.

I began to speak separately to these students, asking questions, looking for ways to discredit growing thoughts of angels-on-earth. But the more I asked, the more the evidence came.

One day in the 1990s, while teaching a Spiritual Development class, a whole process unexpectedly channeled through about angels. Many students were relieved, and helped substantially by the unexpected story about the "Secrets of Angels on Earth". Some cried with happiness that someone at last understood their lives, and could give clues as to their next steps. Whereas others didn't seem to have a clue as to what I was talking about. It seemed that the lives of angels-on-earth were not for everyone.

It became apparent that certain people had angelic types of ways, and were climbing the same mountain of life, but taking different routes. Most of these people were on different staging posts along each path.

It became so evident who was an angel in their prospective final lifetime and who was not, it reached the stage where I could judge, just by looking at someone, the path they were on. Sometimes it was obvious to a point of 100% certainty that I would ask a student, "Do you know what you are?" (I did not ask, "Who?") Usually, the answer would return, matter-of-factly, "Yes, I'm an angel."

Understanding evolved. I developed questions to forge deep

inside an angel-on-earth's heart and soul; if students answered "Yes" to most of the questions they would probably need to know more information to help their angelic development.

Many people cried when hearing the questions, saying after that the tears were because at last someone understood them. I would then support these individuals to understand why their lives had been as they were so far, what they could do now, and where they might aim in the future.

This process evolved further. It seemed as if I was attracting more and more of this type of kinder, sweeter, more loving student onto classes. Perhaps it was imagination, I thought. But no; regular class helpers verified that the energy of students on classes had indeed changed. The majority coming were angels-on-earth.

So instead of sharing angelic knowledge with everyone in a class, which would have included people who may have seemed to not be angelic souls and who consequently might not know what I was talking about, I began to ask classes what I now call the Angelic Questions. Their eyes were closed so they couldn't see each other, and so wouldn't be embarrassed when answering. I simply asked them to raise their hands in answer to each question.

Two things evolved from this.

Firstly, everyone who did not raise their hands to most of the Angelic Questions were politely asked to leave and enjoy lunch.

Secondly, I asked those who raised their hands to most of the Angelic Questions to either leave and have lunch food for their body, or remain and have food for their soul.

Most students attracted to courses by then seemed angelic in nature, and most who answered "Yes" to the Angelic Questions chose to stay behind to hear a 45-minute story, a synopsis of the Angelic Path from pre-birth to post-death.

Those who should perhaps have remained in the class, but left to have food for their body instead, realized they'd made a mistake when they saw the smiles of love on the faces of those who had stayed behind to have food for their soul.

The next thing that evolved was that I noticed each question seemed to have an average response rate. For example, questions about feeling alone, separated and detached were answered "Yes" by almost all angels-to-be, but not so often by those who were not on an Angelic Path.

It became apparent that those who answered "Yes" had probably not had a happy childhood. Whereas those who had not felt alone were probably not angels-on-earth. A few though seemed more likely to have an angelic soul if they'd had a very happy childhood, or a LOving mental attitude. And so understanding evolved.

These free group teachings over lunchtime became, for some, an even more important part of the class than the class they had expected. They were able to put their entire life into an understandable clue-strewn context. Some needed extra support, so certain excellent angels-on-earth became "mother angels", helping those who were still learning painful lessons.

I began to think of running a specialist class just for angels-on-earth.

And so this very First Angel Party was born. I decided to hold it in December, just before Christmas, a time that for many is more angelic than other times of the year.

I chose not to advertise the class. It would be semi-secret, not openly advertised like normal courses. Attendees could arrive only by personal invitation to ensure that, as far as possible, those attending would be angels-to-be. Most angels arrived via one of my international lectures or classes. Some were from chance meetings around the world. By the end of the year, the list had grown long.

The 1st and 2nd of December are dates that will live in the minds of many, a most beautiful experience. That was the first time in their lives they were in a large room full of people who only understood the highest, most perfect LOve.

The turnout surprised everyone. I hadn't asked for confirmation of numbers of attendance, and had hired a smallish room at Regent's College in London. People crammed into every corner. We brought in more chairs until there was no more room for extra chairs. People sat on desks, windowsills, on the floor, anywhere they could, until they squeezed together. It was standing room only.

Eventually, a wonderful angel-in-the-making said, "Leave it to me." Half an hour later we moved into the largest hall in the college, a grand hall with an ornate balcony and majestic paintings, a fitting tribute to what was my first ever large gathering consisting only of angels-on-earth.

This book is about that gathering, the talk I gave, the questions posed, secrets revealed, clues offered, energies felt by those present, and potential ways forward.

The objective is that, like those at the gathering, many readers will find clarification about their past, understanding for their present, and hope to light their future.

For ease of reading, although the book was written up as the two-day lecture, the break-times, and the ending of day 1 and the start of day 2 have been omitted to create a better flow.

Foreword 1

I've had a love affair with mind, body and spirit books for many years, but this book is incomparable to any I have read. It's provocative and an all-embracing experience of an exploration of the mind, spirit and body. Unlike most books, while reading *"Secrets of Angels on Earth"*, I embarked on a life-transforming journey. I tried not to travel too quickly so as not to miss anything. It astounded me how intricate the soul really is.

Being interested in people, I was intrigued about how others coped on their long road to finding peace with their soul. It was at Allan's Angel Party that many gathered to share experiences of their angelic development with Allan's invaluable guidance and words of wisdom. It was an eye-opener and wing-opener to discover that there are people akin to myself who have lost their way on this earth for numerous reasons. Irrespective of their religion, race, or status, their souls develop in ways fashioned and shaped by their daily lives, and maybe their previous lives.

Being a psychology graduate, I have grown into a world of people who are skeptics, but who are also believers of the unknown and unseen. Some people can detect energy shifts in other people, but to scientists the soul's changing patterns are invisible and immeasurable. It has become my prerogative to follow my heart and not my head. There is no way I could ever allow my scientific knowledge to contest my profound belief in angels. To scientists, angels cannot be seen but, like you can't see oxygen, it doesn't mean angels don't exist. What angels do seem to be forms of healing and works of kindness, but there could perhaps never be a defined explanation as to how these healings or good acts are performed. Scientists used to be skeptical that auras exist. Aura cameras now take pictures of the aura so scientists now accept the existence of auras. This was a revelation. Science is now starting to welcome the notion of what the average eye cannot see.

Allan has been known to me for nearly 20 years, and I was fortunate to have been his Reiki student many years ago. In the long interim that we hadn't seen each other, I had always felt his energy and presence near me. It was during his lesson that I was blessed to see his golden aura. I thought I was hallucinating but this was a genuine conscious vision, one to behold that I've never forgotten because other students saw too his golden aura too. He exuded an energy that has remained with me till this day and still brings a smile to my face and tears of joy to my eyes. This vision and these feelings are not uncommon as hundreds of people have proclaimed the same thing.

On reading this book, the words emitted a power of their own and fulfilled every part of me. I felt guided back onto my soul path after feelings of loss and bewilderment for many months. Reading the book for the first time I had an emotional reaction, which increased the second time on reading. Details in the book can be missed, as the soul heals on its journey throughout the book. If, like me, you are unsure of what type of angel you are, you may be surprised to learn there are a variety. It may be bewildering to read why our souls have to endure years of experiences, good and bad, to reach the highest echelon of being an angel. The content is descriptive and apt for those who are striving to be the best angel they can be, and to help others be the same. As Allan said at the end, this book is not to be given to others, but to be carried around to read and read again.

For those who know already and are aware you are angels, this book should take pride of your place in your home. For all you who do not know yet, or who are non-angels, it is a revelation to read, and should be read with an open heart and mind because you are maybe surrounded by, or are close to, an angel right now. It is the epitome of descriptions and examples of what being an angel is.

Despite not fulfilling my dream when I was a child of being a

Christmas angel, one of the most idyllic characters in the Nativity play, I felt my wish was coming true when, on a course, I heard Allan describe what it was to be an angel. I cried on hearing Allan's words that carried me from my seat to somewhere safe on this earth. I felt I was a round peg in a round hole, not a depressed, lonely, desperate woman on a mission to find love. It had been a long and lonely journey on the yellow brick road of doom, gloom, abuse, pain, loss and rejection. I always wondered why my life, like so many others, had comprised of an endless search for the right man, the right religion, job, partner, pet, house and holiday. Nothing seemed right, because my heart had an image of the perfect love that would make me feel whole and fulfilled. This book, thankfully, mentioned all aspects of these social, physical and emotional challenges, and Allan shines a beacon of hope that there is a way to face our convictions, with LOve.

It appears there was no such thing as the perfect "anything" on this earth. This yellow brick road I have travelled down is as Allan describes, my "soul path", so the exploration for perfection became futile. Allan's guidance and wisdom leads up the angelic ladder to the ultimate rung of "LOve", the highest level of God's love. It could take years or lifetimes to go through each "Platformation" or level to reach this Godly love. Allan has proved his doctors' predictions wrong, and cheated death. Life is far too precious to throw away and to ignore a dream to be a healer. He was cured, and his dreams went from strength to strength, visiting countries lecturing and teaching. He came to this realization of what seems to be the infinite experience of love and peace with our lives.

During the love for his work, Allan has met politicians, royalty, celebrities, and sports people. All were fortunate to receive his loving touch ridding them of numerous problems. Children are more open to such phenomena without question or prejudice, and some admitted seeing halos and wings on some people. Some people may think these children are delusional, and I, as a trained psychologist, should consider these visions as figments of wonderful imaginations. However, children can indeed, as have many people, witness this spectacle of people's wings in full glory. Perhaps unbeknownst to them, they have a bedazzling pair too! Any scientist would think I was mad believing this in contravention to what I have learnt, but science has closed doors towards an unseen energy that is immeasurable by any scientific device, but that can be felt with every cell in our bodies and beyond.

On reading this handbook for angels, I went through a roller coaster of emotions, from loss to ecstasy. The "Platformations" Allan talks of are achievable levels of being an angel even though, by oneself without the support of a Group, it might seem like hard work to reach the top Platformation. The experience I could equate to is working your way through every genre of film ever seen at the cinema. Every life is "cinema at its greatest"; it contains horror, death, love, relationships, breakups, animals… the list goes on!

His book is one to take you through what I envisioned to be a luxurious lagoon of the deepest blue water, concealing the abundance of life beneath it. With every page turned, there are sights to behold, areas to explore, new sensations awakening past memories. The safety of the lagoon is protective while moving through each page, and each page is to be cherished. There is no rush to get to the end of the lagoon, or to get out of the water. Be at one with the energy; let it carry you naturally to where you are destined to go.

The mind, body, and spirit are inseparable and are all affected by each other. If one area of the individual is sick, the other areas will also feel that malaise. If all are healthy, then the results will be all three working in harmony. Through my own experiences of ill-health as also depicted in the book, it is without argument that the body cannot heal when the mind is at war with itself and its environment. Awareness of our social environment is conducive to calming the mind in reacting to stimuli accordingly and without detriment. Human interaction, infiltrated with LOve, is the only answer to calm the rapid waters of the mind. LOve, like a pebble thrown into water, will cause ripples to affect everyone in contact with us. LOve begets LOve, therefore dissipating any existence of negative emotions. All our wrongdoings are from an absence of LOve, and Allan's book spotlights on the methods of bringing peace back into ourselves and society. In Allan's words, "The Angelic Path is secreted away from most people's conscious minds," so in the book Clues are suggested that might help alleviate. He encourages us to find love via these Secrets and Clues from his and others' own experiences. They contribute towards our flight along our Angelic Path, with the help of fellow angels in angel Groups, and through Allan himself. He'll never leave us to work through these levels on our own; he has armed us with information not mentioned before in other books, so we can survive as angels in humans' bodies.

Scientists have shown that positivity and love have eradicated illness and toxicity in our cells, and improved our overall health dramatically. It's the simplicity of a smile and an act of goodwill that can turn our lives around. Allan is living proof that this can be done! With gratitude to him and all those mentioned in the book, we can conquer the universe with infinite LOve for all, with Allan's book as our torch to light the way!

Helen Taylor
BSc (Honors) Psychology

Foreword 2

In 2002, Professor Petruska Clarkson attended the author's levels 1, 2, and 3 therapy courses. As a famous psychotherapist, she could not comprehend how psychological conditions can be cured so fast and said she'll test them in her practice. Sometime later, she phoned and said, *"Instead of seeing some patients for two years, I now see them for two sessions. The second session is just to make sure the first session worked."*

Professor Clarkson invited the author to offer his therapies in her prestigious Harley Street clinic for psychology, which he accepted. On hearing the Angel Story, she stated,

> *I have used that (angel) knowledge in my work as a psychotherapist. When the story about an angel's life relates with people who have angelic souls, they can feel comforted and supported. Then negative conditions such as stress, fear, sadness, sleeplessness, anger, and anxiety can be reduced. Also, when my patients realize there are beneficial reasons for their past suffering, there is also an increase in positive symptoms like happiness, energy, acceptance of life, relationships, peace, and love. This knowledge can be used in medical practices to help Angels on Earth.*

Professor Petruska Clarkson

Fellow of the British Association for Counselling, Fellow of the British Psychological Society, Consultant Psychologist, Psychotherapist Supervisor and Management Consultant, author of numerous psychotherapy books.

Acknowledgements

Special thanks go to friends, students, and patients, and to numerous people I have met even just once by chance, without whose openness about their lives as angels-on-earth this book could never have been written.

It has been an amazing journey, with countless stories guiding toward the one obvious conclusion. Angels-on-earth are a reality of God, a truth of life, an honor to witness, and a way of life so astonishingly structured, even with life's immense variety of ups and downs, hopes and fears, and joys and sadnesses, it is breathtakingly beautiful.

Thank you to all who have shared your angelic strengths and weaknesses, human upright and inapt paths, and the different ways people love with their humanity compared to how they LOved with their divine soul.

Thank you to everyone who reads this book, and goes on to share their angelic gifts with others, to help humanity, to reduce suffering, and to make a real difference to our needy world.

Thank you that many people, whether they read this book or not, will enjoy the wonders of soul development on Earth, as they edge ever closer to the glory that is due to all angels.

And I give thanks that sharing what it is like to live a life of an angel-on-earth may help open the wider consciousness of planetary thinking towards even greater happiness, harmony, and peace.

Glossary

Unusual words, terms and phrases are defined in the section in this book in which they first appear. Others are defined here, to help understanding from the start.

"Secrets of Angels on Earth" Groups

a. A "Secrets of Angels on Earth" Group that you start near your home to support yourself and others on your paths.
b. An existing "Secrets of Angels on Earth" Group that you can apply to join who meet regularly to support each other's paths.

Angels-on-earth

a. People whose souls have learned most needed lessons in previous lives, and must now learn how to have and share love and LOve.
b. People whose souls did not learn lessons in other lifetimes, but who did so well in this life and achieved whatever was needed for their soul's progression, they can now learn how to have and share love and LOve.

Clues

Clues, mainly hidden in the text, are options for aspects of an angel-on-earth's life, love, LOve, soul path and Destiny. Clues aim to bring to the fore clues you may or may not be aware of, and suggest possible ways forward.

Helping humanity

Angels who LOve and help humanity, includes LOving and helping animals, plants, environment, anything.

Love

Any version of human love that can be imperfect.

LOve

The highest, most ideal and perfect LOve.

LOve-Based Living

A new approach to life, a love and LOve revolution for everyone, especially for angels-on-earth who reach a way of life that as far as possible LOves everyone and everything, everywhere, to achieve their soul purpose.

Platformation

A level reached in life where a lesson needs to be learned and outcomes formed, usually connected with an aspect of human love, or Godly LOve.

Prospective final lifetime

a. An angel-on-earth's potential not to return for another life if the Contract is fulfilled unless they wish to return.
b. A human's potential to be an angel-on-earth in their last lifetime, even if it was not "meant to be" at the start.

Secrets

Secrets that you may or may not be aware of, are openly revealed, or hidden in the text as ways of life that:

a. Are unknown, unseen, unaccepted, or unrecognized.
b. For personal reasons cannot be discussed openly.

Soul

The part of you that is the total sum of all your lifetimes that lives on after death, and remembers LOve.

Supreme Soul

The Soul of God, of LOve, of highest universal perfection.

Medical Information and Disclaimers

The information herein is not an alternative to orthodox medical doctors' or medical consultants' prescriptions, referrals, operations, or advice.

This book is for entertainment and to potentially help certain types of people.

You should not read this book if you have been hospitalized due to a mental or emotional illness of any kind including altered states of consciousness, schizophrenia, introspection, hallucination, delusion or paranoia within the last ten years.

Do not read if you have seen a doctor or been prescribed medical drugs for a mental or emotional condition of any type, including the ones above, within the past five years.

And do not read if you have felt suicidal, or suffered from a drink, drug, or other addiction in the past four years.

Also, this book should not be read if you may not easily be able to come to terms with yourself or others potentially being an angel-on-earth.

Please respect and accept a doctor's opinion about anything in this book.

Author's note: specific mental, emotional or other conditions may be due to an archetypal conflict between an imperfect body and a perfect soul; or between someone trying to love flawed people with their memory of perfect LOve that their soul unconsciously remembers before arrival on Earth.

However, orthodox psychology, counseling and similar therapies do not currently resolve issues of the soul, so it is best to adhere to the above guidelines.

Future Medical Opinion

Certain concepts in this book address definitive psychological issues. Countless people with standard conflicts in various age groups and on Platformations described herein seek orthodox mental, emotional, counseling, and medical help, only to find after years of treatment that it does not work. They have been helped quickly, often the same day, when they understood the values of their angelic soul.

Some people know they are angels and yet are orthodox medical professionals such as doctors, psychologists, or psychiatrists. They know there is no current medical or other model formulated to help the specific health needs of angels-on-earth, and so realize their therapies can't even help themselves with their angelic developmental issues.

Maybe this book will offer clues for a new therapy that is needed for the coming age of angelic souls, a treatment that has guidelines to help this special soul group who interact like no other soul group on Earth.

Hopes and prayers are that, in the not-too-distant future, a new breed of medical professionals who understand the Angelic Path will take this book seriously. So that one day, angelic workers within orthodox medical, psychological and psychiatric fields can accept these issues raised and expand the knowledge into valid and competent therapies. They can then provide more effective services to help an extraordinary type of people, called angels-on-earth, enter a new age of enlightenment.

Introductions

Aims and Objectives

This book's aims and objectives are twofold.

Firstly, to clarify and support angels-on-earth's thoughts, actions, experiences and goals throughout their lives.

Secondly to attempt to open the minds of other people, especially non-angels, to the existence and realities of angels-on-earth.

Angels-on-earth are not part of a cult, even though many who do not understand may take that incorrect view.

Angels-on-earth have always been merely a necessarily almost-secret part of life, part of Earth, part of humanity's souls' evolution, a pathway to God, the Supreme Soul. But at present, there is little that can help non-angels understand people with angelic souls. It is a lesson for some angels-on-earth to understand themselves.

If you think you might be an angel, maybe the revelation of potential secrets and the clues in this book will help you make more sense of a not-easy-to-understand life. Then you can hopefully achieve soul goals faster, with happier understanding.

Indeed, the Angel Party helped many of those present.

By reading this book, if you find you might be an angel-on-earth, you too can enjoy that Angel Party, find LOve, and discern the differences between human and soul lives.

This book may also give you clues to know which partner to share your LOve with, discover how to use money spiritually, and see signposts leading to your soul's Destiny.

After reading, you can use this book as a permanent reference guide for everything that happens on your soul path, for the rest of your life.

If this book clarifies your path, the differences you feel between human love and Godly LOve, which Platformation you're on and how to overcome it, or your future options, maybe you will soften some pressures away from your life.

If this book achieves just one aim, I hope it is that readers will know that for LOve-Based Living, life is there to be lived and loved, but souls are there to be LOved.

If this book achieves just one objective, I hope it is that readers can move more quickly through the soul lesson Platformations, to provide the LOve and gentleness of the angels above to help themselves, and all they touch.

Clues To Know You're an Angel-on-Earth

Most people evolve over many lifetimes of experiential soul lessons. Eventually, they learn enough to potentially be in their final lifetime, which is the ultimate subject of this book.

But the majority of people are not angels in their prospective final life. They still need to learn from additional, future lifetimes. For this type of person, they can still, in this lifetime, become an angel-on-earth if they do extremely well and quickly learn enough lessons that would normally have needed other lifetimes to learn from. Then they can, perhaps consciously, make another Contract to fulfill a task on Earth, and this book will become relevant to their Angelic Path.

A few people, only a few, know they are in their very first lifetime, but have done so well they have already earned the right to become an angel-on-earth. If they learn their lessons fully enough, after passing on they might be able to choose not to return.

Some people simply know they are an angel-on-earth because they can see, hear or feel certain things that will be explained in this book.

Other angels-on-earth only know they are an angel because others explain it to them, or because clairvoyants have seen their wings.

Some people may know they are an angel because of their constant desire to share highest LOve to help humankind. Often they feel they can't yet die and return home to Godly LOve, because their soul has more LOve to offer.

If you're not sure you're an angel-on-earth, read the section, "The Angelic Questions" to see if they feel relevant to you. Do not try to make them fit you and your life. You can also log on to www.angelsonearth.info and answer online Angelic Questions.

Some people who are angels-on-earth may not be able to

answer the Angelic Questions appropriately. For example, they may have an unusually positive attitude or love and LOve mental ability that naturally overcomes questions about issues on the Angelic Path. Or some people who are angels-on-earth may not be at a level to understand their secret nature yet. So for these types, they may not yet be able to understand and accept the teachings in this book.

However, the percentage of people who pick up and buy this book who are angels-on-earth will be significantly high. Maybe you were attracted to the word "angel" in the title, or perhaps you scanned some chapters or chapter headings, and read something relevant to your life. Or maybe you just knew the book was for you.

A word of warning is in order though. Most people will relate to something in this book. That does not mean most people are angels!

As you read this book, you may realize that you are an angel-on-earth for any of the following reasons.

Did you have tears of joy, sadness, elation, calm, relaxation, relief, peace, healing, or some other intense feeling?

Did you suddenly, unexpectedly understand why you had a good or not-so-good life?

Did you feel positive because you have recognized that angel knowledge has connected within you?

Did you at some point instantaneously realize your purpose on Earth?

Did the clues seem appropriate options for your soul path?

Did you sense deep inside your being, your soul saying, this is the truth?

Did you recognize it's just how it is, you are an angel?

Did the secrets feel relevant to your life?

Do you feel thankful that at last someone understands you, your soul and your purpose?

If at least one of the above applies to you, this book may hold your ultimate truths, and perhaps you are a budding angel.

If you have an emotional reaction, if you felt the messages in the book are relevant to your life, please reread the book. That is because you usually only absorb what is relevant to you at the moment of reading. On the second reading, you should benefit from different wisdom. Consolidate the ideas from within this book to within your being.

Human beings go through ups and downs. If you reread the book a few months or a year later, you will gain support to climb life's hurdles. You have a limited span of life, and rereading the book will help you stay alert to the issues on your path.

As you move up the Angelic Path, continuous rereading will unfold new truths to help your development at each further stage and Platformation of life.

If You Are Not an Angel-on-Earth

The advice here is very simple. Not everyone is an angel-on-earth.

If you are in any doubt whatsoever whether the information in this book is appropriate and relevant to you or not, use the age-old safety saying, "When in doubt, leave it out."

In other words, if in doubt, do not try to make the words in this book somehow fit into your life. It is better for your life, and maybe for your soul and health, to forget this book, and get on with leading your life and finding a path in other ways. Know that are many human and soul paths that could eventually lead you to the same end result.

In any event, you do not have to be an angel to be a moral, beautiful person. Even though you do not feel LOve within your soul, you can still uphold upright values, use great empathy, share your human love, learn about LOve, and then share your human knowledge of perfect LOve with something you see is in need.

If you have the slightest doubt that you are a potential angel, accept that is how it is. Instead, find another book to help your path differently.

You will find choices and chances cross your path, whether you are an angelic soul or not. Everyone on this marvelous planet will always have more opportunities to become angelic. Try to seek harmlessness. Attempt to only do goodness. Practice positivity. Explore happiness. Improve your thoughts, speech, and actions to become a better person. Become moral, ethical, kind and helpful in all matters, as much as you can. Study different human loves and Godly LOves.

If you achieve the ways suggested in the previous paragraph, even people not in their last lifetime, without any type of memory or innate knowledge of perfect LOve, can still gain a logical understanding of what LOve is.

All is well because even if your Contract did not state your Destiny was to be an angel-on-earth, if you wish, your Free Will choices can help you learn all necessary angelic lessons now, in this lifetime.

If you prefer, or if it is relevant, you can wait till another lifetime, and learn your lessons then. That is OK too. In the higher scheme of how the universe works, all is perfect, whatever you decide.

If You Are an Angel-on-Earth

If you are an angel-to-be, each stage of your life may hold something new to learn about a new phase of angelic progression.

But how you tread the Angelic Path to become angelic is not easy to understand by yourself. For example, you might get stuck on a particular Platformation, and wonder what is happening, whether you've taken an improper path, or even that you are being punished for words or deeds in this life, or in a past life.

Each time you do not understand a part of your life, or when you need to find solutions, or if you wish to progress further or faster, your first and perhaps best idea might be to refer to the various secrets and clues in relevant Platformation sections of this book, to see if answers are here.

This book offers hope, and shows the potentials of what to expect. Particularly on early Platformations, you will find there is still hope you can find a better way to interact with others, a better morality, a better existence. Much must be learned and understood to earn the right to become an angel.

Principles in this book can provide revelations about angelic issues and conflicting aspects of human love and Godly LOve to help you live more comfortably, and happier, and to reach soul goals faster.

Be as perfect as you can throughout your life. Develop harmonization of body and soul. Aim to be generous, and truthful. Act spiritually at home, work, and play. Find a teacher of spirituality, love, or soul Destiny development to guide your path. Use your money for your family and the needy. Aspire to LOve those "below" you as much as those "above". Join or start a "Secrets of Angels on Earth" support group to help each member achieve their goals.

It is one thing to do good, and quite another to be harmless. Always consider if actions or words will improve yourself or others. The saying, "Treat others as you would like to be treated by them," is an excellent way to lead your life, especially on early Platformations when you may be coming to terms with a not-so-nice life on Earth.

Due to the nature of a developing soul, some mini-chapters in this book may only be understood in retrospect, after you've achieved the goal suggested in that chapter. It's only when you look down the mountain you have climbed, that you can see the path. You cannot see the path ahead until you tread it.

See life not as a race to be won, but a game with soul reasons to be achieved, where the speed of success is not as crucial as putting into practice positive qualities of LOve, and consequently fulfilling your Contract.

Read relevant spiritual, angel, and soul books, websites, blogs, anything that could help you overcome the Platformation you are on. Study what you need to do, and when you need to do it. Then practice and practice the knowledge. Eventually you might gain wisdom. Then you may be able to move on to the next Platformation, towards your end goal and the fulfillment of your Contract, quicker, and with a great sense of achievement.

Some Platformations need time to overcome them. There is no reason not to progress. That is, unless you lack strength of purpose and perseverance. Always make time for necessary experiments and actions to develop the qualities needed on that Platformation.

Please do not give this book away to another angel. If you are an angel-on-earth, you will probably need to refer to knowledge needed to understand a higher Platformation's new developmental processes.

As an angelic force for goodness, few lessons are easy on your soul path. If they were, those lessons could have been done "upstairs", before birth. But being prepared by the knowledge of this book can make the journey easier to achieve.

If you feel the content of this book is right for you, you may like to start a "Secrets of Angels on Earth" Group of angels-on-earth in your area, an "Angelic Group for Evolving Souls". You will gain beneficial friendships, LOving people, and mutual support for your soul's journey and eventual Destiny. See Appendices 2 and 3 on how to start a Group, and the benefits of being part of a Group.

One thing is certain. When you achieve your lifetime angelic goal, you'll find satisfaction with your life, and beautiful harmony, peace, and happiness.

Secrets of Angels on Earth

It is not surprising that angels-on-earth are not well-known. Human beings who are also angels have probably never appeared as their angelic selves on mainstream TV, or in major newspapers or glossy magazines. It is no secret that most people do not discuss every aspect of their lives openly, especially if their ways or beliefs are not accepted by society's "normal" standards.

It's also common knowledge that most people have secrets they do not tell even their closest friend or family member.

A standard concept, accepted in psychology, is that keeping secrets is not good. That is because most secrets are adverse, and that adversity may increase, and keep eating away at you consciously and unconsciously.

It is like the classic story of one bad grape in a barrel of bountiful fruit, turning the harvest bad.

But in the case of angels-on-earth, the big clue is that you are not keeping an adverse secret. You are keeping aspects of your life secret that are so LOvingly, beautifully different to most people's non-LOving worldly view, that you know others may not be able to accept the sweetness of your angelic comments.

Many angels-on-earth understand, sometimes from a very early age in childhood, that it is best to keep certain things a secret from most people. This realization may occur when you first learned to speak and share conversation, and you mentioned something about this type of subject to a parent or sibling or friend at preschool. And you received a disbelieving response.

Thus you may learn even from a very young age that it's best not to discuss these topics with your friends or family because you might lose them as an otherwise trusting friend.

So keeping the context and meanings of your life as an angel-on-earth secret becomes a positive. It's a way to protect yourself from the disbelieving, prying, spying, trolling, or judgmental eyes of others.

It is important perhaps for some people to understand what angels commonly keep secret. Secrecy is normally only about mystical aspects of life, LOve and the angelic soul. What aspects of life are usually not kept secret is the soul purpose of an angel-on-earth, and the positive difference an angel makes.

Earthly, non-mystical, practical things should not be secret. They need to be openly shared, so more people know the wonderful gifts that can be shared to help others in need. The more people who know of an amazing way to mitigate adversities, the more people that secret angel can help.

What if the angelic nature of an angel-on-earth was not a secret, if instead they told everyone they are an angel? Many people hold personal, subjective viewpoints, convictions, or even prejudices against angels. An angel-on-earth might be "brought down" by unfair or unreasonable gossip. Many people who could otherwise have been helped could be scared away, and the angel-on-earth may achieve less.

Deep down though, most angels-on-earth know that secrecy about their soul, LOve and mystical purpose is an essential part of the path. They know the path must be a lonely one, to be learned and trod with personal views kept within. This loneliness, this secrecy about angelic LOve, and also usually about angels, provides resilience against others' disbelieving thoughts or comments.

Most angels-on-earth realize that even family members do not always stay close; they may turn against each other at some point in life. So why should you risk giving them a reason to not talk to you, or even disown you?

Especially, most persons with an angelic soul know deep within that even a closest friend can become the opposite, instead of sharing love with you.

The classic dissenting types of persons experienced by Jesus, according to the Bible, were doubting Thomas and treacherous Judas. They are unfortunately all too common 2,000 years later, in everyday life.

Many angels-on-earth achieve LOvingly well on their path, only to be brought down by a version of a doubting Thomas who spreads cynical words about them, that other people unfortunately believe, and then repeat. Horrid gossip can destroy someone's beautiful pathway.

It's similar to a treacherous Judas. I know too many people whose lives were crucified by an ex-friend or family member who becomes a Judas type, telling awful stories about them that are at best exaggerated, and at worst untrue. All the goodness and nourishment they had been achieving with their LOve-Based Living and Godly callings of LOve, helping and caring for others, can be destroyed easily by an unthinking, unfair, and uncaring Judas.

So why should an angel-on-earth give their friends or family clues about their need for LOve, how they feel about their path in the world, about their various past lives or Contract for this life if they remember them, about their feelings of sharing LOve in a bigger way one day, or about the potential for them to have a soul that emanates LOve?

Why should they even mention angels, when most people would never believe their best friend in all the world has seen a ghost, at least not until they see a ghost themselves?

What benefit would there be in sharing a way of life that many would view as unscientific and unproven, and could therefore be seen as being irrational. In a worst-case scenario, someone who admitted to being an angel could be viewed as being potentially psychologically unstable.

There are too many dangers in sharing your feelings and knowledge about your Angelic Path. And too few benefits in wanting others to know the same issues about love and LOve as you.

You may want the whole world to know LOve like you, to be as LOving as you, to share as much LOve as you.

But being a secret angel-on-earth is a way to enjoy the privacy needed to grow on your path, and a way to embolden your actions when needed without the hindrance of non-understanding, and possibly destructive, people.

The title I chose for this book, *Secrets of Angels on Earth,* is not because I want angels' lives to be secret. I'd love the opposite, for the lives of all real angels to be public knowledge.

The title includes the word "secret" because the angels themselves may need to keep aspects of their angelic paths secret from friends and family, and potential future enemies. That secrecy will give them freedom and space to live a special type of life, with a secret angelic consciousness, so they can achieve their Angelic Path Destinies. The word "clues" is included in the subtitle because they are options certain angels may choose at certain times.

By all means test friends and family, just a little, about angels above, or angels-on-earth, to watch their reaction. But if you perceive disbelief, back away from the topic. Just enjoy your human relationships and try to keep your friends and family close and strong for the rest of your life. You never know, at some point in the future, they could change their mind about angels.

The more important thing is that you spread your LOving wings, unclipped.

Eventually you can show everyone the true you through your LOving ways. Especially when you make a difference to, and provide joy in, our uncertain but certainly needful world.

Take heart that your inner beauty will win the battle of hearts' desires, and that one day you will lead by brave and joyful high LOve example.

Clues To Inter-National Differences

Angels-on-earth come in many forms, so do human beings. What a human being is like with their character, personality, or in their understanding of and interaction with their life and the world can be relevant to which country they grew up in.

There is historical discussion about nature versus nurture. For example, with nurture, if you grew up in a violent country of terror and civil war, where your family were murdered and friends were tortured, you will probably develop very differently compared to if you grew up in a country of peace as the closeted child of a respected prince.

Or, with nature, if you grew up in a country where over the millennia, genetic inbreeding and inheritance created detrimental genetic inheritances within the population, that may make you likely to portray the same traits. So you will probably develop very differently compared to if you grew up in a country where the people are known to be sweet, gentle, and loving in nature.

I certainly do not name nature or nurture countries, although in recent times, some countries have nurtured their people towards an understanding of, or a partaking in, cruelty through violent regimes or murderous civil wars. Whereas certain other countries in recent years are widely known for their people's sweet and beautiful nature.

Your background of your specific national nature or nurture could probably therefore have an influence on the type of human being you became.

This book is written on the basis of Western influences, how Western culture, nature and nurture affects humans and angels-to-be.

So if you come from, for example, a peaceful Middle Eastern country, where drugs, alcohol and sexual promiscuity are banned, and you are a female raised in traditional Islam, some aspects of this book might not be relevant to your understanding of society. Do not be concerned that chapters on addictions, sexuality, relationships or other subjects seem alien to you, or even shock you. You were possibly lucky that you didn't have those types of nature or nurture to learn from within your country. You may still be an angel-on-earth.

And if you come from a war-torn country, and have been involved in atrocities which perhaps it was truly impossible to escape from, you may also still be an angel-on-earth. You might be able to make amends, and prove your angelic credentials with good deeds.

So as you read this book, be aware of which country you were raised in, and how you were affected with the natural nature or nurture aspects of your specific society.

And try to discern that some chapters might be more, or less, relevant to you depending on which country's traits has influenced you the most.

Simply accept the parts of the book that may be relevant to you, minus the nature or nurture aspects emanating from your nation.

The Difference Between love and LOve

One of the tragedies of the English language is that there is only one word for love. Other languages such as Sanskrit have one word for the LOve of God, and other, different, words for other types of love. Some examples of different loves in Sanskrit are as follows.

affection love	(anurAga)
causing love	(anurAgin)
conciliating love	(anuraJjana)
desire love	(abhikam)
devotional love	(anurakti)
fond love	(anurudh)
in love with	(anurAgavat)
the state of being in love	(anuragitA)
love that cannot vary	(aspanda)

It is right to have different words for these different loves, for they are all very different love-energies. They can be used to explain the type of love you may possess for a sibling, spouse, child, grandparent, lover, neighbor, boss, and so on. These different words can even describe love for chocolate or a pet. But most languages have only one word for love. Is it any wonder we get confused as to what love means?

Many years ago I found that, when trying to type the word love, if the love was about the love of God, my fingers could never type the word in lower case, "love". If I were typing about the natural love of humankind, the word would appear on the screen as "love". But if I typed about divine love, no matter how much I concentrated, the word would come on to the screen as "LOve".

That went on for weeks until one day I thought I had to find out why. So I held fingers over the keyboard and typed in a question. "What is the difference between the spelling of love and LOve?"

Immediately the answer came back. My fingers went stiff as they flew across the keys. It was a strange experience. Peace filled the room, as if high angels had taken my hands. The channeling is on the next page.

One of my students has said that the lettering "LOve" is also relevant to ancient Greek spellings and deeper meanings about Godly never-ending LOve, and that the Greek language used to have five words for love, all with different meanings.

Recently I was explaining the importance of writing the words differently, LOve and love, to a teacher friend. One of her pupils, a 6-year-old girl, tells everyone, "I can see wings on some people, but not everyone." The teacher said that while she was showing her how to write happy and sad words, in lower case as she was so young, the child took the pencil and said that "love" should be written with a capital letter. When the teacher asked why, the girl replied, "Because love is special." Out of the mouths of babes...!

Since using the two different spellings of love and LOve, it seems that the use of LOve helps people free themselves from the thought-shackles of human loves and open to, and concentrate on, the beauty and perfection of the highest LOve.

Channeling on love and LOve

Many people will ask, Why do you spell love, LOve?

First and foremost this is a beautiful God-given opportunity to teach of true, highest, perfect God-LOve. It will make many people think. Initially, they will consider it a spelling mistake. Soon they will realize it is not.

When sometimes the word "love" is spelled "LOve", they will wonder why. That will help human thoughts unconsciously focus onto different types of love, especially the differences of human loves and Godly LOve.

Then explain the lettering to intrigue and evolve their higher thoughts.

L… Always use a capital L to underline the critical difference of the LOve of God compared to human loves.

O… Always use a capital O to portray the circular, all-embracing, never-ending, universal nature of the LOve of God compared to human love.

ve… And you need a small "v" and a small "e" to make the capital "L" and capital "O" obvious and more important.

A Message from the Angels

The day before the Angel Party, while typing notes for the lecture, I was thinking, "What should be the main points of the lecture?"

Suddenly my hands were taken over. The fingers went stiff, and moved across the keys quicker than I could typically type with two fingers. Having channeled and taught channeling since the 1990s, I am used to channeling various guides, masters, angels, and other beings. I could feel the high, light, caring, angelic presence.

I relaxed, and let the following words flow out automatically, without putting conscious thought to the keyboard.

By the time I'd finished, there on the screen was a beautiful message to share with angels-in-the-making, before starting the first day of this Angel Party.

The Message

Tell them (the angels-on-earth) that we are here for them; that they are not alone; that the issues of their hearts are the issues of ours; that the problem with this world is not of their making but the making of their God; that the way forward is to tread in beauty and truth; that if questions are not asked all is still possible; that the only thing that will hold them back is not moving on; but that when the time is right they will move on.

Say that God and the angels are here for their unwanted emotions.

Once they leave your Party, they need to breathe; breathe freshness of ideas; a freshness of approach for the new life to come.

Perhaps the soul's way for some would also be the way for us; quick, simple, painless.

But if that is not the way, if the way is slower or not so easy, blessings may be given to God for making the journey possible in a way that is right for souls even though understanding is impossible.

Perhaps the ending of the two days should be one of LOve. Let them experience LOve. Show them what to aim for within themselves, permanently.

Until then, be aware of the consequences of your actions. Give support. Be kind. Let no one take you away from your task of sharing beauty in the world quicker than it otherwise would have been.

Chapter 1

The Angel Party Openings

Opening

"Welcome to my first large gathering of angels-on-earth. Greetings to this Angel Party!

"In the history of Earth and during the millennial evolution of humankind, every conceivable way human beings can interact within themselves and between each other has almost certainly been considered, explored, and occurred.

"So Angel Parties would have been held elsewhere before, somewhere on our planet, throughout moments of history. For example, the international soul-teaching Brahma Kumaris may have held angel parties since their founding in 1936, albeit, probably at a higher level of their organization.

"Today I have invited a large group of special angels-on-earth, including some people who haven't attended angelic talks or courses before, but who I know are angels. And you angels are meeting together deliberately in one room. That is special.

"So this is my first Angel Party, an amazing occasion to bless the angelic hearts, minds and souls of all angels present. I pray you will enjoy many more Angel Parties in future.

"These will be an extraordinary two days. I've met and invited every angel in this room personally. Many other people asked if they could come, and I've said, 'No.' A lot of you know people you consider to be like you, an angel on this pathway as well, but I again had to say, 'No,' for this year, because it's my first Angel Party.

"It seemed important to be 100% sure only angels on this pathway are here today because then you can make angelic friends. I wanted to ensure you'll not find someone here and think, 'Oh well, maybe they're not an angel,' because then it would be just like any other party.

"And, quite frankly, we don't want people here who aren't angels-to-be, like reporters. I don't know what a reporter would write about today and tomorrow, do you?

(Laughter.)

"So it was a matter of personal invitations, that I only sent out last week. Thank you for coming at such short notice.

"I didn't think such a big room would be needed, but it was. The room was way too small for the numbers who arrived without confirming their attendance. Thankfully, one of the higher angels here did her supportive angelic duties on Earth, and staff allowed us to use this room. It's called Herringham Hall. I think you'll agree that the high ceilings, huge arched and draped windows, and balcony, give this a feeling of a fantastic sense of occasion.

"These will be casual days. Actually, it was delightful just now. I didn't want to start at the time stated on the invitation because everybody's angelic energies were already merging, weren't they?

"Did you feel it? The energy…?

"Can you still feel the energy?

"Everybody was talking, being, moving, thinking together, at oneness, with human love of course, but even more with Godly LOve. Did you feel that?

"Yes, but that feeling of LOve isn't the same with most gathered groups. For example, many of you are medical professionals, and you know almost every beginner's class you ever attend isn't like that because some people there are wondering, 'Will the class be like this?', or 'Is it going to be like that?', or 'I'm not sure about that person over there,' and many other similar uncertain thoughts.

"So the energy before starting this morning was exceptional, abnormal in its most wonderfully gorgeous LOving energy. Every angel connected so beautifully to all others in the room that I thought, 'We'll just let the LOving energy run and flow.'

"I hope this energy will remain throughout today and tomorrow, to enable you to make new and good friends, friends who understand about Godly LOve, friends to last your lifetime.

"Very often, this pathway is not easy. I know some of you dithered whether to come here or not because you still have challenges on this path. So that will be discussed. Today it will mainly be about the predicaments, and offering clues to try to help you. Tomorrow it will mainly be about the wonderful levels you will hopefully reach.

"Yes, wonderful levels. This life can become very special for everybody here because you're all here for a reason; an extraordinary purpose driven by your LOving soul.

"I think the majority of you know deep in your heart you're on this planet for a certain special reason. You may not know the reason yet, but you know there's a definite reason why you're here, that when the time comes to manifest your reason for being, your life will be happy, fantastic.

"I've brought two boxes of tissues today, because touching on secrets and clues of early Platformations might not be easy for some people to cope with. And if there are a few tears, that's OK. It's really OK.

"Yes, that's one of the reasons you're here. To let out tears of recognition of what you truly are. Some angels-on-earth release tears of thanks that at last someone understands. Or they release tears of hope that hardships may have a beautiful reason.

"If tears start to flow, we'll share the tissues around the room.

"When teaching this subject briefly on courses, tissues have occasionally run out. Some of you may remember at my Centre last summer, when almost everybody was crying, weren't they? I think two or three people were screaming, weren't they? They were actually screaming! They were letting out energies that had built up because of the conflict between their human bodily issues, and their Godly soul. After, they told everyone, they felt better than they'd felt for most of their lives.

"Although beautiful LOve is really what an angel's path is all about, there are numerous other types of human interactions, especially in the first parts of life. So please help those around you. And pass the tissues if needed!

"People have specially visited England from other countries, just to come here today and tomorrow. So I'd like to welcome the Danish contingent; thank you for coming all the way from Denmark. Also, somebody has come all the way from Sweden. Where are you? Thank you very much for coming all that way. There are also angels here in this room from America, Uruguay, Russia, Mexico, Spain, South Africa, France, Chile, and other countries.

"So an Angel Party isn't just about this country, England. Angels-on-earth belong to every country, a worldwide influence. Isn't it wonderful that these two days have angel representatives from so many parts of our world?

"And there are angels here who are Christian, Muslim, Hindu, Jewish, and probably from other religions that you've not yet mentioned. And there's a capitalist, a city financier, a communist, and a Marxist. Isn't it wonderful that angels exist in, and can come from, any philosophy on Earth?

"I know some of you think every person on Earth is the same as you, an angel-on-earth. They're not. Angels aren't even in the majority on our planet. There are, in fact, very few. I know everybody in this room is an angel on this path. But you don't represent everybody on this planet.

"Some time ago, on a beginners' healing course, somebody in the class was an angel on the pathway. She talked about angels-on-earth, and this lady, who is here today, thought everybody was on this pathway. I replied, 'I'll ask the group the Angelic Questions.' Out of about 30 people, I think two put their hands up, didn't they? Yes, there were only two out of about 30 students in that room who raised their hands to acknowledge their understanding of the questions, because only those two were on this Angelic Path.

"Still, two out of 30 is quite a high percentage, quite a high rate compared to the numbers of this planet's population. In fact some high angels I know have considered how many angels are on the planet. We all separately came up with the same number, the same percentage. Out of every 300 or 400 people on Earth, there is only one angel. So the chance of you connecting with other angels is small, especially because, probably, both of you won't talk about your angelic nature.

"Sometimes though, soul groups come together. On healing, psychic or spiritual classes I try to feel the energies of people as they arrive. I watch their faces, and read their interactive energy forces. Occasionally I realize there's an Angelic Group soul present. So then I'll maybe tell a brief Angel Story at lunchtime or when the course ends.

"If I tried to tell the Angel Story to a group of people in a bank, science research laboratory, accountancy office, or on a building site, there would probably not be such a high percentage of people in those places who would be on this Angelic Path. I've taught bankers, scientists, accountants and builders who know they are angels, helping in whatever way they can with their LOve. But there are probably not so many angels in those logical, science or trades types of professions, because most angels would be attracted to more caring professions.

"Caring or creative professions offer an outlet for an angel's LOve. For example, it is common for a soul group of angels to be drawn together within the creative arts or orthodox medicine. Angels-on-earth seem attracted by the alternative or complementary health care professions, the arts of healing, intuition, or spirituality. Those who progress higher, seem more likely to be angels. In general terms, the higher the level, the higher is the percentage of angels.

"People who book onto self-help healing groups often have

higher LOve motivations. They want to improve their personal faults, and they want to help other people. They're more likely to be angels on this pathway because helping themselves and others is what the life of an angel is all about. They are about developing their faulty human minds and bodies to be in tune with their LOving souls. And they're about helping to develop other people's minds and bodies, to be in tune with their LOving souls, yes?

"Some of you here today are in a medical, scientific, or caring profession where you are trying to make a positive difference to the world. There are those of you who offer one-to-one support, or teach classes designed to help others, such as with psychology, psychiatry, self-development, healing, spirituality, health care, counseling, and so on. Think of who amongst your bosses, colleagues, or students may be on which angelic level. Then perhaps you can find a way to help their angelic paths, even though it might not be appropriate to discuss angels openly. Helping an angel to achieve means helping the world improve.

"In the higher levels of the caring or creative types of professions, you'll find higher percentages of angels present. That is because angels are often drawn towards a caring or creative career, where they can become or create the change they want to see.

"Angels know deep inside their souls they want to share the highest LOve, the LOve they know consciously or unconsciously that's absorbed inside their soul being. They want to share that LOve with the world, as much as they can. A caring or creative profession, regardless of what the words 'caring' or 'creative' mean, offers an excellent path to achieve the goals of making a difference with LOve.

"But remember not everybody is like you, an angel on a pathway. Perhaps there would not be so many angels if we had a group of tax inspectors here?

(Laughter.)

"Well, maybe there would...

"Godly LOve is a beautiful force that's within everyone potentially. I say, potentially, because every person on Earth is on his or her individual soul pathway. You may be one of the few souls who found the way to develop angelically in the first lifetime. Or there's a minor potential that you descended to Earth to help something specific, and were already an angel. But usually, there are many learning curve lifetimes, as souls grow towards the prospective final angelic learning life, that all angels here today are on.

"After these two days, please, I do hope you don't go out into your parts of the world and start telling everybody what this weekend was all about, that you're an angel, or that you've had fun with a large group of other angels at an Angel Party. It's best to keep your life as an angel-on-earth secret from most people. That is because, quite frankly, most people won't understand what you're talking about.

"They really can't understand what you're talking about because most people are not on the Angelic Path. And then they may start to think, 'Is this a friend or a crazy person?' Or, 'This is too weird!' And then you'll possibly lose friends, and even close relatives may not like you. In an extreme case, an overly zealous non-understanding friend or relative may even call the doctor. If you have a timid character and personality, you'll probably be led to the doctor's without much fuss. And then you could be damaged by people within institutions who do not understand your true nature, treating you in inappropriate ways, instead of supporting you to tread your soul pathway.

"So it's best to keep secrets of being an angelic soul on a special pathway to yourself. Maybe the day will come when you can talk openly about being angelic.

"Not so many years ago, most people thought healers were a bit crazy. Nowadays, the health services of many countries employ healers in surgeries, hospices, and hospitals.

"It might be similar for angels. The evolving knowledge of a growing angelic soul may eventually become accepted. But until those days come, unless you're a brave warrior ready to go to war and battle against disbelievers, maybe it's happier to keep the angelic aspects of your life and goals secret, and not to say you're an angel-in-the-making.

"If you do think someone is an angel, you could simply refer them to the website "www.secretsofangelsonearth.com", or the Facebook page, "Secrets of Angels on Earth", where they can find clues about their lives, ask questions, or answer the Angelic Questions. If it is appropriate, they could join one of our "Secrets of Angels on Earth" Groups if they wished, and gain the support and help of others.

"Always remember that this extensive inner knowing of highest LOve is something most people don't have. Deep down from within the beauty of your soul, your divinely angelic nature will desire to share LOve, and you'll want to get out there to spread Light into the darkness of this world. You will want to tell everybody the truth of angelic power and Godly LOve.

"But if you start talking about wings and halos, it will probably not be appropriate for most of the population on our planet. Please don't scare people. By all means, give explanations where necessary and proper. But discern, please. Find your particular way to share this knowledge only with special, trusted, people. Be conscious of harmlessness. Discern, deeply.

"You know this force of beautiful LOve because as angels you have it inside you. You have the LOving energy of Godliness, of the Supreme Soul. On the higher levels of your path, this type of LOve enhances your life in incredibly beautiful ways.

"I hope these two days will be very flexible, that you'll go with the flow of the needs of everyone here. Because like any subject, the issues of the soul path of an angel could be discussed for months, not just for two days. So I pray flexibility can allow you to learn not only from this lecture but also from your needs.

"Actually, today has already gone with the flow because you'll note the itinerary for the two days has changed. That is because some of you have studied other subjects with me, and are used to lectures. And I thought, 'Well, it would be nice if someone else could do some of the sharing and some of the talking.'

"The idea is this. You are all on the same path here. And on this pathway it doesn't matter what family you've got, what friends you have, what occupation you're in, what religion you are, what culture you're from, what political or social model you believe in, what education you've had, what country you live in, or anything else to do with your human life.

"None of those things matter.

"Those choices you made, or the choices your family made for you, are the human bits and pieces created like a jigsaw called 'your life'. Those things are merely part of leading a life. As far as the soul is concerned, they are very unimportant.

"You see, you could have had a different life, and yet it may not have mattered because it would still have been a similar story, energetically. You'd have felt similar feelings within you, and interacted in similar varied ways with those around you, as you travel along your angel pathway. We will talk about the pathway Platformations you can reach.

"Today will be mainly about the secrets and clues of the early Platformations, mainly from the teens to the 30s.

"Hearing or talking about this can provoke tears because the early Platformations often aren't pleasing, and less pleasant memories may come to the fore. But understand you are safe here. I and many others here today can try to help you. In the whole scheme of God's plans for the universe, all is well. The early Platformations may be tough. But they are simply to help you understand your and others' human strengths and weaknesses, pleasures and horrors. It's about living on Earth fully, and, for some people, that means incarnating properly.

"And then you reach the Platformations of understanding the

rest of humanity.

"Then there are Platformations to share Godly LOve.

"Finally, there are Platformations for finding your soul purpose, your Destiny, your specific reason to be here.

"We'll talk about all these Platformations. What I hope is not that I'm now going to lead your life for you, or that any of you will find somebody here to lead you. Although support from other people can be useful to guide you how to lead your life towards your Destiny, it is only possible to suggest clues on how to overcome a Platformation. Your entire life cannot be led for you. It is up to each angel to use Free Will to choose what they believe are the best options to learn from and progress accordingly.

"This soul path you are all on, quite frankly you'll have opportunities to fulfill that path whether you were here today and tomorrow or not. Your God, your angels, your masters, your guides, your inner soul knowing, would all have conspired beautifully to develop you. You would have been led down the pathway to the understanding of why you are here on Earth, where you have to go, and what you have to achieve. So even without these two days, you would have got there, I pray.

"I say, 'I pray,' because you all have Free Will. So maybe some angels do not recognize the signs, or choose not to do their path. And then, of course, you may have to return to Earth again after moving on from your physical death, for another attempt at something that, with a bit more thought and action, could have been achieved in this lifetime.

"So although I pray and believe most of you would have found your soul purpose anyway without this course, the primary goal for these two days is to speed up your progression, and open your eyes to your amazing potential. Hopefully, less of you will have to come back to Earth for another life; unless of course, you choose to.

"I intend to help you understand the various levels of the

path, and what you could or should be doing on those levels, to help you overcome hurdles, and to reach your Destiny quicker. That, in turn, can facilitate you helping improve a part of our world faster. Because that's what it's all about. And this is done through finding your unique reason for being alive on Earth, and how you can support your version of society in a particular and often huge way.

"So whatever Platformation you're on, if I can offer clues to help your understanding of your Platformation, I may also automatically help your development on it. This may be explained practically later, when one of you angels, someone to be chosen at random, comes up to speak. When others listen to how you dealt with Platformations yourself, maybe they can relate to your angelic experiences.

"Perhaps during the breaks, or maybe after this weekend when you have finished here, you can connect with people who understand your energetic Platformation. It will be exceptional to meet other angelic souls who understand not only what you are feeling energetically on your Platformation. They have also previously found ways to cope with your types of angelic love or LOve issues and so may be able to help you evolve on to the next Platformation level. There are many ways your understanding may evolve, but listening to others who have 'been there, done that', and then making your Free Will choices as to whether their comments are ideal for your life or not, is one of the best ways forward.

"As many of you know, I don't provide name and address lists on courses because some people do not want to be on them. But for these two days, because you are all from the same soul group, I would like you all, if you don't mind, to put your names and addresses down on a piece of paper. You are all connected in LOve. So if you could do that at lunchtime? Two of you have kindly offered to type the list and bring it in tomorrow. Then maybe you can network afterward and help each other evolve on this pathway. Please include email addresses if you have them.

"So, you are gathered here first and foremost to understand your lives, yes?

"On the early Platformations, there's usually a great feeling of being alone. But you'll realize during these two days you are not alone. You are, at least for these two days, all angelic friends on the same LOving path.

"And understand that, especially if you've successfully gone through a Platformation, you can give support to somebody stuck on that same Platformation. If possible, if you have experience of a specific Platformation, could you please help those people on those early path levels? But please speak gently. Allow their Free Will to choose whether to act on your suggestions or not. Thank you for that.

"Lower does not mean worse. It's just an evolutionary rung on a ladder that almost all angels go through. You'll pass the early Platformations of life. Simply accept that they take time to pass. It might not feel like you'll get through them sometimes, but you will rise toward happy phases.

"So do help others if you see a need, and you have the ability and experience.

"There's one other reason why you shouldn't talk to too many people about this afterward. Especially, you should be very careful about talking about angels-on-earth to someone who you think might be on this pathway.

"Think about this. What would happen if you found a little cocoon and inside was something ready to evolve into a butterfly?

"If you take the butterfly out of the cocoon too quickly what will happen?

"Maybe it will fly away, a perfectly attractive butterfly. But a more likely outcome of premature birth is that it wouldn't be able to use its wings, and it would never fly. And then it would die without fulfilling its butterfly Destiny.

"That's the clue to how it may be if you find a potential angel amongst your normally loving family or friends. If you talk about angels-on-earth in a way the person cannot understand and accept, they may end up energetically flopped out of the cocoon too soon and never spread their angelic wings.

"Please remember that fundamental reason why it might be better not to talk about these two days to most people outside this room; why it's best not to talk about angels to someone even if you think you **know** they are an angel.

"If you find a potential angel-on-earth is struggling like a fish dangling in mid-air, and they're wondering what the heck to do with their lives now, please phone an angel from your list who went through the early levels. Try to phone someone experienced, someone who can offer clues on what to do because they have walked up that part of the soul mountain, and can look down the path. Find someone who has already seen how to overcome obstacles barring the way up to the next Platformation.

"So please try to find someone to adequately support the person you think is an angel. Your friend will hopefully be helped to understand parts of their life they may be stuck on, or need guidance for, in gentle, caring LOving ways.

"Then your friend's soul evolution may be able to progress, without plunging them, potentially, into further chaos because they could not have coped with much angelic knowledge at that time. A higher angel will know what to say to them; but also as importantly, what not to say.

"You have three choices if in doubt whether you could adequately explain the Angel Story.

"First, you can refer potentially angelic persons to our website www.secretsofangelsonearth.com.

"Second, refer them to our "Secrets of Angels on Earth" Facebook Group.

"Or third, a transcript of these two days will be made into a book. Give them a copy of that book. If it is relevant it will support their love and LOve lives. It would be a book they can refer to again and again, for life, as needed.

"All options give others enough information so they'll not just leave their cocoon of safety and flounder. They're more likely to be enhanced through adequate understanding to grow more perfectly on their Angelic Path."

The 22 Angelic Questions – Clues To a Potential Final Lifetime

"So that is the introduction.

"Let's now start properly by explaining the Angelic Questions. It is a series of questions used to ascertain the likelihood of whether someone may be an angel-on-earth or not.

"These Angelic Questions and the reasons I'll give you for asking them will also give you clues to, and a summary of, what the Angel Path is about before going into it in more depth.

"After, I'll try and help you understand the various Platformations you may be on, and what you could do about them.

"So please could you put your things on the floor and get into a comfortable position. That is usually placing your feet flat on the floor, one hand on each leg, base of the spine against the back of the chair, and then close your eyes gently.

"If you're going to tell this to friends, to family, to people you meet because you feel the person is an angel-on-earth, please ask the person this series of Angelic Questions first. Don't just say bluntly something like, 'Hi, I'm an angel, and I think you are too.' That is not appropriate.

"The answers will provide clues as to whether you might consider they could be an angel-on-earth and therefore you may perhaps talk more about the Angelic Path. If you don't get enough positive answers that are relevant to the person potentially being an angel, then you don't go further. Change the subject. Keep your secret, and keep them as a friend.

"Please also understand that, although I'll explain the reasons for each of the Angelic Questions, due to possible confusions very few people you talk to should be told these reasons for the questions. That is, unless you have determined for sure they're an angel-on-earth, or unless, when it is published, you have a copy of the book of this Angel Party as backup.

"If you are in doubt whether to discuss with someone about them perhaps being an angel-on-earth, simply ask them to log on to enquiries@angelsonearth.info where they can assess for themselves their angelic potential.

"The first question I always ask is, 'Have you ever felt alone?'

"If you have, can you please put your hand up?

(Hands raised.)

"If your eyes were open you would see that probably everybody put up a hand. Yes, that's how it is. Probably everyone on this planet has felt alone at some point. Especially if a parent or loved one dies or leaves, most people may feel alone. But the motivating reason for feeling alone for an angel on a pathway is different, a secret from the conscious mind. Unless you've had a perfectly cozy and loving childhood and life, the clue to your feeling alone is that you are away from the LOve of God. It's a different feeling compared to being lonely. Feeling alone is always the first question to ask.

"To ensure the person isn't feeling alone because of events such as bereavement or divorce, the second question is, 'Have you felt alone most of your life?'

"Again please raise the hands.

(Hands raised.)

"Almost everyone… There are often a few less angels who have felt alone all their lives including from childhood.

"The few less are probably the types of angels-in-the-making who are lucky enough to have had wonderfully caring parents who protected them from the evils and terrors of the people and events on our planet. Then the angel-on-earth will feel loved, and not alone, from an early age.

"If love from parents is unconditional, that love will feel similar to the knowledge of Godly LOve from within the soul; then harmony and compatibility between body and soul may reign beautifully. Also, if someone has a natural positive attitude toward life, they also might not feel alone.

"The third question I always ask next is, 'Have you felt separated or detached?'

"Again, please put your hand up, but this time if you've felt separated or detached for most of your life.

(Hands raised.)

"And that is how it is. Virtually everybody put a hand up for that question as well. Probably it is the same angels who raised their hands to the previous question. Because you **are** alone, separated or detached. You are away from the ideal oneness of the LOve of God, where you at one time felt so connected to everything in such comfy ways.

"Perhaps someone who has lost a loved one may also feel separated or detached. But if somebody has felt alone most of their life, due to being an angel away from perfect LOve, they will usually also feel separated or detached from the beautiful LOve of God. That is the same clue as feeling alone, a very different proposition compared to temporary, event-related feelings due to losing a loved one.

"And then the fourth question, just to make sure you are going to talk to somebody who would accept this story, ask, 'Do you think you have a soul?'

"Please raise your hands to answer this question.

(Hands raised.)

"Everyone! Nowadays most people believe they have a soul. If I'd asked that question in the 1980s, not many people would have replied, 'Yes.' But nowadays, perhaps in cohesion with the progression of spirituality and angelic consciousness throughout the world, most people agree that souls exist.

"If somebody doesn't believe they have a soul, then there's no point in telling this Angel Story to them, because they almost certainly wouldn't accept the concepts within the story.

"Atheists also usually won't understand about souls even if they're on this angelic soul pathway, because their concrete belief pattern has focused their thoughts away from the inner soul of Godly LOve, towards the outer world of human existence. Atheists may become angels too, but through unconscious interaction with life events.

"A fifth question you could ask is, 'Do you believe that at one time before you were born, your soul was with God, or with whatever you call God?'

"Hands up, please.

(Hands raised.)

"More than three-quarters of you. Please excuse the use of the word 'God'. I always use that word, not as a religious word. 'God' simply represents something I don't understand. Spiritual and angelic organizations such as the Brahma Kumaris use the word 'God', and the phrase, 'Supreme Soul'. Some people say, 'The Universe', or 'The Light', or whatever. You can use any word you like, but God, or Supreme Soul are the words I use.

"Over three-quarters of you know that your soul was with God at some point before birth. That is a very high percentage. It is almost certainly way above the percentage rate you would get if you asked people at random outside on the street.

"The sixth question is, 'Do you understand your soul is here to learn lessons?'

"Please raise your hands if you do.

(Hands raised.)

"Everyone here... But if a person replies that they do not believe their soul is here to learn lessons, they probably won't understand the story. Almost certainly there would not be much point in continuing, because they wouldn't agree what the lessons are, or couldn't understand why a lesson should even exist.

"'Do you believe in past lives?' Maybe it's not a question that's quite so crucial to the understanding of the Angel Story, but it can be. You can also phrase the question, 'Do you remember past lives and their connecting thread?'

"Put your hand up to the seventh question. 'Can you remember any of your past lives, and perhaps also their connecting threads?'

(Hands raised.)

"Not many people can remember this. About one-fifth of you today can remember past lives, and the common thread that connects all your lives.

"But again this is probably a highly significant percentage compared to members of the general public. The connecting thread is a very relevant force because, if you can remember it, it will give you clues as to how you can evolve. From this, you may understand your lesson or lessons to be learned in this life, and then maybe your ultimate goal as well. You will learn about this in more depth tomorrow.

"There's an eighth question to ask, whether the person believes in angels. Hands up if you believe in angels.

(Hands raised.)

"That's all of you, 100%, who believe in angels. Of course, that's why you're here, to learn about angels-on-earth. But if you'd just met someone and are trying to determine whether they are an angel, and if they say they do not believe in angels, there really isn't much point in continuing. You might as well talk about the weather.

"If someone has answered 'Yes' to all questions so far, the ninth question to ask is, 'Do you remember the Contract you made about the life you could lead on Earth?'

"Hands up if you can recall a Contract you made.

(Hands raised.)

"Not so many people recall making their Contract. It's not

such a crucial question to the understanding of the story. But some angels do remember.

"I will discuss this later. It's most interesting that those angels-on-earth who remember making the Contract, remember quite similar happenings.

"That is because Contracts for angels-to-be are usually about the life-path of sharing angelic LOve.

"Memory of making the contract normally extends only to the point where they agreed contractual terms, not the terms themselves. Memory commonly only recalls glimpses of details of the life to come.

"Because complete answers are not given, Angels need to find a way to fulfill their Contract in this life. That's what life is about. That's what Free Will is about. It's about finding a way through conscious and unconscious decisions to fulfill the Contract.

"Although not many angels-on-earth remember their Contracts, those who do commonly have something special to achieve. On their higher Platformations, when sharing their LOve with a part of the world that will lead to the angel's specific Destiny, it is most intriguing how dissimilar each angel's ventures can be, but how similar their contractual pathways are.

"It's also interesting that, if someone is not an angel-in-the-making, and they probably still have other lifetimes to come, their very different soul pathway would almost certainly have very different contractual terms, not connected to LOve.

"A tenth question you can ask, again not always crucial, is, 'Do you feel or have you felt suicidal?'

"You've all got your eyes closed, so hands up if you've felt suicidal.

(Hands raised.)

"There's maybe over three-quarters of you today who have felt suicidal, and that's typical. Not everybody on an Angelic Path feels suicidal, but around 80% do. Research by the mental health charity, 'Mind', suggests that only about one in three of the general population think of suicide. So human beings with angelic souls are almost 200% more likely to have suicidal thoughts.

"Yes, on this pathway it's complex on early stages when you're away from highest most perfect LOve.

"You who are in orthodox medicine, psychologists, psychiatrists, healers, counsellors, you who are teachers here, those of you who maybe have become Samaritans or who have helped people in the suicidal stages of life, maybe this is an area of 'reasons for suicidal thought' to examine more closely in the future?

"Maybe an event provoked and caused the suicidal feelings. Perhaps it's far more profound than that. Maybe the clue for an angel-on-earth to understand is, it could be an issue of the soul wanting to get Home, back to perfect LOve and not wanting to be here, wanting to get away from the evils of humanity. Let's talk about this. And please don't worry. Help is available for anyone whose suicidal feelings are because of their desire to return to LOve, and who are still in need of support.

"Another question to ask, the eleventh, is about relationships.

"'Have you had troublesome relationships?' Hands up.

(Hands raised.)

"Everyone! Of course, almost everyone on this planet does.

"But the reason angelic souls have relationship setbacks is different. The big clue is that they feel beautiful, wonderful LOve deep inside their souls, and expect and want the same LOve within their relationships.

"Permanent LOve from relationships is usually impossible though, because no one can always be LOving. So relationship dilemmas develop, and maybe one day you will split up with your friend, partner or relative thinking they don't understand you enough, can't understand LOve enough.

"A follow-up twelfth question that might help you differentiate between the people with angelic souls, and those that don't have an angelic soul yet. 'Do you know inside you what real, perfect LOve is all about?'

"Please raise your hands.

(Hands raised.)

"Everyone, again, knows real LOve inside.

"And put your hands up to this subsidiary, thirteenth, question. 'Do you expect everybody to have the same force of LOve within them, and they don't?'

(Hands raised.)

"And everyone again! So angels on this pathway have complications with relationships. Almost always angels have very different relationship misfortunes compared to other people on other pathways, very different. Of course, relationships are demanding. But this is a special type, connected between love and LOve, that I'll talk about more fully in the Angel Story.

"To some people, certainly not to everybody but to those who have said 'Yes' to almost all the other questions, I also ask question fourteen. 'Have you felt pains in your shoulder blades?' I do not wait for an answer, and immediately ask the next question.

"Question fifteen is, 'Or, have you felt pains in-between, in the center of your shoulder blades?'

"Whether or not you have experienced your wings somehow is an understandably secret topic for most of you, but you are all on the same path, and anyway, you all have your eyes closed.

(Raised hands.)

"Probably much more than three-quarters of you have felt pains in your shoulder blades, or in the center of the shoulder blades.

"Most of you know that with any issue, I always 'come down to Earth first', to look at grounded, practical reasons for something that could be mystical. If practical reasons cannot be validated, then the mystical reason is more likely to be true.

"So in this case, I always say to the person, 'Let's get realistic.

Maybe you have a physical ailment. Maybe there's something to be healed. Perhaps you should see a doctor.'

"You have to 'come down to Earth' and check it out first with a doctor. Then if the doctor cannot find a diagnosis, I add, 'Maybe there's another reason for these pains. An energetic reason.'

"There is a good clue if you wish to discover whether pains in the shoulder blades are associated with either a physical condition, or an energetic wing. Ask the person, do they get those pains when they share angelic LOve in any way at all; or maybe sometimes even when they just think of LOve? Or do they feel those pains when they share LOve, or meditate on LOve, or whatever else they do with LOve?

"Question sixteen is, 'Is it when you interact with LOve one way or another that you feel the pains?'

"Raise your hands if that's the case with you.

(Hands raised.)

"Probably about two-thirds of you have recognized that pains in the shoulder blades are somehow connected to you and your LOve.

"Most of you who felt pains in your shoulder blades have eventually realized that is where your wings are growing. And it's painful because this beautiful, energetic winged force has to squeeze through a little hole, or a small energy gap, which isn't big enough yet, which hasn't developed yet. The wings are sprouting.

"There's a seventeenth, allied, question to ask, not because the answer is essential to whether or not I tell the person the Angel Story, but because the answer is interesting. 'How long ago did you start to feel pains in the shoulder blades?'

"The exciting thing is, if a person is not diagnosed with a physical condition, that started say three years ago with pains in the shoulder blades, then almost certainly it was three years ago when they started to develop their angelic LOve. LOve spreads wings.

"Then you can ask the eighteenth questions. Ask, if at the time when they first felt the pains, did they undergo a change? Did they gain more acceptance, a career change provided a more caring way, an attitude change to a more LOving one, or an interest in providing therapy or helping others in deeper ways?

"Almost certainly they will have shared their angelic LOve in the appropriate way that causes the wings to sprout.

"The nineteenth question to ask is, 'Have you known deep inside that you have a special, important or big role to eventually play to help our world?'

"Please raise your hands if you've known that you have a big role to play to help others one day.

(Hands raised.)

"Yes, everyone here knows they have a big or important role to play for our world.

"The follow-up twentieth question is, 'Do you know your soul purpose?' Or in the same vein, 'Have you found your singular reason as to why you are here?'

"The twenty-first question is, 'Are you starting to share your soul purpose with the world?' I don't mean a simple sharing of unconditional human type love, which starts as an early though important Platformation; I mean sharing your real reason for existence.

"Hands up if you think you've discovered that.

(Hands raised.)

"There's maybe about a quarter or a third of you like that today. That means about three-quarters of you know you have an important soul purpose to achieve, but do not yet know what it is. It's a secret to uncover. Later I'll explain the differences between sharing your unconditional human love in a general sense, and doing your soul purpose of Godly LOve.

"And lastly, the twenty-second question that perhaps you could ask, if the person has replied affirmatively to most of the other questions, is, 'Do you believe or know you have a purpose beyond your soul purpose?' Few will answer 'Yes' to this question, as most angels you meet will still be learning about purpose.

"Those are the questions to ask. Don't ask all of them to everybody. If somebody says, 'No,' to the feeling of being alone most of their life, and of being detached and separated most of their life, unless they had a happy childhood or positive mental attitude that resolves feelings of being alone, there's no point in going further and asking more questions. Keep the secret questions and clues for someone who might genuinely benefit.

"If someone is still on the early levels of the Angel Path, they will not understand, nor be able to answer, questions relevant to those on higher Platformations.

"If someone answers the angelic questions affirmatively, and it seems right that only good can come to you or them through sharing the angelic secrets and clues to their lives, you can relate the Angel Story.

"But only if it's right."

The Angel Story Introduction

"I'm going to tell you the Angel Story, an outline of the path an angel treads on Earth. Some of you have heard part of it. Some of you have heard only a tiny part.

"Although I've told the story privately, one-to-one, with someone I've met by 'chance', a synopsis of the story is usually told to many at once during a lunchtime or evening break for about 45 minutes, when it seems as if an angelic soul group has arrived for a therapy, spiritual, or other course. But the story is only told to those on the class who answered 'Yes' to most of the previous questions.

"I've also lectured on the Angel Story in Beverly Hills, USA, Malaysia, Australia, UK, Dubai, and so on, and at Mind, Body, Soul Festivals. For example, in Mexico City's World Trade Center, so many people lined up for the lecture entitled, 'Angels on Earth', over 100 people could not get in. Organizers had to create a cordoned-off area for a second 'Angels on Earth' lecture. It just shows how many people are interested in this subject. Interestingly, a high proportion of attendees were angels-on-earth, attracted by the lecture title.

"Due to lack of time in a busy diary, though, I haven't yet had a chance to explain the Angel Story fully to anybody.

"From this story, you can evolve. You can share knowledge, secrets, and clues on how to progress. You can share various Godly LOves and human loves, and try to help other angels develop.

"From this story, you'll peek at the peak of your souls' paths."

Chapter 2

Pre-birth

At Oneness With LOve

"The story starts with explaining how, at a time before this lifetime, your soul was with whatever you call God.

"Before you came down, your soul was with oneness, with the Supreme Soul, with ultra-perfection, with the highest, most perfectly divine LOve. Your soul was with the wholesome beauty of God within the universe.

"Not many people remember being at one so far back in time, but a few do.

"Hands up if you remember being with the oneness of God or the universe before making your Contract.

(Hands raised.)

"Yes, very few remember that far back, but some of you do remember the beauty. You've probably kept it a secret from most people though, because you know they almost certainly cannot understand, and are likely to laugh, or make a condescending comment.

"The clue for you though is, of course, you didn't feel alone when you were at one with such beautiful perfection; of course, you didn't feel alone. How could you possibly feel alone when you were with so much that was as supremely LOving as you and God being at one together?

"At that time, you felt and experienced only gorgeously comforting sensations. There was relaxation, calm, peace, happiness, joy, bliss, ecstasy, rapture.

"How could you possibly feel separated or detached when you had a connection to everything ultra-positive in the universe?

"Everything was perfect then. You felt LOve of divine forces.

"Although you had no wants, you felt LOvingly wanted.

"Although you had no needs, you felt LOvingly needed.

"There was no yearning for Godly LOve because you were at one with Godly LOve.

"You felt the ecstasy of freedom within a Godly framework.

"Then, one day, you feel it right to accept to break away from your loving group. You do so willingly, happily, knowing that somehow this is important to do, not yet understanding what it means to be human."

The Semi-Secret Contract

"At some point you make a decision, a life Contract, to come down and be born into a human body on Earth.

"The contract is semi-secretive because although not many of you remember making the Contract, I've talked with some of you privately who do remember making your Contract.

"Normally three other beings are there. They know about the life you are due to lead. Those of you who remember, could see. They might be your three chief lifetime guides, yours, your Earth-mother's, and your Earth-father's. Sometimes, the one for you is called your Guardian Angel, or Doorkeeper, or Gatekeeper, whose responsibility becomes to guide you towards fulfilling your contractual terms and in so doing to facilitate relevant and necessary experiences that will help your Destiny unfold.

"Occasionally a fourth being is present who will become an essential human guide to you on Earth. In some circumstances, you may have additional guides with specific responsibilities to help you along specialist pathways.

"The beings explain why you are about to be born on Earth, and what your previous lifetimes, if any, hadn't resolved, that need to be resolved in this next and perhaps final lifetime. The beings then give clues to the life to come. They may explain the tasks you need to achieve, goals to reach, people to meet, interactions to have, important pathway choices, and your ultimate purpose of this life.

"Hands up if you remember something along those lines.

(Hands raised.)

"About 20% of you remember making your Contract. That is a very high percentage. For most angels, the Contract is a hazy unconscious memory. But for the 20% who remember, I expect you've kept it secret, and maybe told nobody, for fear they wouldn't understand.

"Those of you who remember your Contract may also remember the feeling you got with it; a knowing that you had to make this Contract, but wishing you didn't have to.

"Hands up if you remember that.

(Hands raised.)

"That is normal. All of you who remember making your Contract also remember that awful feeling of not really wanting to, don't you? And probably you've kept that a secret from at least most of your friends and family too?

"Yes, you had a feeling of knowing you had to come down to Earth but wishing that you didn't have to. You ideally preferred to remain in the LOving safety and security of divine oneness.

"But even though you do not fully understand, there is a slight, deep-knowing realization that to leave the all-embracing LOving warmth has an importance. Even though you do not understand, you sense that there's an imperative task to be fulfilled.

"Yes, I know from conversations with you, that is how you felt."

Déjà Vu Clues

"Once on Earth, glimpses of your Contract may give you sudden insightful clues to help your life. It's called, 'Déjà vu.' Déjà vu is when you are, in this lifetime, thinking, doing, listening, saying, or otherwise interacting with something, and it seems to be a repeat of something you've done previously.

"It is a repeat, a replay, a glimpse of the Contract you made.

"Déjà vu is a momentary touch into the fact that you've made it this far into your Contract, that whatever the déjà vu was about was pre-required for your soul to reach its goal, predestined by the forces that help you, a part of your pre-birth memory.

"Most angels-on-earth can't remember the Contract. Therefore they can't remember what the precise purposes of their lives are for. They do, however, almost always retain a deep inner knowledge that they're here for a reason, a higher purpose. They may feel as if the purpose of their life is to help humankind or our planet.

"Please raise your hands if you have a deep inner knowing that you have a higher special calling, or a big mission, to help humanity or our world.

(Hands raised.)

"Yes, you said that just now. All of you know you have a special calling or big mission to do. That is a semiconscious remembrance of the Contract, allowed by the higher forces to keep angels-to-be, 'On their toes.' This unconscious remembrance ensures you don't forget completely, and waste your life in hedonistic pursuits. You've been there, done hedonism in other lifetimes, you need different life experiences now.

"Your Contract can therefore be an immediate cause of a deep feeling of being alone and feeling separated and detached, away from LOve perfection.

"Déjà vu about these feelings, your Contract, or the Destiny for your human-soul life is very common, but without the understanding of why.

"Science explains déjà vu similarly, saying it's an experience through one of your senses that connects to an unconscious memory of something you experienced in your past, and that this provokes familiar feelings of having been there, done that. Well, these scientists are partly right. But I doubt many such scientists would take into account memories of the Contract made before birth.

(Laughter.)

"We've already found that only about 20% of you remember your Contract.

"But if you remember, please raise your hands if you've also had déjà vu.

(Hands raised.)

"Yes, it's the same 20%.

"And hands up if you know your déjà vu was a momentary vision of something shown to you in your Contract.

(Hands raised.)

"Again, that is the same 20%. Everyone who remembers their Contract, even though they've probably kept the memories as their own secret thoughts, knows déjà vu is a momentary glimpse of an important milestone on the path, a recognition that you're on the right track, that something to do with the déjà vu may be of crucial importance for your ultimate goals. And therefore, you should sit up and take notice. Is that correct?

(Hands raised.)

"Yes, those who know your Contract, you all understand this truth.

"There's another angle. Often there's also déjà vu of a part of the Contract when you had a huge feeling of being upset. That is because making the Contract causes a sudden realization that it's essential to come down to this beautiful planet called Earth, with all the non-LOving things going on down here, that may happen to you.

"Hands up if you remember being upset about this.

(Hands raised.)

"Yes, most of the 20% of you who remember your Contract felt upset at the prospect of the unLOving life you would have on this planet. You usually keep these thoughts secret, because who do you know who would accept that your déjà vu experiences take you back to that moment when you realized your Contract would take you away from LOve?

"Déjà vu can also be a sign that you are on, or not on, the right path. Whenever you have a déjà vu experience, immediately stop anything you are doing and contemplate the picture or thought in your mind for 30 seconds. You may then be able to embrace a strong feeling, a clue as to whether what you were about to do or say at that moment would take you down the best path. If necessary you can then use Free Will to change your words or actions to stay within your Contractual terms.

"If you remember your Contract, and remember that you didn't really want to experience lessons that are not about LOve, you may also recall your karmic thought."

The Karmic Thought

"Some of you have thoughts like, 'I have to go down to Earth. Oh no!'

"Hands up if you remember the Contract and remember thinking, 'Oh no!', or a similar type of exclamation.

(Hands raised.)

"That is just how it is. It's interesting, isn't it? Almost all of you who remember the Contract remember thinking words like, 'Oh no!'

"It's interesting it's never opposite types of words. It's never, 'Oh yes please.' It's never, 'I'm excited to experience non-LOving things on Earth.' It's only ever words such as, 'Oh no!' It's as if there's something karmic in phrases such as, 'Oh no!'

(Laughter.)

"But that's how it is. Perhaps it's the karmic realization of the necessity to release all of your karma, all of your unwanted stuff from your souls' lifetimes.

"Karmic issues are usually your secret because people can't comprehend something so mystical. It's not taught at school. How can they conceptualize something that might be a radical thought? What framework do most people have to fit you in?

"Some people remember choosing to come down to Earth as

opposed to having to. A few of them remember being elated at the prospect of experiencing a new life on Earth again, as their soul Contract was agreed. So far, I've met very few people who still felt elated down here on Earth. It's usually the opposite.

"Most persons who refused a chance to progress on to the next realms of existence, and who chose to come back down again, now wish they hadn't, and say that their lives have been not as easy as they'd expected when the Contract was agreed.

"Some people though are happier. Especially those who eventually become leaders, game-changers, inspirers, planners, or organizers for the new and better world to come. Although the first learning parts of their lives are still more often than not imperfect, one way or another, imperfections will be far outweighed by the joy they will feel being in service, helping others."

Clues To Past Life Relevance

"Somewhere between being at oneness with the most perfect highest LOve and making your current Contract for this lifetime, most people have other lifetimes. During these lifetimes you can learn a variety of lessons.

"Hands up if you believe you had past lives.

(Raised hands.)

"Almost everybody... And hands up if you remember any of your past lives.

(Raised hands.)

"That is about a quarter of you; good. But if you asked that to the average person off the street in a Western country, a high percentage would not even believe in past lives, let alone remember them. Although maybe there might be a higher percentage of reincarnation believers from a country like India?

"Because past lives are not within common knowledge or acceptance of the majority of the population of most countries, even if you remember some of your past lives, you probably keep them secret from almost all friends and family. You have no wish to be laughed at by people who could not understand, or who have not had similar experiences and memories.

"Angels-on-earth are sometimes allowed to remember more about past lives because remembrance helps your understanding of the soul task you are trying to achieve.

"Past lives may provide clues about your lessons to be learned during this life. They may also provide clues as to your soul's highest purpose in this life. I'll discuss specific issues about this later.

"Remember, a Contract is made before each lifetime. The point of this for all of you who have been specially invited today is, in your previous lifetimes, you learned your lessons well.

"That's an excellent clue. That comment should have an exclamation mark. You learned your lessons well!

"It's the opposite to what many angels initially think. You haven't entered this lifetime because you were not good enough in your previous lives, so you are now experiencing some type of karmic punishment.

"Maybe you still have a few lessons left, but in general terms, your past lives have achieved almost everything you needed to learn, and all that is needed for your soul's attempt at achieving the ultimate purpose in your potential final lifetime.

"However, for your prospective final lifetime, because you've done so brilliantly in your previous lives, one particular clause is added to the Contract."

Clues of Precise Conscious or Hazy Unconscious Memory of LOve

"The one extra, particular, special clause in your current Contract for your prospective final lifetime is about divine, Godly LOve.

"The Godly LOve clause is part of your Contract because in your past lives you've done so well you've earned the right to remember blissful LOve, to remember the pre-all-lifetimes perfection when you were at one with everything.

"Some people can recall LOve consciously, exactly, as if they were still there.

"Most people recall LOve 'unconsciously', as a hazy memory.

"Please put your hands up if you have a precise conscious or hazy unconscious memory of this perfect LOve deep inside you.

(Hands raised.)

"That is everybody.

"Hands up if it's an explicit conscious memory. In other words, do you remember making your Contract and, prior to that, consciously remember being at oneness with the perfect LOve of whatever your version of God is?

(Hands raised.)

"About one-fifth of you can consciously remember both making your Contract and being with LOving perfection. And that is about the right percentage. Although you are confirming that here, with other angels, you are likely to have kept that memory a secret from friends and family.

"Of you, hands up if you've had a generally good and kind life.

(Hands raised.)

"Almost all of the one-fifth of you…

"Do you see? There are two clues to help the understanding of your life.

"If you have a conscious memory of highest LOve and you remember the Contract, you will usually have had a calmer, happier life because you consciously understand the differences between the highest Godly LOve, lower human loves, and your life lessons. That means you will interact on Earth in relatively harmonious ways.

"However, you'll most likely have a very different and not such harmonious life if you have a hazy unconscious memory of at one time being with that perfect LOve.

"Hands up, please, if you've had a hazy unconscious memory

of being with the perfection of highest LOve, and that hazy memory has created dilemmas.

(Hands raised.)

"Probably the rest of you...

"Hurdles usually occur if you have a hazy memory of Godly LOve because there is almost always a contraindication with human non-loves.

"The combination of hazy unconscious memory of perfect LOve, and the conscious attempts at human love are baffling, because you don't desire lowly, human loves. You are unconsciously craving to get back to the Godly LOve.

"Hands up if you have a hazy unconscious memory of perfect LOve, and your life has not been good. Maybe you've kept secrets about angels from family and friends, but the essence is that you can't accept non-LOve and imperfection.

(Hands raised.)

"It seems almost all of you with hazy unconscious memories of Godly LOve have had a complex life, especially with friends and family. That is because you don't fully understand, and so can't rationalize, the inner conflicts between Godly perfection and human imperfections.

"And that is how it is.

"If you have precise conscious memories of being at one with Godly LOve, you'll almost certainly lead a happy life.

"But if the memories are hazy unconscious, an angel-in-the-making's life is likely to be more secretive, because they can't quite grasp the realities, and life can become more reactive than that of the average person.

"Let's discuss these issues."

When the Soul Enters the Body and Makes a Contract

"There are different opinions amongst spiritual leaders about when ensoulment occurs. Ensoulment is the moment the soul enters the body, and maybe also when the soul makes a Contract.

"For example, the Brahma Kumaris' founder stated that a Contract is made with God, in the womb, before birth.

"Paramahansa Yogananda taught in his *Bhagavad Gita* that the soul joins this plane of existence at the moment the sperm and ovum unite.

"These two seemingly incompatible teachings could be compatible. Paramahansa Yogananda's teachings suggest the soul 'joins this plane of existence' when the sperm and ovum unite. He does not state that is when the soul enters the womb, or makes a Contract, only when it joins this plane of existence. The Brahma Kumaris' teachings are also correct, that the soul 'makes a Contract with God' in the womb.

"So diversity of thoughts about ensoulment may not be incompatible with each other. Some of you in this room today have said you remember your ensoulment. And according to you, your soul has entered the body, and made the Contract, at different times to others of you here.

"So although Brahma Kumaris' and others' views may all be true, also try to respect the realities of you here. Because you have differing experiences and realities about when ensoulment occurs, diverse options might also be true."

The Contractual Soul

"Some spiritual teachers suggest that, during the Contract, the soul's spirit form becomes human, a male or female with hair and features prepared as it will grow in the life it has accepted. After the Contract, good clairvoyants or mediums may now see the human-looking soul waiting around one or both of the couple it allowed or seeks as its parents, with the same looks it will have at a certain Earth age.

"If only one of the couple consciously wants a baby, the soul might wait around that person, with the understanding that the other potential parent may or may not accept the soul as their child at some time in the future.

"The soul's learning has started. It can see and hear, and use all senses it will have as a human being including emotions, and understand attitudes. It can experience what it's like to be angry, sad, afraid, and so on.

"Emotional reactions and attitudes are an angel's biggest Earth lessons of how to interact more LOvingly with all of creation. And these lessons start in earnest as you view the interactions of your future parents.

"If a parent senses that you are around before you have entered the womb and made a Contract, a parent may become anti-parenthood; or the opposite, and become broody, and want to make love to conceive. Or some parents may sense you during the pregnancy, waiting nearby to enter the womb and make a Contract.

"During ensoulment, an intuitive parent-to-be may detect the incoming soul, and at that moment know whether their child will be a boy or a girl.

"Your chief lifetime guide may take a back seat after the Contract, when you're probably guided by the two other beings who were present at your Contract, the main guide of each parent-to-be. They help you understand who, why, where and how the lessons will be learned.

"Then the beings may leave you, only returning when there's an important situation that needs their help. You're alone, alone learning your lessons. And if you have connected to parents-to-be that aren't as perfect as you'd expected, thoughts of not wanting to fulfill your Contract might start seriously.

"Some people remember watching, feeling, sensing, or even hearing their time in the womb, and knowing whether they were conceived in love, or lust, or by accident. It is sometimes not easy to live with these memories. You may suddenly feel alone, separated and detached from the perfect LOve and beauty you preferred.

"Fears of your future may then start to rise, or anger may

manifest why you can't be with LOve, or depression may occur that you'll live in an imperfect world.

"Such feelings may also arise because you have not incarnated fully yet, and so you still have strong connections to the previous life. You recall previous life events, and may sometimes not wish those events to occur again."

Chapter 3

Childhood

Entering the Womb

"After making the Contract, there are various classic stages when it is possible to have a sudden memory of perfect LOve. Then a consequent realization can arise of being separated from that perfect LOve; and having to live on Earth in human ways with human challenges.

"The first of these impactful insights of suddenly being away from divine LOve can occur in the mother's womb.

"It seems common agreement amongst organizations that teach about the soul that the soul enters the womb somewhere between three months to the fifth month of pregnancy. Brahma Kumaris say during the fourth or fifth month of pregnancy. Some Islamic philosophies state that the soul enters the womb after about 40 days of pregnancy. Many of you today, though, have different memories of the point in time you came near to your mother's womb, or at the point of conception. Some aware mothers-to-be, like some of you here, feel the soul entering. It's the moment when the mother-to-be feels a quickening, a surge of life force inside her.

"Most of you angels-to-be won't remember entering the womb, and some that do will remember it as a joyful experience. But others will remember the feeling, 'Oh, why am I here? What am I doing here?'

"Hands up if you remember that.

(Hands raised.)

"About 10%...

"And put up your hand if any of you 10% remember thinking at that moment, 'Oh no!' or similar words.

(Hands raised.)

"Almost all of you at the Contract think, 'Oh no!' or something like it for the first time, when you realize that soon you will not be with LOve. The second realization commonly comes as you enter the womb. That's when you can also remember separation from highest LOve. There's a momentary realization as you enter the womb that this isn't divine LOve, this isn't perfection, and this isn't what you want.

"You feel the imperfect physical, emotional, mental, and spiritual speech and action interactions of the mother-to-be.

"You feel the genetically inherited faults your human body will have, due to imperfect chemicals in the brain and imperfect hormonal imbalances.

"You feel the ways you'll interact, the silly or inappropriate things you might say and do. You'll realize that you'll not be perfect enough, that you'll never be good enough in the eyes of the perfection of your God's LOve.

"And you know you'll have many other natural human imperfections.

"And then some of you realize that this life will not be so easy.

"For those who know this truth, your life may not be simple because you cannot connect your thoughts to the Contract. Thoughts are in the present moment. It's a moment of sadness, anger, depression, of some emotion that may last until you realize how to evolve away from human issues and into angelic Godly ways of life."

The Birth Process

"Some people remember being born, and as they are being born, thinking, why are they here, why should they come down to lead this life? It doesn't feel good. They suddenly feel separated, suddenly feel detached, and suddenly feel alone.

"Hands up if you remember being born and having those feelings?

(Hands raised.)

"There are almost 10% of you who remember being born and then realize you're going to have a demanding time, away from LOve and goodness. Do any of you remember having the thought, 'Oh no!'? Or similar language?

(Hands raised.)

"All of you who raised your hands to the previous question, you also remember thinking, 'Oh no!' or something like that. It's that karmic thought again, a thought that you've probably kept secret because you can't find anyone, even a family member, who could understand.

"It's just how it is.

"Sometimes the realization you're about to have a laborious life comes from traumas during your birth, the mother's pained anguish, the pulling, pushing and tugging, that doesn't feel anything at all like perfect LOve.

"Psychic midwives or mid-husbands say they can see small, bright, fluorescent colored lights circling above the baby being born. They say the lights are in beautiful harmony, as if part of the baby's soul group conversing with each other, having last-minute conversations with the 'chief' guide who will stay with the baby throughout its life.

"Occasionally the awareness of being away from the connection to highest LOve comes from your experience at the time that is similar to that of psychic midwives. You may know your ancestral hosts are circling just above, chatting to your chief lifetime guide for this lifetime.

"At that moment you may realize that the guides aren't even perfect themselves, that they are also on a learning curve, that they could potentially make mistakes.

"You know also that your imperfect guides may let impure things in and out of your life, sometimes by mistake because they haven't learned enough to resolve every issue that may arise in a lifetime of chaotic events.

"You may also grasp that when extreme needs to help you arise, they have authority to deliberately let fatalistic things into your being to teach you positive lessons, especially if you are not learning those lessons fast enough.

"Some newly-born souls realize lifetime guides have permission from higher sources to put your life in danger to help you find ways to reconsider your soul's reason for existence, and even to give you a near-death experience to help you understand and find the right track.

"I know many of you have almost died numerous times. Of course, organizing a potential death is only as an absolute last resort when your guides consider that, after many opportunities, you're never going to fulfill your Contract, and you need time to review your life, time to take stock of what you've done, and time to discover how you can change for the better. Those issues will be mentioned later.

"You, as angels, have probably figured out that normal human connotations of death do not apply. You realize that within the higher reasonings for the evolution of life in the universe, death is just part of a process. Death is simply to ensure you'll do your angelic venture on Earth faster next time around, or achieve your soul's Contract for this lifetime more quickly. Either way, death helps to achieve God's good works to prevent more suffering.

"These realizations and the conflicts between your new human perception and your higher soul understanding can provoke unconscious responses such as fear, sadness, or anger, which may last until you've gained an acceptable harmony between human love and soul LOve.

"So those times are the earliest moments that angels-to-be are most likely to realize the enormity of their life's goals, and their potentially grueling earthly tasks.

"Then start the Platformations of your prospective final lifetime, from birth to after death, the first being your incarnation period from birth up until you are two years old."

The Two-Year Incarnation Period

"After birth, you can't walk, talk or interact fully within your given environment for a period of perhaps two years. That is no accident of nature. It's by design.

"Most people have little memory between the ages of zero and two. It's a period for most of forgetting the past, forgetting the past lives, forgetting the Contract, forgetting the perfect LOve, and forgetting why you are here.

"This is a much-needed part of your evolution, for if you remembered too much, there would not be a lesson to learn. You would find easy tasks to solve, and everyone would know every answer to life. The lessons could have been learned 'upstairs'. You would not have had to be born.

"There's a more serious reason for not remembering the Contract. It's the simple fact that, if some people remembered too much, they might be adversely affected. And then perhaps they'd never do their soul purpose.

"Not doing your soul purpose is not an option. So, for your soul to come into your body, forget past lives and your Contract, to incarnate fully, takes about two years. You have to learn to get away from the feelings of being with perfect LOve, and more completely leave behind the freedom of being connected to everything positive in the universe. You have to learn how to move your new human body. And you have to understand what it means to be dependent on your imperfect human body, and other imperfect human beings.

"It's as if past life memories, including for most people those of ideal LOve, are frozen in time, and you're only allowed to learn the fundamental rudiments of human living, like moving, eating, drinking, and dressing.

"And although these restrictions may not be agreeable, most people don't understand or even realize the issues, because it's a two-year, unconscious, near oblivious state of growing into a beginner human child.

"Some babies scream, kick and are a quandary for their parents to keep calm. Of course, most are not yet in a potential final lifetime and are interacting on human levels, with baby-human needs of love.

"But others who are in their prospective final lifetime, some of you angels here, may unconsciously kick and scream against the incarnation period, wanting to get away from all this need for food, this changing of nappies, this earthly rituals, back to perfect peace and Godly LOve.

"I recall tantrum babies whose parents could never calm them. I would pick them up, and talk directly to them, soft words about their soul and the reasons why they had to be born. The words were gentle but honest. I talked of the horrible life they might have on Earth, the fun they'll enjoy, the beauty of helping other people, and doing great to help others, or to improve something, one day.

"The amazing thing is, every baby I talked to like this became immediately silent. The baby would stay completely still, and stare into my eyes until I'd finished. Parents were always astonished. Even though the baby could not talk yet, it was as if they knew, understood and appreciated every word.

"I anticipate that, one day, many parents will understand that a much-loved baby is not only beautiful to look and coo at. The baby needs their love, and LOve. Because even non-angels would feel better if they are LOved. And that is a far nicer start to their lives."

Two Years Old

"Most two-year-old kids are adorable. They came from God's LOve, and interact in simple innocence. They don't yet have adequate sensory development or human experiences. They may not remember or comprehend the sensation of feeling alone, separated, detached, or anything from their past lives, Contract, entering the womb, or birth.

"Instead they explore, see, feel, listen, touch, and smell. All senses are alive to new experiences.

"They don't yet consciously understand non-LOving humanity.

"They are beautiful souls, halfway between the Supreme Soul's highest LOve, and lower human loves.

"There are exceptions to every rule, but most two-year-olds interact with other humans in such beautiful ways that make almost every adult who sees them smile.

"And the adult's smile isn't just a smile. It's a recognition. The next time you see a two-year-old child toddling about, taking first steps towards human incarnation, watch how you feel. See how you feel while that child is acting his or her drama of the halfway house between God's Heaven and humanity's Earth.

"If it makes you smile, think of your smile. Does your smile hit you beautifully, deep inside your soul? It probably will, especially if you're an angel-on-earth, with memory within you of that blissful state of LOve.

"In fact, this state of being may need to be developed later in life, after going through the early experiential platforms.

"As a two-year-old child needs LOve, so an adult angel needs to learn to be like a two-year-old child, a halfway house between human loves and Godly LOve."

Three Years Old

"The next stage when people may realize that this lifetime may not be perfect, and they suddenly feel alone, detached, or separated, is about the age of three years old. At about three, as a beginner human, you start interacting more fully with your parents.

"You might have had beautiful, exceptional types of parents who tried to help you, to be kind to you.

"The thing is, you'll almost certainly compare one or both of your parents with the perfect LOve that you semiconsciously or unconsciously remember, the highest, most ideal LOve from before you were born.

"So childhood becomes complicated.

"Even almost perfect parents can rarely match up to that truly perfect LOve you know deep within your angelically developing soul. They often have to discipline you, shout or even smack, maybe to stop you putting your fingers in an electric socket, or to talk sternly to prevent you running across the road into danger.

"Discipline is not perfect, is it? That's not the LOve your soul remembers, is it?

"Then, many angels wonder what's going on. It's not the highest LOve you consciously or unconsciously know and want.

"For some angels, even from that young age, it can seem as if the land will slip away, as if there's nothing to be gained from being amongst such non-LOving people. You start to unconsciously crave a return to the perfection and connectedness of oneness of universal LOve. Then tantrums can start as you wonder why you must put up with this lack of perfection.

"And it doesn't matter, you know, with your parents, how good or not-good they are. Most of you angels-in-the-making are still going to have the same feelings, that the parents aren't good enough.

"Hands up if you felt your parents weren't good enough for you.

(Hands raised.)

"The vast majority of people here today… That is the truth of an angel. That is how the Angel Story is.

(Sounds of sobbing from the audience.)

"People sometimes scream when they hear these things. That is how it is. You can recognize the truth deep inside yourselves when you hear this story. You know deep inside your being this is how it is.

"Few angels accept that their parents aren't perfect, yet be 100% happy to have them as parents.

"Occasionally, an angel-in-the-making is lucky enough to be so LOvingly cocooned by their parents, so beautifully wrapped cozily away from earthly horrors, that they do not feel alone, separated or detached. They are immensely lucky to be able to feel connected and attached and at one with the family and the world at that young age.

"Feelings gained from your unconditionally LOving family will be akin to the conscious or unconscious feeling their soul remembers of pre-Contract LOve.

"Some angels are loved so beautifully, that their thoughts are programmed into LOve and goodness, and they rarely feel anything else.

"For the majority of those lucky angels-on-earth who had a happy childhood, it may not be until later in life when they can feel aloneness, separation, and detachment. Often this is in the teens or 20s when they start to develop relationships and realize they can't easily find a satisfactory replacement for a high LOve feeling outside their happy family."

Clues To Helping Three-Year-Olds

"Do any of you know a three-year-old child with tantrums? Do they otherwise seem a special child, bred with the ability to achieve, portraying an aura of love? Most parents would say, 'Yes,' to these questions. But children who are angels-on-earth are so unique you'll feel their angelic nature emanating from their bodies.

"What does an angel consist of? Divine LOve. And the highest possible human love is all these baby angels need. They need cuddles, reassurance, and gentleness. And then, even if they kick and scream because they are not enjoying their human experiences, they need more, and more, and then more cuddling, reassurance, and tenderness.

"To scold angels who desire LOve may affect them too deeply.

"Kind thoughts, kind words, and kind actions are the only

ways forward, to provide confidence that divine LOve is still around, that they can still feel a connection to beauty and perfection.

"Talk gently to them as if they are already an adult, because unconsciously they may hear and listen. Talk about anything, especially what it means to be a human being, in a soft, soothing voice.

"Explain your role in their life, how you won't always get it right, just like they won't always get it right either. Say that if possible, throughout their life, you will do your best to help and support any of their needs until they succeed at their chosen ways of life. Chat, even if they can't understand, or when they are asleep. Say anything that is truthful, and that could bring unconscious peace, understanding, and happiness."

Four To Six Years Old

"There's a particular time of life when most angels-on-earth realize they're different. That is when they first go to school.

"There you are, at school or preschool, playing with kids, and realizing these kids aren't Godly LOve, these kids aren't sharing LOve in Godly ways. That's not what you expected from other kids like you. And you start to realize you're different.

"Hands up if you realized you were different from other kids when you were at school.

(Hands raised.)

"Almost everybody here! That is standard. Other kids play, and laugh, and have fun. In a human way, this loving fun could have been good for you. You know you would have enjoyed this harmless, loving interaction.

"But other kids also taunt, fight, and tease. And you can't. Your type of LOve is idealistic and perfect. So you stand back, not wanting to take part, not wanting to hurt or be hurt.

"It's confusing to play, laugh, and have fun in one playtime, and then see teasing, taunting, and fighting in the next.

"This isn't your memory of LOve. It's especially confusing when your memory of LOve is hazy unconscious. You've no conscious reference point as to why you feel you can't play with the other children in the same ways as they enjoy.

"So without understanding why, you realize you were different in your school.

"Actually, this was almost certainly true. You were different from the other children because there probably weren't many other kids in your class on the same Angelic Path as you. Here's a massive clue as to why you feel alone, separated, and different. There is probably only one angel out of every three or four hundred people. So maybe there were no angels in your school at all. Maybe no children in your school understood LOve in their souls.

"Perhaps, just perhaps, you were lucky and had a soul group there. Maybe you found other young angels-to-be. But it's much more likely you were the only angel in the class.

"So you were different. And that's why you found it confusing on how to interact. That's maybe why you kept your thoughts of being different secret. You were different, but who could understand?

"Maybe you couldn't even understand your own angelic LOve nature.

"It's awkward being the only one around who understands and feels true unconditional LOve deep inside the God-nature of your soul, and who wants everyone and everything to be as equally LOving, when it is obvious they are not.

"At school you might have had few friends, or been a loner, an outsider, watching and not participating much, as others play, laugh, tease, and fight.

"If you were lucky enough to have many friends, the likelihood is that you still felt different. You still felt alone, even in a crowd. Somehow, despite enjoying fun at school, you also felt separated and detached away from the groups.

"That feeling of being different, being alone, could last most of your life, until you realize the reason why you are different.

"You are one of the few people around, maybe the only person you know, who can sense highest LOve."

Seven To Twelve Years Old

"As with many aspects of the Angelic Path, parts of this section may not apply to you. You may have been able to come to terms with the issues of living in an imperfect world. Or you might have shared your soul LOve in a way that didn't cause you inner conflict with the educational, family, cultural, religious or ideological programming that often goes on for a child of this age.

"Maybe you remember how you interacted from the ages of seven to twelve? For example, can you remember being processed into a system of education, family, culture, religion, or ideology, and although maybe you kept your thoughts secretive, you inwardly thought, 'This is not me. This isn't what I want to do. This isn't what this life is about!'?

"Do you recall being processed into education, and told to learn this or learn that, inwardly knowing that the knowledge you'll need for your life is different?

"Do you remember being given options to choose between different systems, lessons or philosophies, offered by different parents or teachers, and choosing the one likely to create most LOve and peace for each situation? Maybe it's not until a long time later you discover whether you made the right choice.

"Do you remember not wanting to be part of a system, not wanting to be part of a crowd, and struggling with how to get out of the processing that other children seemed to accept without a murmur?

"Do you remember being put into small groups, and trying to find friends in the groups, and discovering it impossible to stay friends too long with anyone because they're different to you?

They tease and make others cry. You know inside you the school groups are artificial, they don't understand nor cater to how you are, or the kind of LOve you feel.

"This processing into a system can be any system. It need not just be a school system. I've met angelic soul people whose parents were strict Muslims, Jews, Christians, Hindus, Fascists, Marxists, and other faiths, philosophies and beliefs. And they tried to bring up their child into their religion or belief-system. They do not realize their child is an angel-on-earth and has his or her own inner knowledge of what's suitable.

"Parents and teachers and others in authority, who teach a particular belief, religious, or knowledge system to an angelic child, rarely realize the child may only go along with the beliefs, not because they want to, but to keep the angelic peace.

"Or maybe the child's lack of mature adult understanding and discernment lets them believe that the system will provide the kinder way for the world, the better way for humanity. After all, they yearn for that superb experience. And sometimes the child will choose an option that might not be the best.

"Occasionally the child is 'brainwashed' into a political or religious belief-system by a parent who thinks they know best. Then the child with angelic potential continues to believe the brainwashed thought patterns. That is, until one day, maybe in their 30s, they realize that the unasked-for childhood-given system is not the main point of view they should consider, or need, for their own personal goals in this lifetime.

"Ultimately, whatever system the parents, school, politics, society, religion, or culture and the like try to impose will rarely be good enough for an angelic child. Consequently the child will often rebel openly, or rebel subtly without complaint from within. Because the angelic child knows, on delicate levels, whatever they may be taught is not the ideal, perfect Truth. They know that their way forward is through a different path.

"Even when so young the child can know, albeit hazily and

subtly, they have an undertaking, and that attempts of adults to program them into a way of life are not connected to their soul's ultimate lifetime goal.

"Some children are brainwashed in too-forceful a way into accepting programming. So it's also about this age that some children rebel.

"They refuse to communicate with some teachers, or to attend lessons, inwardly knowing their lessons are irrelevant to their lifetime's goal.

"They argue relentlessly with one or both parents, with their angelically pure understanding that their parents are trying to dictate worldly things that will be irrelevant to their Godly LOve path.

"They shy away from the attempt at being programmed into a religion or doctrine or belief-system and may become confrontationally aggressive, hyperactive, or attention deficit, or be diagnosed with a medical condition that is not medical, it is spiritual, emanating from their soul.

"You see, it's the Angel Story again. Behind all their interactions is the subtle, inner realization that these human lessons are about the LOve they desire and remember from pre-birth.

"In a severe case, aggression, hyperactivity and so on can become the norm. The angelic child can't explain to adults why they're aggressive, because the child does not have any conscious understanding of the differences between LOve and love.

"Anyway, the adults would not understand because the reasons for needing the highest LOve for a soul purpose are not part of any parental, teacher, priestly, medical or other training. And with no adequate communication comes childhood frustration and eventual despair.

"I'm not saying that every child like this is an angel-on-earth. There are of course many categories of children who are irritated by authoritative teachings.

"What I'm saying is that some children have a memory of real Godly LOve in their souls, and an inner knowledge they have a vocation in this world. Then they'll very likely interact in non-ideal behavioral ways because the only thing that matters to them is perfect LOve and how to share it.

"Then they'll choose the option that will most likely help them share their angelic LOve, based on knowledge from their upbringing. As most children don't understand their soul LOve, the most likely option is they will choose an injudicious option.

"In an extreme case, the angelic child will seem to adults as if they are the opposite of an angel. Their tantrums, their lack of respect for authority, their lack of interest in human tasks all combine to make adults think the child needs help.

"Serious help is only forthcoming from so-called professionals: school truant officers, school counselors, psychologists, social services, or even psychiatrists.

"This supposed support may not help the angelic child, because how many of these types of professionals have any training in matters of spirituality, the soul path, or the memory of pre-Contract LOve? And how can they advise on the LOving project that a child angel may know they need to achieve, a project that has a different motivational force behind it from any other 'normal' job on Earth? How can they assess that the child may be an angel? How can they diagnose issues with the soul?

"The worst stage is reached when some children even consider suicide. This type of angelically soul-filled child may believe consciously or unconsciously it's a way to release from the negativities of humankind.

"Unwittingly, the child may feel that suicide could return them to peace, get back to their real home where the only thing that exists is highest, beautiful LOve.

"Thank goodness, most children also realize that this is not the way to resolve their situations. Because somehow, even subliminally, they understand that they still have an important place to fill.

"Some angelically-souled children try to deal with non-LOving parents, teachers, and school friends. They try to make friends of their enemies, be kind to teachers other children dislike, and follow parental guidance even when it seems unfitting.

"This type of child is amazing. They are already doing at their tender age what most angels-on-earth try in their 30s or 40s.

"Even though they are not receiving highest, perfect LOve, they are sharing their LOve. They are ahead of the game, with a greater chance of achieving their soul path Destiny quicker, bigger, and better."

Clues To Helping Seven- To Twelve-Year-Olds

"There are standard ways to help angelic children with contrary types of thoughts. The first is to discern, to recognize they have a different understanding of how the world works. Their needs are different because of a deep sense that the world should be different. The world should be LOve and only LOve, in every diverse aspect of life. Therefore they may respond differently to discipline or therapy compared to other children.

"Although there will be suggestions for clues on how to help seven- to twelve-year-old angels-in-the-making, these issues apply to any childhood age group. That is because all ages of angels need two things more than all of the other types of soul groups on Earth.

"One, they need unconditional love shown to them at all possible times. They won't understand LOve-Based Living, but they will almost certainly feel the need to receive that warm feeling of higher LOve from others.

"And two, they need to be able to express or share their more Godly, caring LOve.

"Of course, everyone needs love from others. But if an angel does not receive beautiful Godly LOve enough, it can break their hearts, or create depression, anger, sadness, and so on. And strong feelings of being alone, separated, and detached.

"Deep within they know how they want LOve to be, how it **should** be, how they unconsciously recall it.

"Some angels-on-earth in the seven- to twelve-year-old phase, and some zero to six-year-olds and teenagers, can be helped by being offered constant and excessive amounts of LOve. It's mainly teens and preteens who are so LOve needy, but some angels on any Platformation could also be desperate for LOve. It's one of the few ways to help them stay in balance.

"No matter how much teens and preteens cry, or rage, or do inappropriate things, to discipline them, even if you consider the discipline to be gentle and well within the limits of socially allowable punishment, just a little discipline may make some angels worse. They feel worse because they see the futility of trying to find perfect LOve. After all, if they are disciplined, they are not getting LOve, are they?

"There are other ways, the ways of the pacifist, of negotiation, of peace. There are ways of acceptance, or of explanations about any human ways. A child like this needs to tread any road that will not lead to even the mildest types of confrontation, but roads to higher LOve instead.

"An angelic child on an early Platformation needs to find someone to share thoughts, ideas, action, and chat. Parents and teachers need to possess unconditionally accepting and loving ways, yet keep boundaries of good behavior. It's not an easy balance to keep. But if that balance can be achieved, then perhaps, maybe, there's a chance to overcome the hurdles.

"I've seen many pre-adult angels-to-be. Two were little terrors, belligerent and moody. I watched in admiration as the parents never complained. The troublesome children were LOvingly cuddled, kissed, and hugged until the unenthusiastic reactions to this life on Earth were kindly and sweetly nurtured away. Not once, but time and time again. Those children grew up happily, well adjusted, still with a confusing time ahead with the necessity of learning their soul lessons, but without any memories of childhood exasperations.

"I've also seen the opposite. I remember two friends who constantly confronted their young children, and argued with them, as if the parents will, one way or another, force good behavior into the child's character. And I've seen this not help. Not once, but time and time again. The angelic child is much more likely to rebel, to become worse, to fight with parents, to want to run away. One did run away.

"The clue instead is to help the child find peace within at least one relationship, somewhere, somehow, with a person who can offer human love, to explain human issues, unconditionally. The child knows God's LOve, but now needs to know about humanity, with all its goodnesses and faults, in a caring, soft manner that they can accept.

"Unfortunately, everything in life has different sides. Offering unconditional LOve to an angelically-souled child may not help the child's soul path growth in the longer term. That is because positive human love lessons on early Platformations may not have been learned. Then maybe, as adults, they will be shocked to discover the world is not as rosily tinted as they'd thought. This issue will be discussed later.

"So perhaps the best option a parent, or a psychologist or similar professional may choose to help a child who craves LOve, is to describe the wider variety of the faults of humanity. Miss out the ultra-worst bits of humanity though. That may be too shocking. Especially, explain softly why they may feel different to other children, and why other kids maybe are not so LOving. Explain with gorgeous, cuddly love and gentleness.

"At least the LOving child may gain a secure base within their thought processes about the world, from which soul pathway type lessons can be learned from future, not-so-nice human relationships.

"Another option for Please review whether a dash is needed

after 7 both here and in other 'age instances' in the text because there is already the word 'to' meaning the same as the dash? 7- to 12-year-olds is to help them express or share angelic LOve, even in tiny ways.

In other passages you have allowed numbers to be typed in full, such as:

'"Although there will be suggestions for clues on how to help seven- to twelve-year-old angels-in-the-making…'

As I am unsure which you prefer, please adjust in the final edit. The query about the use of the dash and the word 'to' also applies.

"I taught healing and spiritual classes for this age group. Occasionally a child would take to the class as if it was their soul reason for existence on Earth.

"One such girl studied healing when she was nine years old. She was gentle, kind, and absolutely LOving. Her mother is an angel, so recognized her daughter's need to share LOve. She gave her opportunities to do so, without being overly ambitious or out of balance with school or childhood play. This girl wasn't repressed from sharing her soul beauty and LOve. Within two years she had patients, including her teacher's best friend. She became known as a healer. If other children had fallen over and hurt themselves, or were upset, teachers would let her sit at the back of the class and use non-touch healing to help. She even came to one of my exhibitions and gave healing on the stand to a religious skeptic, who was dazed by experiencing her energy of LOve.

"A similar angelic child was a girl of seven who attended what she called a 'foot school' in her dreams at night. Each morning she explained to her mom that she'd learned a new foot point to press to cure another illness. One day she told her mother, 'Mommy, last night I learned about a point to press on your foot. If I press it gently clockwise for about two minutes, my night teacher said it will cure your back pain.' And it did. Her mother and grandmother did not discourage or encourage her dreams. They simply let her explore her way to share her soul memories of LOve, her Contract, and unconscious teachings. And she grew up as a delightful, happy girl, with the ability to help almost anything she decided. Her parents had nurtured her angelic soul needs, with love.

"I met another angelic child, a seven-year-old girl from Botswana, who knew color therapy deeper than all adult color therapists I've met. She was calm, intelligent, self-assured, and quietly confident. She explained that her knowledge about color therapy came during dreams at night from her true master. She said, matter-of-factly, her job on Earth was to master her master.

(Laughter.)

"Her knowledge and expertise was heightened because she saw colors inside people, and could tell from the shades of colors whether they were angry or sad. She said she knew when to run from a child because she saw red fire burn inside them that meant they were about to be horrid. She chose all her friends deliberately because they had pretty pinks or lilacs inside, and were nicer children.

"She knew what each shade of red meant, each shade of orange, and many others. She said she was now studying at night the meanings of different shades of purple. She has a vision.

"When she's eight, three-year-old children will come to her home where she'll teach them about color. She knows that the children's parents should teach two-year-olds the names of the colors first. Then when the children are three, she'll teach them how to stack colors on top of each other, to play with energies.

"Four-year-olds will learn the color that's best for their health, or to improve at schoolwork, and so on.

"She had an objective for each year. Eventually, eight-year-olds would be able to teach color healing in her school. Surprisingly this child hadn't told her mother, or any adult, of her gift, but could see I would understand. My task was to guide her mother into helping her child evolve her angelic LOve path, yet keeping the balance of childhood.

"These three children were different. They knew they were different, like most school-age angels. But they'd found a way to share their angelic nature, and were encouraged in different but appropriate ways by understanding parents. All three became far happier compared to angelic children who had zero support or no LOving understanding from adults.

"One that wasn't helped was a ten-year-old boy, a natural healer, and an angelic child. So I allowed him on an adult healing class. He said he was better than all of them. He probably was better than the adults so gently I suggested he might be better, but that everything on Earth can improve.

"Carefully chosen, soft words gave confidence to share his higher LOve in the class, and the adults a motivation to improve.

"His parents didn't care for his healing potential, or about his gift or interests, and ignored his need to share LOve. He became dissatisfied with school and life. Eventually he was confrontational then uncontrollable. I feel he would have had a different and better young life if he'd been encouraged to share his brilliant gift of LOve. He'd have had deep inner satisfaction within his soul that he was being of use, achieving his unconscious LOve reason to be on Earth.

"Look out for these special children. There aren't many around. But when you find one, without pressure of any kind, help them to understand how to share their memories of Godly LOve in a carefully coached way. It's just to help them. It's also to help the myriad people those children could help, even at their young age."

Chapter 4

Teens To 20s

The End of Dependence and the Start of Independence

"For most angels-on-earth the path starts at some point in the teens. Until then, most of you would not have had much of a genuine opportunity to express your Free Will, your angelic being, or your memory of perfect LOve. You would not have had much chance to share your Godly LOving nature with others outside secure enclosed environments such as your family home or school.

"Because of that, many of you may have felt imprisoned, confined, and have yearned for the time when everything can change, and you can be independent.

"Throughout the world and within the diverse interactions of all peoples, any changeover period has inherent chaos, until changes are understood and alterations to ways of life are implemented. For example, divorce usually creates chaos within a family; and the fall of the Berlin Wall created temporary chaos in East and West Germany. Eventually, the resultant repercussions become understood and steps are taken to resolve everything.

"Similarly, there are changeover periods in children. Perhaps the biggest change comes from when the child's needs change from being dependent to wanting independence. It's the change from the dependence of pre- and young teens on their family, for food, clothing, everything, to the independence of mid-late teenagers who often want or even demand to make their own choices in life. For some families this can be a chaotic time, a time when feelings run high and when parents and children do not understand each other adequately.

"It can feel worse for the average angel-on-earth child. That's because they don't only have to cope with complex issues of the hormonal changeover to beginner adulthood. They also have to cope with the knowledge of LOve glowing from within their souls, and perhaps according to their perception, the feelings of non-love showing from their family. •

"Children with angelic souls have additional burdens.

"They have thoughts or feelings of the LOve of God, the Supreme Soul, and how that conflicts within themselves.

"They may believe that they are not thinking, acting, or speaking like the perfect divine LOve they know.

"They probably think whether or how they can accept themselves as an imperfect human being, a being without LOve.

"They may begin their search for what eventually becomes a near-impossible hunt for idealistic LOve outside them.

"And they often feel lost, unable to cope, with no guidance of how to fulfill the unconscious yearnings of their souls.

"It's so tricky, a jigsaw of conscious and unconscious thoughts. Somehow angelic teens need to re-piece their lives into a new pattern, to understand the best possible way forward. They are trying to become adults, non-loving humans, yet feeling the Godly pulls of their LOving soul.

"This Angel Story probably cannot help most angelic teens. It's almost impossible to tell them the story, to explain their Platformations and soul tasks in a way they could understand and accept. It is so mystifying to describe how they could become an angel themselves, maybe it is best not to try any angelic explanation whatsoever.

"Firstly, the transition from childhood is confusing enough. For many teenagers, adding angel knowledge could confuse their already overloaded brains. The result for some could be inducing or exacerbating various adverse mental health conditions.

"Secondly, teenagers have not yet gone through experiences of life as adults. They probably have no context to relate to about the adult angelic Platformations they need to overcome.

"Most teenagers go through archetypal perfect angelic souls versus imperfect human bodily conflicts. That creates a lack of understanding that few can overcome, even with spiritual styles of guidance or counseling.

"One method to support such lost souls is to help them put the pieces together of transition from childhood to adult. It may not give them an instant cure, but it will probably provide them with a focus, a way forward, a process to aim for, to take the pressure away from the previous confusion."

Clues To Jigsaw Guidance for Teens Who Are Searching, or Feeling Lost

"The clues to help teenagers progress is to explain their lives at present are like a jigsaw.

"A jigsaw is a good analogy because the process may include memories from childhood, yet provide a method of positive creation for the future.

"Start by explaining you'll give them some clues about their life. Say, they need to make a jigsaw of their life. Ask, how would they like their lives to be in the future? Because they have choices.

"To complete their lives, to complete a jigsaw puzzle, they need to find the right parts of life, the right pieces of a jigsaw.

"They need to accept that solving a jigsaw puzzle is not always easy. And they need to accept that constructing a life might not be easy either.

"Like constructing a real jigsaw, some pieces of teen life may be missing and must be found.

"Some pieces of life may be unfitting, like from a different jigsaw, and can be thrown away. Some pieces of teen life may be discarded completely.

"And so the analogy continues.

"Some pieces of the jigsaw of a teenage life may be undesirable colors or patterns, and need to be changed. The teenager may change to a less, or more, colorful daily pattern for a better way of life.

"Some jigsaw pieces may be perfect, but are in a wrong position, and need to be moved around somehow to fit more comfortably. It's the same with teenagers who may need to review parts of their life they need to change, and to reposition their aims and objectives, their hopes and dreams, more happily in their future.

"Another piece may be the right piece of the jigsaw, but other pieces it needs to fit into aren't in position yet, so this piece should be put to one side for a while until other pieces are ready. Similarly, a teenager may have wants, desires and needs that may have to be shelved temporarily until something happens to facilitate their dreams.

"Then, after giving an overview of how to complete a jigsaw, explain each jigsaw step in more depth, in the context of that person's life. Explain it perhaps in the following way, but use language you feel that person may understand.

"'You're about to lead a life as an adult, and have many options of what type of life you'll lead. Do you want a busy life, a happy life, a relaxed life, an exciting life, or a life where you help others?'

"'It's like going to a toy shop and choosing a jigsaw. You can select one with dark colors and horrific images, or you can choose one with bright colors, and a beautiful scene. You just create the beautiful jigsaw you want.'

"'To create a jigsaw, you need to experience different pieces, see if they're right for you, and if they fit into the ideal jigsaw you'd like.'

"'Many pieces may be missing, so you need to experience as much as you can. How do you know a piece fits until you try it?'

"'For example, start new hobbies or recreational pastimes such as collecting something you're interested in, or any type of sport or music that you feel you might love. Search online and read through one of the many lists of hobbies or things to do.'

"'You might be pleasantly surprised at the hundreds of opportunities you'd never thought of before. Try something. Try anything. You'll never know how good you'll be at it, or how much you'll enjoy it, until you try. It might not fit your life and you'll then try something different, very quickly.'

"'Don't waste too much time on something that's not good enough for your life. Alternatively, you might find something that exceeds your expectations in amazing ways, and you could end up an expert.'

"'Other pieces of your jigsaw of life can include meeting new friends. Check out clubs and societies where you live, or online, and find people with similar interests to you. Again, it might not fit your life, but it might fit perfectly. You could find a friend for life. You'll never know unless you try, try, and try again.'

"'Consider ways to earn pocket money or wages. Even part-time work can teach and help you become the adult you'd like to be. You'll learn about other people's LOving and non-LOving traits, and discover how to deal with all sorts of misfortunes. You'll have a head start as a beginner adult because you'll have learned lessons about people early in life, in your teens. Even if it's waiting on tables in a cafe, you'll learn about all types of people, and how charming you have to be to get the best tips!'

"'Continuously think of new ideas of how to lead your life. There are many options. Maybe try different ways you could volunteer to help those in need. To help someone, to do good, is a wonderful way to feel good.'

"'From all of these, decide which you would like in your life immediately, which you want to throw away without further thought, and which you may put to one side and maybe use in the future. You can't find the right jigsaw unless you experience all of the pieces.'

"'Accept that things will happen in life, things you don't want in your jigsaw. Discard those options as soon as possible, so you can move on to find more beautiful, more appropriate pieces for your life jigsaw.'

"'Do not hang on to pieces that aren't LOving enough. Be aware though that, sometimes, what may seem like a non-LOving puzzle piece was only non-LOving at that moment. It might be more relevant later on, in ways you could not currently imagine.'

"'So you will need to be careful, and discern, as far as you possibly can, what is right for your life.'

"'As you experience different aspects of life, check each piece thoroughly, how relevant it is to the beautiful picture you're trying to create.'

"'Think about each aspect deeply. Meditate on each part of your life. Feel each piece powerfully from inside you. Then act appropriately to keep building the picture you want.'

"The jigsaw analogy needs to be continued in as much depth and creativity as required until the young person has understood.

"This is unlikely to mean they're cured. The beginner adult still may have to resolve numerous issues, and will still need support, guidance, healing and so on to help their development.

"At least they now know that unwanted aspects of life can be discarded, and they can keep searching for appropriate pieces of their particular beautiful jigsaw of life.

"This gives many angels immense inner peace. Angels may know they now have a method to find their soul purpose, and they can eventually complete the jigsaw unconsciously or consciously, to fulfill their reasons to be on Earth."

The Teens and 20s Search for LOve

"This element of the angelic path, that usually starts in the teens, may be relevant to angels of any age or Platformation.

"Certainly in early Platformations, depending on how you interacted with family and other figures of authority, your life probably won't feel like the perfect LOve you know inside you.

You are still mainly dependent on others, without any true Free Will. You may feel that something is not perfect, but you can't understand why. So you feel alone with your thoughts or feelings about God's highest LOve and the non-LOves that humans have on Earth.

"In younger childhood, most of you will not have understood the issues of Godly LOve and human love interaction. The teenage years are when, for most, this understanding starts.

"In your teenage years, there you are, starting to find an agreeable boyfriend or girlfriend. Many angels on the path unconsciously try to find a boyfriend or girlfriend who understands LOve, the highest LOve, not those human, dictatorial, ideological early earthly loves experienced in earlier years.

"Let's talk first about those who consciously remember LOve, what highest LOve was all about, and especially about those who remember when they were connected and at one with God's LOve. How does all that affect their relationships?

"Commonly, relationships are easier for most on their Angelic Path if they are able to interact adequately with the memory of being with LOve, and use that memory with conscious awareness in their relationships. They can be so aware of their memory of the perfect LOve, they know already they'll never permanently be able to repeat such a beautiful experience down here on Earth. Various relationships usually become more bearable, because they won't be seeking LOve they know they can't get.

"Although those luckier types of angels consciously remember and know LOve, and therefore they know what they're doing with relationships of all types, most angels-on-earth don't understand why their relationships aren't easy.

"That is because many more relationship mishaps occur if the awareness of being connected into the perfect LOve of the divine is unclear, if it is a hazy unconscious remembrance.

"That leads to the stumbling block of angels-on-earth trying to find a good friend or ideal partner. Usually, they want a partner like the idealistic LOve they hazily recall, but normally it's not a consciously-made decision. It's more commonly an unconscious interaction, with zero understanding about why their potential friends or partners aren't LOving. They think everyone they meet should be as LOving as them, but of course, they can't be. Most people are not in their last lifetime, and won't experience the feelings of highest LOve at any time in their lives. So there's a mismatch in the desires of what a relationship should be like.

"So there you are experimenting in your teens and finding boyfriends or girlfriends who don't interact with LOve in that perfect way you unconsciously remember and therefore expect. So some of you might split from your first partner, and try another one; and another; and another one; and another; and another one; and another. And so it continues. Splits might even happen with friends and relations.

"Most teenagers in the majority of countries go through more than one, maybe many partners searching for their ideal mate. That is how life is. But an angel's motivation for seeking a partner is different. An angel doesn't usually try to find a partner with whom to share normal human activities.

"For an angel, it's a different search. Human activities mean little in comparison to divine LOve.

"So here's the clue to your search; you unconsciously seek a friend or partner who's compatible with Godly LOve, to take the place of connectedness, unity, oneness and absolute LOving perfection.

"Hands up if you've searched through that process.

(Hands raised.)

"There are maybe two-thirds of you in this room today who went through that. It's like you're on a journey of an impossible holy grail search for highest LOve.

"Unknown to the angel-on-earth, repeatedly attempting to repeat the God force within, through a partner without, is special. It's a soul lesson, a way to show different paths of human loves and Godly LOves.

"It doesn't feel special in early stages though because you don't understand that a search for a perfect relationship is an unconscious search for highest LOve.

"You do not yet realize your life will probably ultimately unfold not through the human types of love to be found in a partner, but through your soul purpose of divine LOve.

"Anyway, when you meet someone, they're on their best behavior, and so are you. You interact LOvingly, trying to impress. Their best behavior may feel like LOve to you at the start. But they can't keep up their show of perfection, and soon have no choice. They reveal the imperfect human being they are. So you soon realize the person isn't perfect, the person has faults, and they're not enough like perfection of LOve.

"Now please put your hands up if you had many, many friends or partner relationships, nothing satisfied, nothing was enough perfect LOve. The relationships couldn't satisfy your soul needs.

(Hands raised.)

"That is normal for angels-on-earth; it is about the same two-thirds of you.

"This lack of satisfaction in a relationship is not easily controlled. You need an acceptance that you can never find permanent Godly LOve from a human; and skills to negotiate relationship hurdles. Otherwise your lack of LOving satisfaction may lead to many relationships or even many marriages.

"Some angels are very lucky and find a suitable partner fast. But they're in the minority, as in this group today, about one-third.

"The clue for most angels is to accept human faulty nature, to study ways of others, to care for those less fortunate, and to seek human love values.

"Practice those human love values. Then your angelic beauty

can LOve their humanity.

"Most angels don't realize that's the clue. Instead, when they understand that they can't get idealistic LOve from a person permanently, they find another partner only to repeat the pattern until, eventually, some people seek Godly LOve outside one-to-one personal relationships in many good or not-so-good ways.

"The different types of relationships in your 20s and 30s will be mentioned in more depth later. But before then, these issues create the potential for additional lessons."

Teens and 20s Hating Their Imperfections

"As with certain other lessons, this Platformation could be relevant to some younger angels-on-earth, or those in their 30s or even older, especially if they do not learn their lessons early or well enough. But if angels need to pass a soul lesson on how to LOve their human imperfections, usually the lesson starts in their teens.

"Teen angels are learning to be adults, yet have conscious or hazy unconscious memory of perfection. So they might develop spots, acne, blackheads, and other facial imperfections, and compare themselves to models, or try to look at least as refined or defined as their friends.

"Girls frequently compare themselves to pop stars or other kids at school with a better shape, nicer skin, cuter nose, fuller lips, or bigger eyes.

"Boys may look at sports stars or boys with bigger muscles, taller stature, or more handsome features.

"Developing teens soon see they're not as perfect as memories of perfection suggest they could be.

"All teenagers may go through such thoughts. But for most angelic children it's tougher to accept.

"Less secure angels can feel unworthy. They're not as perfect-looking physically, or not as perfect emotionally and mentally as they know they could be. How they look, feel, and think is not LOve, so they soon lose confidence in themselves and their abilities.

"Consequently, when such angels look in the mirror and consider their personal flaws, they may dislike or even hate themselves.

"They can detest their looks so much they deface themselves with facial pins, strange hairdos, unusual clothing, anything to take away thoughts that they're not perfect naturally. Of course, many people do these things for fun or fashion, but for angels, the potential motivation is a hatred of not being perfect enough.

"Some angel teens dislike their looks or life on Earth so much they end up with severe over- or under-eating disorders knowing it could affect their health adversely, and have possible risks of death. They want to die because they're not perfect, and nor is anything around them, and they unconsciously wish to return to perfection. But they often keep their fears and dislikes a secret, inwardly thinking nobody could do much about it anyway.

"Others repeatedly cut, deface, and deliberately injure areas of their face, limbs, or bodies. Some risk their lives by cutting their wrists or arms and are sometimes hospitalized, not caring if they die. Death would be an escape from dislike of their imperfect selves, and from the non-LOving people around them.

"Yet others hate themselves or this world so much they contemplate, or even attempt, suicide. An attempt at committing suicide is often a cry for help. But for angels-on-earth, it is not in the normal sense of the words, 'a suicidal cry for help'. Rather, it's a cry for help for someone, anyone, to understand their secret soul urge for perfect LOve. And if they can't get LOve on Earth, they'd rather return 'home' to where everything is LOve. Suicidal thoughts due to a lack of LOve will be talked about later.

"Of course, other types of people who are not yet angels-on-earth may also go through these issues. But the motivating factor for an angel-in-the-making is that your looks, height, weight, personality, whatever, are never going to be perfect enough. You want more.

"So you may self-harm, somehow knowing you can never be as perfect as the LOve you crave.

"You want to be a perfect specimen of a human being, but do not yet comprehend that perfection can only materialize permanently in God and Heaven, not forever in humans on Earth.

"Even stunningly beautiful or handsome angels find their flaws, maybe a tiny facial blemish that they blow up out of all proportion in their minds because the blemish doesn't match up to Godly perfection.

"If someone is beautiful or handsome, and is an angel who hates themselves, I say quietly and deliberately something I know from experience may help. Something like, 'Yes, you are very beautiful. But actually, you're just a bit of rubbish really, aren't you?'

"There is often a stunned silence. I'm maybe the first person to call this beautiful person a bit of rubbish.

"So then I continue, 'Yes, you're rubbish because your beauty will be discarded like an unwanted piece of clothing, and thrown out to be buried or burned. Your beauty is temporary, and inwardly you know the temporary beauty will not last. The only beauty that will last is the beauty in your soul.'

"And they usually nod wide-eyed but smiling, happy that at last someone understands.

"This issue that they are not flawless is mystifying for many angels, as the knowledge within their souls of how perfect everything can be makes it tough to accept the early, lesser forces of human love and human imperfections.

"So how can you have higher LOve for yourself?"

How To LOve Your Imperfections

"These exercises are suitable not only for angels-to-be, but also for people who do not yet feel they are angels-on-earth and who would like to develop their spiritual nature, or a deeper love for themselves.

"Look in a mirror. Do not look superficially. Inspect yourself. See every wrinkle or pimple, every patch of different colored skin, every hair or mole, and every sagging shape. See all parts of yourself as exactly as you can. For many people, this will be the first time you've ever seriously inspected every part of you.

"Then look in your eyes. Inspect them. Look through and beyond your eyes, deep into your being. And say to yourself, with the highest and most perfect thought possible, 'I LOve you.'

"Ask yourself, 'How did that make me feel?' If it made you feel good, repeat it the next time you look in a mirror or see a reflection of yourself. And then repeat again; and again. Keep reaffirming the affirmation that you LOve yourself deep inside your being, until you do. You will ultimately have reprogrammed your unconscious mind to accept you are worthy of LOve.

"But for some angels, looking in the mirror and saying, 'I LOve you,' does not make you feel good. You feel unworthy of LOve because you know you're not as perfect as you could be. How can you LOve yourself with such feelings of unworthiness?

"If you feel unworthy, try this. Look at yourself in a mirror and repeat, 'I LOve you!' three times, with deep feeling. But use a different emphasis on each occasion.

"First place emphasis on the word, 'I'. Repeat three times, '**I** LOve you!' Think about it. '**I** LOve you!' Think about it. '**I** LOve you!' How does that feel?

"Then say, 'I LOve you,' again, but with the emphasis on the word 'LOve'. 'I **LOve** you!' How does that feel? 'I **LOve** you!' Does it feel different from the first time? 'I **LOve** you!'

"And then say the three words a third time, this time with the emphasis on the word, 'you'. 'I LOve **you**. I LOve **you**. I LOve **you**.' Maybe that emphasis felt best?

"Analyze your feelings. Whichever emphasis felt best, that is the emphasis to use in the future.

"In the future, whenever you look in the mirror, feel deep within your being, and say to yourself, talk to your body, speak to your soul, with emphasis and passion, your favorite emphasis such as, 'I LOve **you**.'

"Maybe add phrases such as, 'I **am** beautiful.' 'I am **God's** child.' 'I deserve **LOve**.' '**I** am worthy.' Choose an appropriate emphasis, to one that feels strong enough to empower you.

"Write your affirmations on paper and pin them in prominent places. Each time you notice the writing, affirm the statement by repeating the words three times, with feeling. Absorb the words deep within you.

"Accept that this process may not achieve quick success. Persevere.

"Accept please, though, that you can reprogram your unconscious thinking habits by repetitive affirmations of thoughts that you are a real beauty.

"And one day you'll discover you've changed. You may suddenly realize you're different, and that you're like a butterfly coming out of a chrysalis. You are turning into a being more amazing and astonishingly gorgeous than you can currently imagine."

Teens and 20s Suicidal Platformation

"The suicidal Platformation could affect any age group. For some sad souls who were damaged by abuse, or who cannot find their path, suicidal thoughts may occur throughout their lives.

"Suicidal thoughts arise most commonly though in the teenage years and early 20s. That's when angels enter adult worlds, away from parental dependence. It's also when angels suddenly discover independent life isn't like the Godly LOve felt inside their souls; they feel horrible.

"The world is horrible. Horrible people with horrible emotions doing horrible deeds. Horrible everything! No one else seems to understand that LOve could replace everything horrible. So they keep their LOving nature secret. They simply want to get out of this world, back to the unconditional LOve they hazily remember.

"Some angels-to-be find life so burdensome they attempt suicide, not once, but many times. I'm sure some people do commit suicide, sadly, thinking they'll get away from Earth, and return to peace.

"Even if you're lucky, and are found alive and hospitalized, hospital staff cannot understand your real reason for the suicide attempt. How can they know you want to escape from what you perceive to be horrors of life, and return to a LOve? Maybe they can understand the 'horrors of life' part of your story, but how could they understand the perfection of LOve you crave to get back to.

"Even psychologists and psychiatrists can't appreciate your soul-driven motivation to return to perfect LOve. So nurses and doctors often give you little time, preferring to concentrate on other people, textbook cases they were taught how to help at university. Then you feel even more alone, even more misunderstood.

"Thank goodness almost everybody here is over the suicidal thought process. About 80% of you answered earlier that you have felt suicidal, wanting to get back to peace. Most of you 80% will have got through this suicidal Platformation. You rejected the suicidal thoughts because you knew that even if you succeeded in committing suicide, it wouldn't help you. You knew you'd have to return down here to Earth anyway and do it again.

"Hands up if you felt like that.

(Hands raised.)

"Yes, about 80% again…

"No matter how suicidal you felt, or how many failed suicidal attempts you've had, you knew that if you'd killed yourself, you would have had to return anyway, to come back down to Earth to start again, to learn essential lessons for your soul's progression.

"So what's the point? You might as well go through the process in this life, no matter how trying it is.

"Hands up if you've realized that.•

(Hands raised.)

"Almost everybody has. You can, through perseverance, get through this awful phase. You can release suicidal thoughts. And you can evolve to a higher Platformation.

"You all have your eyes closed. How many of you are today still feeling suicidal?

"Three of you… Let's chat after, to discuss the issues. You won't be alone now, not anymore. You have people around you who understand; angels around you who have been there, tried that already. I will connect you and provide all the support you need.

"It doesn't matter how you feel now; know you'll go through this Platformation to reach higher and better levels. There's a natural evolution to the Angelic Path.

"If it's almost unmanageable for you right this moment, remember these angels-on-earth around you today who have gone through very similar feelings.

"Like you, they may not have had non-angelic people's reasons to attempt suicide. They're more likely to have had energetic LOve reasons for not wanting to be here anymore, to get away from the horrors of humanity, and to return to peace and highest LOve.

"If you're an angel-on-earth, remember that, energetically, it doesn't matter about the human causes of your thought processes. It doesn't matter whether your suicidal thoughts are to do with your family, friends, trade, religion, culture, disaster, war, or this, that, or the other. These are just the superficial reasons that make you wish you were back with the harmonious LOve you knew before making your Contract to come down.

"The important point is, you do somehow go through this suicidal Platformation, knowing you have LOve to share. And you will eventually reach the next, higher Platformation.

"I hope that if you still feel suicidal, acceptance will come from today and tomorrow, that you need to stay here, to do your mission on Earth. Maybe form a "Secrets of Angels on Earth" Group to help each other after these two days, and gain support from those who have come through this challenging phase."

Clues To Overcome a Suicidal Platformation

"I'll repeat a few issues just mentioned because suicidal feelings are not always easy to deal with. Angels may wish to escape from any human issues they feel are unworthy and unloving.

"As there's only one word in most languages to describe all types of loves, an angel-on-earth is often confused. They somehow know they have perfect LOve inside their soul, a memory of what Godly LOve is like. But that doesn't seem like the love of their mother, brother, neighbor, boss or whoever else they connect with. And they can't understand why.

"So when other people can't provide ideal LOve, an angel may feel depressed, sad or another emotion, that may lead to suicidal ideas.

"On this Platformation, to make things worse, when angels-on-earth try to find perfect LOve in one form or another, they are rebuffed because the heavenly LOve they seek does not exist permanently on Earth.

"So they want to try to get back to where they usually hazily remember being in total calm and peace.

"The angel-on-earth is still living too much in the pre-birth memory of being connected to the perfect universal LOve. They have not incarnated fully as a human being. They are still operating as a soul of LOve.

"This can be a conundrum because, until suicidal angels-on-earth incarnate appropriately, they will not be able to lead a fully human life. So they cannot learn human love lessons, or properly share Godly LOve.

"One student who is an angel-on-earth said that her father was suicidal and in a psychiatric hospital. No amount of counseling, drugs or therapy had dissuaded his suicidal thoughts. Last week I suggested she ask him the Angelic Questions.

"Today her email had good news. At least, it may be the beginnings of goodness in his life. He answered 'Yes' to all Angelic Questions. He is a potential angel.

"I say potential angel, because maybe he's stuck. Perhaps he hasn't fully incarnated. Even at his advanced age, he's too much with the memory of Godly LOve. He hasn't grown through the Platformations, and his human life has made it too much for him to cope. He can only see the futility of human life without permanent LOve.

"He needs to get away from those idealistic thoughts based upon pre-Contract memory, and into his human body. He needs to incarnate fully.

"So how can you incarnate more fully? The clue is that, for some people on the Angelic Path, for those who consider committing suicide so they can return to peaceful coexistence with the universal LOve, they have to disconnect from Godly thoughts for a while.

"It's the opposite of what we try to do for most people on Earth who are on other pathways, especially those who aren't angels-on-earth yet.

"We try to help non-angels find their God, the Supreme Soul, to understand perfect LOve, because they do not already have an internal memory within their soul of what true LOve is. If we can teach them LOve and LOving ways adequately, they may overcome their Contract, and be able to step onto the Angelic Path.

"With suicidal angels, it's the opposite. They already know what highest LOve is. Trying to teach them more about LOve may make matters worse. By providing tastes of the previous

LOve existence, they crave LOve more, and it can sometimes lead to more severe suicidal thoughts. That is because the Godly LOve experience can't last permanently. And when they can't get LOve, suicidal thoughts may rise.

"The clue is to seek Earthly love, to reincarnate properly, and forget Godly LOve for a while. Hands up anyone here who has been through that process.

(Hands raised.)

"Maybe a quarter of you did that. It's the typical response. Thank God most of you here have found the way to incarnate fully and naturally. Thank God most of you here have found a way to progress on your soul paths.

"And, as a quarter of you found, how to progress is to stay away from anything that may remotely remind you of idealistic LOve. If you can stay away from LOve in any form, you'll not have reminders of perfect LOve that may make you consider suicide again.

"By staying away from LOve, instead of being too much at one with God and not wanting to live on Earth, you'll eventually reincarnate fully into your body. You will interact with other humans to learn lessons of love and non-love that will lead automatically to a better understanding and acceptance of highest LOve.

"This should not take long, though it depends on how deep your craving to return to LOve is. For the deepest cases, the remedy is to stay away from Godly LOves for two years. After all, it takes about two years for a baby to incarnate, so it will take up to the same amount of time for an adult who did not incarnate adequately to ensure integrated incarnation has occurred fully.

"During these two years, please have nothing to do with Godly LOve in any form.

"Do not say prayers, do not go to a church, temple, synagogue, mosque or the like.

"Do not do spiritual meditation, give or receive spiritual

healing, practice yoga, or listen to Gregorian chants or spiritual music. It would be good not to read the Bible, Koran, or other religious or spiritual books.

"Do not even wonder at a sunset, or God's creations in nature.

"Do not do anything that may provoke glimpses of LOve, or tastes of the beauty of where you'd prefer to be.

"Instead, do Earthly things, good things of course, but things without potential for experiences of LOve. Take up a new hobby, sport, or recreation. Join a club, society, or organization. Ensure it is fun, enjoyable, exciting, but has nothing to do with Godly LOve.

"Angels-on-earth will not like being told to abstain from LOve for two years. They will want perfection, they will desire divine LOve. They will want to continue with whatever 'helps them feel good', or gives them their highest feeling, the closest to LOve. They will crave to be back with the best form of LOve in the universe. And they may even hate you for suggesting they stay away from what they know is the best feeling ever, LOve.

"But do persevere. After explaining that, to stop feeling suicidal, they had to stay away from all types of Godly LOve for two years, some people disliked me.

"A typical case is of a lady at a Mind, Body, Spirit Show in Colchester, UK, who exclaimed, 'There you are! Two years ago I felt suicidal. You said to stay away from anything to do with God's LOve for two years. I hated you! But I felt terribly suicidal. Psychiatrists could not help. So I tried it. Thank you so much. I feel great now!'

"Another case was of a man who asked to attend courses to help his suicidal thoughts. After testing him with the Angelic Questions, I politely refused, saying he needs to stay away from anything to do with the highest LOve for two years, because the course may give him feelings of LOve and, consequently, suicidal thoughts to get back to LOve. He could have studied and used a system of healing that provided early, more down-to-earth frequencies, but he wisely decided not to do any healing at all, and incarnate properly.

"Two years later he phoned, saying, 'Allan, I feel great now. After having no God-stuff for two years, I don't have suicidal thoughts now. It's great. I'm ready to do your course.' I accepted the man immediately.

"Both these examples were from suicidal people from whom I'd asked the Angelic Questions. They'd answered appropriately, showing that the issue was not suicidal thoughts for human reasons, but for soul reasons of wanting to return to their angelic memories of LOve.

"This is how to resolve this angelic Platformation. If someone is feeling suicidal, providing they answer affirmatively to the Angelic Questions, if they stay away from Godly LOve in any form for up to two years, and if they explore the early, earthly forms of love, they should within the two years have incarnated fully, and be able to take up their human roles and begin to progress on their Angelic Path.

"Explain to them that, when they have come back into human balance, it will be good for them to seek their God once again and learn how to share that LOve with those in need.

"This lifetime for an angel-on-earth is all about creating the balance between human love and Godly LOve."

Clues To Relieve Suicidal Thoughts

"In the UK I was a Samaritan, available on the phone to help suicidal people. Common reasons for suicidal thoughts include grief, a medication side effect, or an attempt to escape from a non-LOving life.

"But an angel's suicidal thoughts are less of the human world, and more about the LOve life after this, the next part of existence, to be with nothing but LOve.

"It often doesn't even matter whether your friends, relatives, colleagues and so on are kind and loving towards you or not.

If you feel suicidal, your focus may be on how to obtain even better LOve from 'above'.

"So how do you know someone is suicidal?

"You listen to them during normal conversation for 'key phrases' like, 'I've had enough of this life,' 'There's no point in living,' 'I'm giving away all my possessions,' or 'I want to be in heaven with my dead parent.'

"There are numerous similar phrases that give clues that someone is considering suicide. Of course, it might be just chat, with no connection to suicidal thoughts. But you can't take a risk. Why risk their lives?

"So if you hear any such phrase, even though most people feel uncomfortable discussing suicide, it is worth exploring whether or not the topic is relevant.

"Here is a process that might save someone's life.

"First, in a caring, loving voice, reflect back the phrase they used, using a slower, deeper, quieter voice. For example, 'You said you've had enough of this life?'

"Wait for an answer.

"If they don't answer, pause, giving space to think.

"Often the person will respond by repeating back the same words again, but with the additional words that should have been there to start with. Such as, 'Yes, I've had enough of this life because (whatever the story is).' If they pause, wait for them to speak again. If they pause for too long, add softly, 'May I ask what you meant when you said you've had enough of this life?'

"Many scenarios could occur next. If needed, refer them to a doctor or suicidal specialist for help.

"If you feel comfortable, and if they are starting to discuss what's causing their suicidal thoughts, ask non-leading questions about why they made the comment. Their response will usually recall an event that they cannot cope with, and need to get away from.

"You now follow a simple two-step process.

"Firstly, ask questions about those events, but not because it interests you. Ask questions only about their comments. Keep asking questions. When they pause, you pause too, giving them time to think.

"Secondly, when it seems there's nothing to add, gently ask, 'How do all those events make you feel?'

"Asking those questions brings them close to their feelings. They may cry, and release the suicidal feelings.

"I've briefly discussed how to relieve suicidal thoughts because a suicidal Platformation is common for angels-on-earth. But, a BIG but, don't take risks with a life. If suicidal thoughts seem real, or if the events seem genuinely disturbing, encourage your friend to visit a specialist, or phone a suicidal helpline. Or search the web. There are many options available online.

"And contact an expert yourself, as soon as possible, for further advice if you have suicidal thoughts, or if you wish to help a friend.

"A life is worth saving. Saving an angel-on-earth's life, who could one day create a big project to increase others' happiness, might be even more worthwhile."

Teens and 20s Negative Addictions

"No part of the Angel Story is relevant to all angels, though many go through drug, alcohol, tobacco, food or another addiction phase. Sexual addictions can be a poser for some angels too, so I will talk about that when discussing relationships.

"The teens and 20s are the common times of life when angelic addictions occur. Addictive phases at later stages of life are more likely due to reacting to the loss of a loved one, or other event.

"In many countries nowadays it seems almost a normal occurrence for teenagers to smoke, take drugs, drink alcohol to excess, or have eating disorders. They do so for a wide variety of psychological reasons.

"For example, peer pressure encourages teenagers to do the

same as their friends, and take legal or illegal substances they may not have taken normally.

"Escapism feelings from a family or neighborhood is common. It's also common to want to escape from a non-LOving childhood. Using substances can seem to be the easiest escape option.

"And there's also the teenage need to experiment, including being anti-authoritarian. In a teenager's mind, it can feel they are trying to create independence.

"So, debatably, smoking, taking drugs and alcohol or having extreme food fads can be a regular, but maybe unhelpful part of teenage life. Even after teens take illegal substances, most grow up as normal human beings, playing a good role within their society.

"There's a clue here for teenage angels-on-earth who often have a different reason to smoke, take drugs or alcohol, or have food fads. It's because smoking, drugs, alcohol and food are ways to get fixes of LOve, to feel at one with the divine.

"Getting a 'fix' of LOve might seem strange if you have never felt like that. But it's how it is. The fix is a quick fix. It's not a fix like cuddly human love from one person to another, that might not be perfect. It's a high, a feel-good factor that's the closest feeling they've had so far to the feeling of Godly LOve within their soul. It's a fix for their lack of LOve. And they love it.

"They love the feeling so much they experiment more, drink more, eat more, take more drugs, continuously, unconsciously, unwittingly trying to regain and repeat the ecstasy of oneness with the highest divine type of LOve.

"But it's a quick fix. It doesn't last. Because, no matter what type of high this type of person gets from taking their substance, they will afterward have to come down to Earth. They must afterward live in this real world, interact with real people, people who aren't Godly, who don't understand the beauty of the Godly LOve they're trying to rediscover and readmit to their lives. So then comes conflict.

"There may be a conflict with parents, social workers or others around them who don't understand what they're unconsciously trying to achieve.

"Or there may be conflict with authority that only sees drugs as illegal, or alcohol as an abuse of bodies. How can they see the high LOve an angel seeks, or the Godly LOve reason for them trying to escape earthly complexities?

"Some angels-on-earth then flounder, and are trapped by their craving for repetitive high LOve connections."

Clues To Help Teens and 20s Negative Addictions

"Teen angels with addictions, such as to tobacco, drugs, alcohol or food, need a different type of support to non-angels with addictions.

"There is always some sort of overlap, but on average non-angels need logically structured programs that may help them find solutions that wean them off their addictions.

"Whereas angelic souls need a specialist who can use loving support, or a wonderful human friend, able to reassure that LOve will enter their lives. They need to know that their future will be happier, with better friends, better business, better life, better whatever. They need to know LOve will come their way.

"It is not easy to find a specialist or good friend who is competent enough to help when humans can only offer a lowly love, and these teens only have tobacco, drugs, food or alcohol, to give the highest LOve feeling.

"Teens need help to move on, to find any positive type of love instead of tobacco, drugs, food or alcohol. They need a type of replacement therapy, replacing unfavorable ways to obtain LOve, with positive human love options.

"Replacement therapies are special for each angel. Some seek community love through a church, mosque, or other place of LOving worship where they hope to find LOving friends. Some try a sport, hobby or recreation they love, to make friends to love. Some volunteer their internal LOve to help the needy, elderly, infirm or disabled. There are countless options. Find a replacement therapy that seems ideal and relevant for each individual.

"Some angels with an addiction that boosts their LOve systems can feel the conflict within, between their need for permanent LOve, and their need for an addiction that is not LOve.

"Then eventually they realize they should not keep trying to achieve an addictive temporary high. Instead they start to understand they can seek LOve of the divine outside of their being. And so one day they find replacement therapy options that make them feel better, that help them.

"For most angels-on-earth with addictions, the smoking, drugs, food and alcohol Platformation is a temporary way to seek the highest LOve. They can be helped by loving friends or professionals, or finding a hobby, sport, or recreation they love.

"Once they realize they can't permanently gain that highest LOve feeling through addictions to tobacco, drugs, food or alcohol, and when they find a replacement for the addiction, the inner soul knowledge of most angels will drive them forward to the next and higher Platformation."

The Dangers of Transference – Clues That May Help

"There are common overlaps with hating oneself, self-harm, and suicidal thoughts, compared to addictions such as smoking, drugs, food, and alcohol.

"It's common for angels to overcome an addiction, but then transfer that addiction to another way of life, to another, then another, then another.

"And always for angels-on-earth the underlying issue is a hazy unconscious memory of perfect LOve, and how they and the world around them interact with early loves that are far from perfect.

"So solutions may be to learn how to improve interactions with early types of loves.

"Although the guidance given on resolving this phase of addictions, and suggestions on how to move on from each phase, is what seems to be most useful with each solution, you may seek and find other options that may help, or try a cocktail of solutions to resolve the issues.

"Above all, if you or someone you know is an angel-in-the-making, and seems stuck on one of these early Platformations, maybe try to help them with one of these two options.

"Firstly, help them to understand their non-LOve humanity. They are a human being on Earth, not a piece of LOve in the 'heavens'. They need to get stuck into a human way of life. Whether they like it right now or not, it's worth a try to get them on track to better ways of angelic life.

"Whatever country or culture they're in, enjoy the positive things from that way of life. Try to fit in with their area of the world, and help and support people trying to improve ways of life for their population.

"Teens and 20s do not need to know they are angels. Knowing might bewilder them at a time of life when they are probably too young to understand. Instead, just support them in transferring their paths towards a recognition of a call to action. Help them with the caring, loving call they will eventually see, to help their fellow human beings.

"It might take some time for them to find their positive soul pathway, to choose how to help people in need. Just explain, time is something they have lots of. There's probably a long life ahead. They just need to start sharing their natural caring instincts.

"Secondly, help them know that sharing a human type of love with themselves and others is the way ahead, a learning curve to be achieved, before they can eventually share their Godly LOve.

"It may not be easy at first. It might take a while for your words to transfer their ways of life to positives. But if you choose your words carefully, and speak gently about the angels-on-earth sharing human love, angels will usually at least unconsciously understand.

"Without you even mentioning angels or souls, your humanistic words about helping others can provide personal confirmation to the teen that something bigger and better awaits.

"For inwardly, angels know they have a particular function. They must help something, somewhere, and that to do it, they will have to move on."

General Reminder To Study and Practice

"Regardless of what exists openly or secretly in your life, the clue is the same. You need to research different options to find solutions. And then you need to practice the options to see which solution suits you best.

"In the teens or early 20s most angelic people have not yet had enough life experiences to understand spirituality, or the LOve emanating from within their souls. Although a few may start contemplating such matters.

"But if you study well, and practice lots, you might understand that spirituality can help your life, and that you are simply a sweet soul learning lessons from life, as you climb your soul's mountain path to attempt to succeed in the search for your Destiny.

"Practice of the perfection of virtues can be an aim. That can open your divine self to the highest possible virtues. Those virtues in turn can provide willpower to beat negativity, doubts, and lack of confidence. You can be liberated to become who you were destined to be.

"Remember, some people will have similar experiences to angels, but that in angels there is a motivating force of LOve that others don't have. The Angel Path is a standard life path that others can't easily appreciate if they're not on the path. That is, unless they achieve their non-angel Contract, and subsequently join the learning curves of other angels-on-earth.

"But also remember, everything is how it is only for most angels-on-earth. Not every angel will go through every part of this process in its entirety.

"If you cannot understand how your inner LOve affects your interactions with others, or if you never use your LOve to help others, then, quite frankly, you may need to return for another lifetime. Luckily, most angels-on-earth recognize their caring, helping nature. Even without knowing they may possess an Angelic soul, they can usually find creative ways to use their sweet nature wisely, and tread their paths with flair.

"Some angels are quite lucky. They miss out some of the perplexing lessons, or even miss a complete early Platformation.

"Maybe they have already learned these lessons in a previous life and know how to accept or resolve that Platformation's lesson issues easily.

"Perhaps inner knowledge helps them learn their soul lessons of a particular Platformation faster than is common for most angels, and they can automatically move on more quickly.

"Or the country, society, religion, family or explanative help from someone they've met, or something they read or hear, shows them the immediate way forward. They might then have the ability to develop and act faster than other angels.

"Similarly, spiritual or soul courses that angels-on-earth attend, or "Secrets of Angels on Earth" Groups, can help them overcome the experiential lesson issues more easily than if they were by themselves.

"With one method or another, some angels gain the ability, willpower or strength of mind to take the appropriate action needed to resolve a Platformation almost immediately. They are lucky enough to then be able to move on to try to achieve the next Platformation on their Angelic Path.

"However, most angels have to experience the lessons of each

Platformation. Research, study and practice then become an important way of life to learn how to climb the pathway towards the peak of success.

"In general terms, that is a brief summary of the early Platformations on the Angelic Path.

"As you wander through your life you'll start to interact on your path automatically. God's LOve deep inside your being makes you feel different to most people you meet. So you will interact with humanity in a special and exceptionally LOving way that no one probably understands, including you.

"Although the early stages your LOving interaction with others might not show positive results, and could create issues, the latter Platformations of your life will be absolutely wonderful. I will explain that later.

"Yes, try to understand that the later stages of your life will be wonderful.

(Sounds of gentle crying.)

"Some of you have tears in your eyes now. Some of you may cry every day. But most of you somehow understand the later stages of your life path will be beautiful. These are beautiful dreams you can hold from now on.

"Hold onto those dreams with all your strength of mind. Because dreams can become reality, providing you overcome the early Platformations. Beautiful phases will be discussed soon."

Chapter 5

The 20s To 30s General

The Late 20s To Early 30s Counseling

"Regardless of whether they are angels, most people try to make sense of their lives. Counseling, therapies, psychotherapy, psychology, or psychiatry, can be needed at any stage of life. It's common to seek psychological help when a person, angelic or not, reaches their late 20s or early 30s.

"Angels-on-earth may hope therapy can uncover how to discern LOve versus love, or help them seek the objectives, plans, and Destinies of their lives.

"It is classic that therapy is needed in this age group to 'uncover why parents were not nice'. Angels want to understand struggles with parents when they were children, why their parents did not understand perfect Godly LOve, why their parents were so imperfect.

"Please put up your hands if you sought therapy about the relationship with your parents.

(Hands raised.)

"About three-quarters of you. So only about a quarter of you are happy with your parents or didn't bother to seek help.

"Hands up if you did seek therapy, but that therapy did not help.

(Hands raised.)

"The same three-quarters of you, the normal response for angels. Therapy has not helped you overcome problems with your parents. I am not talking about a child's adult needs to resolve mental or emotional scars due to abusive parents. I am talking about feelings that your parents were not good enough because they didn't give you enough LOve.

"Counseling or therapy for an angel-on-earth about their

parents will rarely help. The clue as to why traditional therapies cannot help is because the training of psychological therapists almost never includes the potential that it was the child who caused the relationship to falter, not the parent.

"Did your therapist explore whether you were the non-LOving stumbling block? Did they consider you interacted with a lack of unconditional LOve for a parent's natural human ways? No... Children seem sacrosanct, like innocent lambs raised by non-caring shepherds.

"Maybe you needed therapy about yourself, not about your parents. You needed to understand that you had a LOving soul that your parents could not possibly have understood, and that children cannot possess adequate language to describe LOve. You needed to know how your LOve can interact with a non-LOving world. And you needed to comprehend what types of human love you can expect, or not expect, to receive.

"But therapists are trained to analyze a patient's past. They rarely guess that they should not discuss issues of being human, and instead talk about the soul's remembrance of LOve from before it was born into this life.

"Orthodox therapies cannot accept that some children's Godly LOve in their souls creates conflicts. It is not taught on conventional medical university courses.

"Anyway, interactions between love and LOve are secrets even to most unconscious minds. So you can't help therapists understand your issues of lack of LOve.

"So therapists can't even dream about exploring a soul's loss of LOve, and how lost LOve makes children feel sad, confused, depressed and so on. Instead the therapist compounds their patient's thoughts, confirming that parents were to blame due to them not being 'nice enough'. No one yet considers whether matters emanate from a rare child, a child whose angelic soul desires the perfect LOve it unconsciously recalls from before birth.

"I repeat, I'm not talking about criminally abusive parents. It's just that, even if an angel had the best parents in the world, you might not like the parents.

"Even if you had the best parents, you would not like the discipline they may need to use to keep you as part of a good society. Discipline is contrary to the unconditional LOve your soul remembers.

"You would not like advice. It's contrary to the oneness of knowledge your soul comprehends.

"You wouldn't like constriction to a playpen, room or house. It's contrary to the freedom your soul wants.

"Also, with so much divorce nowadays it's common that one parent or another manipulates a child. But the child is not wise enough to see through these antics, to see the manipulation of one parent who is using the child as a nuclear weapon to destroy their ex-partner. The angelic child is forced to make a choice and may take the route of love, not LOve.

"Therapy helps you understand that outside forces are only symptoms of non-LOve. So seek support if needed. You may find helpful solutions.

"But usually therapy fails to resolve outer conflicts between parents and others. You eventually need to become introspective with different, angelic thoughts.

"You then look at yourself and the inappropriate ways you interact with other people and the world.

"Then one day you start to realize that your need for perfection is unrealistic because your soul knows true LOve, of which others can usually only dream.

"This kick-starts understanding for many angels."

Clues To the 20s and 30s Search for LOve Through Religion, Philosophy, etc.

"Compared to addictions, a more positive way that angelic souls seek LOve is to study and practice positive ways of life, options that lift their thoughts and spirits higher towards LOve. For example, interests in a religion, yoga, art, meditation, philosophy, martial arts, or therapy.

"Some people flit from one to the other. For example, it is common to move from religion to religion, thinking that one day they'll find a religion that gives the LOve they know inside. But sooner or later they realize that people in the church, synagogue, mosque, temple and so on aren't very nice. They're not LOving. And if the people aren't LOving, the religion can't be the LOve they sought. Then they try the next religion.

"The same process goes for philosophies like Marxism or communism. Many people flirt with such philosophies trying to find the perfect option that will provide the LOve they seek.

"It is not uncommon that some angels become for example Christian, then Marxist, then Muslim, then Buddhist, then acupuncturist, then communist, then Hindu, then herbalist, then a Brahma Kumari, then a Jew, and then something else. Any or all religions or beliefs may be tried, in no particular order.

"It's not to say someone shouldn't be a Catholic, capitalist, therapist, Jehovah's Witness, or whatever. Some angels might find the wonderfully amazing LOve they seek, in a community that fulfills idealistic values. They might stay with one or another way of life.

"All ideologies, religions, therapies, whatever, can be vehicles to journey along your soul's road. Everything can be a sublime path to be LOvingly experienced.

"But here's a clue for you angels-on-earth on this part of the path. Don't attend a meeting once a week and then forget it for the rest of the week. Enjoy a daily commitment to your chosen path. That will improve the self, achieve God's needs on Earth, and fill you with human love worldliness.

"Open up discussions. Discuss human types of love and non-LOve with those close to you. Discuss the aspects of people in world news. Discuss love in a pub, coffee bar, disco or nightclub.

Discuss love with colleagues, or in sports with partners and opponents.

"From these discussions, a greater understanding of the differences between love and LOve will develop within you, that will help your soul path in divine ways later in life.

"Glimmers of realization that your personal knowledge of love and LOve is different to most other people may peek from your consciousness.

"Whatever you choose, serve society throughout your life. Try your best. Do things well. Achieve the maximum you can under the limitations of the body, mind, and background you inherited from your parents. Succeed for your soul, and for your LOve of humanity and God.

"Find what works for you. Any faith or belief could be wonderful if you use it to share LOve. You may even try to convert family and friends into what you believe is so wonderful and LOving. It's gorgeous when that happens, because you have found a way of life that is LOving, providing you are not dogmatic and refuse to accept others' points of view if they disagree.

"Finding a way of life that helps people in need makes an angel-on-earth's heart sing with happiness.

"What though if, instead of using the positive views of the organization they LOvingly joined, they become a fundamentalist who denounces those who don't believe the same as them.

"If the person's viewpoint becomes dogmatic, they may refuse to countenance any view not compatible with their own, and eventually dislike anyone with different views.

"That can achieve the opposite of what their soul needs. They may not be promoting LOve.

"Then they may consider that people who are supposed to be Christians, Jews, Buddhists, Marxists and so on, they probably don't have LOve inside them, do they? They are human beings, on different lifetime pathways, with zero understanding about

LOve compared to you.

"Most of them chose their religion and so on because of a crisis in their lives. They found something that could act as a crutch, to prop them up from their period of disaster. They are not like you. They did not choose their religion or path during a search for perfect LOve. They just wanted to support their moment of need.

"So most of you angels-on-earth soon realize that the religion or philosophy or whatever you join may not promote LOve. You'll soon find people there who aren't LOve, who gossip, fight, and cheat, and do all the awful things you hate so much.

"So what's the point of staying with this lot? You might as well try a different system where the people are more like the LOve you know.

"Hands up if you've felt like that.

(Hands raised.)

"Probably about three-quarters of you today. And so you keep moving around the religions and philosophies until one day you begin to realize that you can't find God in any of these religions or philosophies. If God was there, the people would be Godlier, wouldn't they?

"So some of you begin to understand that religion or philosophy may not be the answer to your prayers to find LOve in your life, and your thoughts turn away from these forces and towards spirituality.

"A big clue for most angels is to start to realize that the higher force of LOve that you know exists inside you will have to be found from a different source.

"On this Platformation, you might even think you may have to find your own version of spirituality…

"Hands up if you thought like this.

(Hands raised.)

"Yes, the same three-quarters of you.

"That is just how it is. This is a milestone on the Angelic Path to true awakening.

"You may begin to realize that each person has their own soul pathway. One key is to understand and practice some type of faith, maybe almost any type of faith that portrays goodness and love, in order to find their highest spiritual values. And that can include dogmatic fundamentalist teachings. As long as their hearts are in a positive place, and they do good works, all might possibly be well with their soul's learnings in their version of interaction.

"You may also start to realize that every angelic soul, regardless of any religious or other belief, is shaped by their individual version of a spiritual relationship with their God. It might not be your spiritual relationship. You might disagree with their chosen route and they may disagree with yours. But you slowly see they are enjoying their path, in their way, and it does not need to be anything like your path.

"You begin to realize that spirituality of one sort or another has potential to open the doors of your heart to restore and renew peace and harmony within all levels of your being.

"Then, utilizing the highest values of your learned religion or philosophy, you can start to tread your personal, unique path of light. You have begun to understand and know how LOve differs from love. You start to see the sweetness you could become. You can see ideal behaviors you could learn. The universal spiritual principles of God within your soul are stepping out of the shadows to be at one with your personal humanistic ideals.

"Spiritual lifestyles, including the study and practice of the chosen discipline, eventually become normalized, at an individual speed that feels good and relevant for each one of you.

"Studying daily nourishes your body, mind, and soul. Eventually you may realize, even if it is only within a few glimmers of light, that you are a spiritual student at the beginnings of understanding, and that you can one day seek opportunities to put your spiritual learnings into practice to help increase health, happiness and welfare of others, in a bigger and more effective way."

Clues To the 20s and 30s Search for LOve Through Meditation

"Angels-on-earth searching for LOve commonly try meditation. Initially, it's a way to focus their thoughts, free themselves from sentiments about events, and raise their consciousness toward the LOving almighty God.

"Depending on the style of meditation chosen, that's what happens. Meditation helps raise them to a higher level, toward a perfect combination of the highest energies of the Supreme Soul.

"Think about it. If regular meditation can help you be physically relaxed, emotionally calm, and mentally at peace, you'd automatically feel spiritually happier, wouldn't you? That will automatically equate to spiritual happiness.

"Then you'd be freed from being dragged down to earth by your imperfections. You are freed to rise to the higher, joy-full, bliss, oneness, or even ecstasy levels of existence.

"You may find a meditation that's right for you from three main sources.

"The first are Apps, YouTube videos and such like. Apps can guide your being into a calmer, more relaxed, more peaceful way of life. Search online. You might be pleasantly surprised at how professional and effective some Apps and videos are. They are often free, so you can try as many as you like until, hopefully, you find something that helps your inner need exactly.

"The second main source of meditations is via private classes. Countless different types and styles of meditation exist, including chanting spiritual or compassionate words or phrases, blanking the mind by gazing at a candle flame or imagining just one dot, and creating visions in the mind to reprogram your being to a better way of life. Breathing techniques are also often taught for meditation, such as holding the in or out breath for a certain number count, diaphragmatic breathing, or breathing for capacity oxygenation. There are numerous styles for each method.

"Private courses to learn meditation may cost nothing, a little, or a large sum of money. Experiment with as much as you can afford. Stay with what makes you feel great. You may find a breathing meditation class, for example, where the technique is just what your body, mind and spirit needs, for the rest of your life.

"The last main source of meditations is global organizations' meditational methods that are often ancient, or historically renowned and refined. These include Buddhism, Mindfulness (in psychology), Transcendental Meditation, and the Raj Yoga of the Brahma Kumaris. Many are free, and worth the effort for angels to check out, to discover if something will support their needs and lay a foundation for future progress.

"Angels often find LOve through meditation.

"Either first, perhaps the meditation itself can lift them from their early versions of life towards the higher LOve of the Supreme Soul.

"Or second, they might find LOve and love from other people learning that style of meditation. Students are often attracted to a meditation because they are seekers like them, even angels like them.

"It is a great blessing if an angel-on-earth can find friends like them who hope to free themselves from the shackles of their human lives, people who desire Godliness within themselves.

"That can give an understanding they're not alone, that others may go through similar lives. Their lifelong feelings of being separated and detached may be partially dissipated by the sweeter feelings of being connected to others who seem to be on a similar path.

"Try all meditations you're drawn to, if you have enough

time and money; try them until you find the best method that provides physical relaxation, emotional calm, mental peace, and a sweeter, kinder, happier, more spiritually fulfilling way of life.

"The Brahma Kumaris' method suited me the best, because it wasn't just about meditation. The Brahma Kumaris also teach about the soul, how to overcome human failings, how to be at one with the Supreme Soul, and how to achieve perfect, ideal values.

"Also, although Brahma Kumaris recommend their philosophies and practices, they do not attempt to tie anybody to them. They may have various philosophies they ask you to follow if you can. But essentially they allow you to walk any path you choose, including Buddhism, a religion, atheism, or whatever your developing heart seeks to try.

"So although you can try other systems of meditation, and perhaps gain a wonderful effect on your life and soul path, I will talk next about the Brahma Kumaris' version of meditation, Raj Yoga.

"Raj Yoga is a meditation that provides a direct connection to the Source of all things, to the energy of God, to the highest purity of the Supreme Soul.

"Raj Yoga helps your soul synchronize with God's LOve power, to gain resilience to an imperfect world, and embrace spiritual abilities to house your goodness."

The Brahma Kumaris' Raj Yoga Meditation

"Raj Yoga means king yoga, maybe because an aim of Brahma Kumari teachings is self-sovereignty. That is just a little joke. You need sovereign control of your being, to raise daily awareness toward the LOve of God.

"Early in their soul paths, beginner angels' human traits are mainly sovereign over their LOving souls. Depression, anger, frustration, ego, sadness, fear, jealousy, or any human feeling or want can take precedence over more Godly LOving traits.

"Raj Yoga meditation includes learning spiritual and soul knowledge. Personally I enjoyed the teachings, because they encourage regular study and self-practice at home. Eventually, you self-master human traits, and understand the better values of your and others' humanity. Then it is almost automatic, done without much conscious consideration or decision making, that you can evolve, and become the LOving force you seek, using the Godliness of your soul.

"When I started Raj Yoga meditation, rising to meditate at 4am seemed weird. I'm a night person. I did not enjoy rising for 4am early mornings. That was, until I could feel the silence, the sublime feeling of peace, in the atmosphere at 4am when most people are asleep.

"I began to realize that at 4am there is less chatter fighting for the airwaves. It felt like the frequencies and amplitudes of the numerous waves traveling through the air were lessened. It left space for thoughts to travel through, to seek and find LOve. I'm so glad I persevered, and discovered universal truths.

"I was taught how to meditate when talking to friends, riding a bus, or being noisy. Before two Brahma Kumari years had ended, I became automatically more spiritual, almost without trying, apart from simple daily practice during whatever I did, wherever I went.

"One day I realized that I was spontaneously more aware and alert, less tolerant of personal thoughts, and more tolerant of others. I was more connected in Godly attitude towards myself in particular, and humanity and the world in general. It was like magic.

"I recall that before meditating, I used to regularly see a businessman who had defrauded me. I would hope his business would fail. Horrible, huh? But I was young, a beginner angel-on-earth, learning lessons.

"One day, I saw him, and thought, 'I hope he succeeds in everything he does.' I was shocked. The thought was not cultured, not a logical decision. It was spontaneous, automatic, rising like a pillow of spiritual comfort from the unconscious mind.

"Through meditation I learned to focus. Every moment of every day I was elevated to more purity in thought, and more Godly wisdom in actions. I had, without really trying much except for the meditation, naturally become a kinder and sweeter person.

"Regular meditation raises you from early self-consciousness that traps you with doubts, fears and negativities. Through a self-realization of understanding true angelic soul nature, you reach the higher self-consciousness that automatically connects to the Supreme Soul, and a relationship with God.

"If you struggle with life or seek access to LOve, as Earth transforms its consciousness to a higher plane of divine perfection, you may find that meditation leads your true LOving self towards your Destiny.

"Through the numerous benefits of Raj Yoga, or the meditation you find best for you, you can be at peace, at one with universal God-consciousness."

How Do You Feel If Not With LOve?

"It is possible for human beings to reach a high frequency similar to LOve. That was shown scientifically, and described well in layman's terms, by the brilliant United States biophysicist, Valerie Hunt, in her pioneering book, *Infinite Mind*. She showed that anyone who reaches above a specific very high frequency in their energy body spontaneously has a type of Godly experience. Meditation, she showed, is one way to achieve a high-LOve frequency state of being.

"Some angels, though, have illnesses, duties, or ways of life that keep their vibrations low. They can't raise their vibration near the high frequency perfection of the LOve of God. So they may feel unloved and unLOved.

"That is similar to angels-on-earth who can raise their frequency towards the divine, but can't stay with highest LOve for long enough.

"Manic depressive persons, or persons with bipolar disorder, are examples. It seems to be a potential hypothesis that, when their frequency is high, perhaps through meditation or prayer or whatever, they are with the highest LOve they seek, and they become manically excited because they feel above the top of the world.

"But when they come down to earth, they are away from the high frequency LOve feeling. They sense they are separated and detached from LOve. That can create consequent feelings such as depression because they know they have to come down from the high Godly frequencies to live in a non-LOving world.

"It's similar to other scenarios, such as angels who seek, but can't find, flawless perfection from others.

"Then as a result, some angelic persons feel alone most of their life because they're away from the source of LOve that once connected them to everything.

"Other angels become depressed most of their life that they cannot feel delightful divine LOve permanently. Yet others feel angry most of their life that they're here on Earth and can't return to LOve.

"Or they feel frustrated, or sad, or some other feeling, most of their life.

"I have already asked if you felt alone most of your life. But what about such things as sadness, depression, anger, manic depression, frustration?

"Hands up please if you felt one or more of these **most** of your life and you feel, albeit subtly, it was because you couldn't find Godly LOve permanently.

(Hands raised.)

"Yes, almost everyone, about 90%...

"And hands up if you've tried counseling, psychology,

psychiatry or some other therapy, and they have not helped you.

(Hands raised.)

"The same number, about 90%. That's more than the 75% of you that were not helped with your childhood plights. You probably kept your lack of help a secret, not wanting to admit weakness or failure.

"That's right, standard psychological therapies usually can't help because no current therapeutic model can help soul urges and LOve desires, or the emotions and thoughts you have when you can't find LOve.

"Think about this though. It is easier to admit your personal emotional feelings or thoughts today, because you are in understanding company with people with angelic souls who have felt the same or similar as you.

"It's not so easy to admit the same things to a counselor, therapist or similar professional because you know they almost certainly cannot understand you and your feelings of LOve, or your soul's desires to reconnect to Godly LOve.

"Those comments are shown to be right by the 75% of you who disclosed your childhood and family LOve issues to a therapist, and are not understood or are rejected by them, yes?

"Other potentially angelic people who cannot feel LOve from outside them permanently for long enough, and who also cannot learn how to progress from one Platformation to the next, may not learn enough lessons to become fully-fledged angels in this lifetime.

"They may need to return for another life. In the whole scheme of the soul's learning in the universe, to return for another lifetime is not such a big deal. It is simply part of life's lessons, a process to be undergone, until beauty and oneness can reign supreme within them, and in all their interactions. This will be considered later.

"Angels-to-be need to get on with their lives on Earth. They may often need to go back to basics, to become more human than Godly, to lead a human existence they can learn from. Only when enough human lessons have been learned, can they move to the next Platformation.

"It is all too common that some angels-on-earth undergo emotional and mental health conditions due to not enjoying enough LOve. But you can rest assured that, one way or another, most angels do learn their lessons on this non-LOve Platformation, and improve dramatically.

"Even though angels-on-earth cannot release thoughts of the beauty of LOve from when they felt at one with perfection, one day they will learn their love and LOve lessons adequately. Then they can move on to a better, happier life, and attempt to help increase LOving perfection.

"This Platformation of feeling as if you are not with LOve is supported by groups such the Brahma Kumaris, who can provide understanding support of love and LOve.

"But angels often go on a maverick search, a long search for perfection. It's the legendary quest for the intangible Holy Grail, unconditional LOve.

"For most people who are not angels-to-be, this Holy Grail search can be personally sensational, revolutionary. It could help them achieve their non-angel Contract, and could lead to them making another Contract to become a potential angel-on-earth in their 'prospective final' lifetime.

"But those who are already angels-on-earth, searching for how to stay with the highest LOve permanently, occasionally increase their angst about being away from LOve.

"A search that is not satisfied, where you are seeking the holy grail of LOve but it cannot be found, can make you feel more alone, more detached, more separated, more angry, frustrated, sad, depressed, and so on. Of course you will feel worse if you know LOve inside you but can't find LOve outside you, despite all your best efforts to try.

"Anyway, for most of you searching, even if you reach the

Godly heights of LOve, you can't stay there. You have to do earthly things. You have to go shopping, cook, eat, go to the toilet, and communicate with people who aren't perfect. Even if you do those things perfectly as a human, it's human love, not Godly LOve.

"It's actually easy to connect with Godly LOve. I have techniques where almost everyone here could connect into that LOve-feeling within minutes. Many of you would cry in ecstasy.

"But that blissful feeling might only help someone who is not an angel-on-earth, who does not have LOve as a deep soul memory. It would give them an insight into how LOving they can become, and perhaps help them onto the Angelic Path.

"It would not help any of you angels today very much, because techniques of being connected into LOve could just become like a drug, making you want it more and more.

"Many methods could temporarily satisfy your hunger for getting back to perfect LOve, but because it's impossible to stay at the same level of LOve as the divine, you probably would feel more and more alone, depressed, sad, angry and so on.

"There's a crucial lesson here. The lesson is that angels do not need to search for the highest LOve from sources outside themselves because, like all of you here, they already know LOve deep in their souls.

"It's not the LOve from outside them that needs harnessing. It's the LOve within. This is such an important level, a staging post of realization between one Platformation and another.

"Understanding that it is LOve within you that can be focused on and developed is another milestone on the path to sharing that gorgeous LOve you have inside."

Chapter 6

The 20s To 30s – LOving Imperfection

The Imbalances of Humanity

"So you are searching for ideal LOve. Probably you won't find it through addictions, people, religion or philosophy. One day, you get it. You can't stay with LOve permanently. Your soul is LOve, unlike your imperfect human body. You may also realize that everyone are just souls inside human bodies, and, like you, all human bodies are imperfect. You get it, that nobody is perfect. No human can be the same as Godly LOve.

"Such ideas may arise as an enlightenment, that may shift your consciousness towards higher and better Platformations. Until you accept that you can't permanently stay with LOve even when you know LOve inside, because you and everyone have imperfect physical bodies, you can't progress to bigger and better ways of life.

"You need to understand that every person on the planet has chemical imbalances in their brains that will sometimes make them think, say and do stupid things.

"You need to understand that all of us have bodies of flesh with hormonal imbalances or monthly cycles that make us think, say, and do silly things sometimes.

"You need to understand that all people have physical, emotional, or mental weaknesses from genetically inherited traits that will make them think and say and do silly things sometimes.

"None of us are perfect. We all have chemical, hormonal, and genetic weaknesses creating myriad conflicts inside us. The imbalances aren't perfection, so angels often consider they, or people they know, are not angelic, not compatible with Godly LOve. You only see your or others' human faults and wish they weren't there.

"You wish that only perfection exists."

Accepting the Imbalances of Humanity

"The clue to resolving this Platformation is to understand and accept that because everyone has faulty human bodies, you and everyone may think silly things, or say inappropriate things, or do foolish things daily. I do. Everybody, everywhere will.

"That is unless your body isn't human, but entirely the body of a God and you are the one and only true God, which I suppose you're not?

(Laughter.)

"So all of us are faulty human beings, and will all fail sometimes unless someone is a God.

"Even those on the highest Platformation are going to fail sometimes.

"Even if you're the most spiritual and LOving being on this planet, you'll fail sometimes.

"Failure is a natural and permanent part of the lives of imperfect humanity.

"Until you LOvingly accept that imperfection is OK, it is just how it is, you can't have higher LOve permanently for yourself or others. You won't be able to move up to a higher soul pathway Platformation because you'll always be looking for, and criticizing, your or humanity's faults.

"Unless you have deep understanding that you and everyone are simply souls with bodies, human beings with faults, you'll not be allowed to progress easily.

"You need to admit you're learning how to accept your interaction with the Godly LOve that's inside your perfect divine soul, while accepting the fallibilities and silly things the faulty human bodies will make you and others do.

"Accepting your frailties and faults, and the imperfections of humanity, is as essential a staging post on your path as accepting you can't stay up high, connected with LOve permanently.

"You are a human being with divine nature inside you. But because of the numerous potential faults with the flesh and blood of humanity, while you are still in a human body, you and others cannot be Godly permanently.

"It's critically all-important to recognize and accept non-LOving speech, actions, anything, because no one can always control their body's chemicals, hormones, and genetics that can unexpectedly sometimes make them do or say imperfect things.

"Until you accept that imperfection is a natural and normal part of being a human, comparisons between love and LOve, and between you and others, will always be made. For sure, your thoughts will likely be unfairly imbalanced. You will unfairly compare your and others' human, early, imperfect loves, with the perfection you remember inside you, and cannot even strive to achieve. That means you can't love yourself or others in ways needed to achieve your soul's pre-birth Contract.

"And this unbalanced unconscious interaction with LOve creates puzzles in your life."

On Hating Imperfections in Others

"When you can eventually accept the natural imperfect nature of yourself, then it's time to try to accept others' imperfect human nature as well, because you probably perceive others' imperfections too easily.

"You can feel people's unLOving emotions, hear unLOving words, see unLOving actions, and you don't like it. You don't like any person not being perfect, not being LOve.

"I'm not talking about persons such as terrorists or abusers. I mean normal people, going about a normal way of life, where you too easily notice the slightest imperfection in their character, emotional interaction, or personality traits, and so on. You may even notice and dislike some aspect of their body.

"You desire perfection from others because you expect

everyone should be like the memory of Godly LOve and ideal perfection you know deep within.

"But of course, if you compare imperfect people to idealistic LOve perfection, few people will ever be good enough. And then your relationships will fail. I have only met a few angels who are lucky enough to find and enjoy brilliant relationships that satisfy their LOve cravings.

"On this Platformation, your LOving acceptance of humanity and all of its faults should include everyone you interact with, parents, children, brothers, sisters, grandparents, and other family members.

"Try to LOvingly accept your partner, neighbors, friends, colleagues, and those you meet through hobbies and pastimes. Everybody you meet, even casually in the street or at a party, deserves your LOve and praise, not your dislike and criticism. That includes angels, who also need your LOve. No matter how much LOve angels have, they will have human faults too.

"Some angels find snags with every boss. The boss tells them what to do, and the angel thinks, 'That isn't LOve.' Thankfully they usually keep their thoughts secretly to themselves and don't tell bosses to their faces.

(Laughter.)

"But some argue with bosses and get sacked again and again.

"Your nonacceptance of human faults is especially relevant to those who are nearest and dearest to you. They will portray their faults right under your nose. Their imperfections will be so obvious, you will easily spot how unLOving they are. Also, close relations have a habit of telling you how to lead your life, while doing nothing about their own. And that, of course, will not give you a feeling of being LOved.

"As part of your angelic learning curve, you may tell them their faults too. And that could lead to arguments, tears, fights, shouting, anger, sadness, or depression. In some cases, the person you love may not want to see you ever again. Sadly, choosing never to speak to a loved one again is all too common in families, often without attempting adequate discussion and resolution of conflict.

"The acceptance of humanity is an intricate Platformation. Rather like the suicidal Platformation, it's not easy to rise above. It could take many interactions before you eventually realize there has to be a better way to communicate.

"Acceptance is what you must achieve. That will be explored later.

"Hands up here anybody who cannot usually accept the faults of humanity.

(Hands raised.)

"The vast majority of you are like that. Of course, everyone, everywhere, interacts with other people. But for an angel-on-earth, the instigating cause of interactions, secreted away from your conscious mind, is that you expect people to be as LOving as your knowledge of perfection.

"So when angels-to-be like you are on the Platformation of searching for the highest LOve outside you from family, friends, colleagues or whoever, the search often makes you feel worse because neither you nor they can stay permanently in a rapturous LOve state.

"So then you start to feel sad most days of your life or feel angry most days of your life, or frustrated or whatever most days of your life. Some people cry almost every day of their life because their relationships aren't as ideal they were with the God force of LOve.

"Perhaps more sadly, most angels-on-earth in that situation don't know why they feel so sad, angry, tearful, depressed, or whatever because they cannot consciously compare lowly, human, imperfect love with the highest most heavenly permanent LOve that is only hazily remembered.

"Hands up if you've done that. Hands up if you've had a feeling inside of you that your partner or family or friend or boss or whoever can't match up to the LOve of God permanently.

(Hands raised.)

"And that's how it is.

"Everyone!"

The Worst Imperfections To LOve in Others

"In the course of leading a life, angels-on-earth will regularly meet, interact with friends, lovers, colleagues, spouse, family members, neighbors, sports partners, or whoever. Regularity of contact makes it easy for angels to notice others' weaknesses and non-LOving faults. If someone's darkest nature manifests in front of an angel, in the angel's mind, it could seem as if their world has collapsed.

"Everyone's faults and imperfections have to be, must be LOved as far as LOve is possible for you as an individual.

"But what about people who you do not know personally, yet are in the public eye? What about those who are regularly in the news and are disliked by many? Maybe you end up disliking or even hating them?

"Perhaps you hate the present head of the nation that's currently the most powerful on Earth. After all, it's historically fashionable to hate the most powerful country around at any given time. Maybe you would like to see that country brought to its knees. Perhaps you'd like a regime change.

"What would you do then with the next nation to dominate the world? Would you instead be against them and their leader?

"Perhaps you dislike or hate the people of a country close to yours who have fought you many times over the centuries. When will this dislike of neighboring nations end?

"Maybe you're against particular religions or ways of life, because they're not your belief. But how many times do people change their religious belief during their lives?

"Or you may dislike a sports team who are rivals of yours. What will you do if your team loses so many matches that they get relegated? Dislike opponents in the early division?

"Perhaps you hate the latest terrorist group because the atrocities they commit are against your ideals.

"Or maybe you support a terrorist group, at least sympathetically, because they hate the same regimes you hate.

"And so forth...

"Can you see? For a LOving angel, whatever disliking thoughts you portray are not the perfect LOve you seek.

"If you dislike or hate, you are entering a new Contract that is not LOve. It is a newly rewritten Contract, one you have created, from your non-LOving human thoughts and beliefs. Hate becomes your lesson in your new Contract. It's not like your original Contract for your soul, all about LOve.

"For some angels on Earth, these early human Platformations are the least easy to overcome. You can easily see what isn't perfect, and think you'll change things for the better.

"What you do not realize is, LOving the things you dislike is more likely to produce the positive effects that are so craved by your soul. LOve begets LOve.

"If you have a soul purpose to do, and if a part of the future of the world is in your hands, how can you resist the need to accept everyone and everything, everywhere, with a LOving embrace, in order to help them?

"But resist some people do. They resist for myriad reasons. In fact, for every human being that exists, there's maybe a different potential reason for them not to accept people's flaws.

"Try to understand, these reasons you create not to LOve others unconditionally are darkness. You're coming down to their level.

"By not LOving everyone unconditionally whatever their faults, you are spreading a lower thought energy than LOve. And that thought will ripple out to others who may unconsciously pick it up. Your lower thoughts of not accepting someone's faults may not bring LOve.

"These stages aren't easy. A soul path isn't easy. Your soul's reason to be here isn't easy. If it was easy, you could have learned everything up there with your God, couldn't you, yes?

"That's why you had to come down here, because it's impossible to learn these lessons up there. That's why it's a bit intricate for some people.

"But life becomes lovely later. Life will be even more lovely than you can possibly imagine."

Why LOve Others' Imperfections

"One clue to solve your dislike or hatred of others' imperfections is to accept that each imperfect person is, like you, on their individual soul pathway. It might not be your pathway. It might not be your path of LOve. It might or might not be the path of an angel. You might not agree with their human choices and ways of life. But they're on their learning curve, and need to resolve their own issues and find a route to their own unique Destiny.

"We'll analyze what you could do about this Platformation, because until you accept every aspect of humanity, no matter how good or not it seems, you cannot possibly have unconditional LOve inside you.

"Your soul may have perfect LOve. You may know LOve within you. You may want everyone in the world to be as LOving as you recall from before you were born.

"But if you can't accept others' faults because you can't LOve them enough, you cannot possibly have pure unconditional LOve on all levels of your being, can you?

"And you end up being as unLOving as them, thinking, doing or saying unLOving things about them. Do you really want to be like those people you dislike?

"Remember, you have sides to your nature that you are trying to analyze and resolve. Similarly, it may be perfectly OK for people you dislike to have a side they are trying to resolve.

"For example, someone who appears on the surface not

to be LOving may actually be an angel-on-earth like you, but learning lessons on an early Platformation compared to yours. So, perhaps you should not judge them, because you were on that Platformation once. Once upon a time you had to go through similar to get to where you are now. Maybe instead of criticizing, you can try to teach or help them, try to support them to rise higher towards your Platformation?

"Or maybe they haven't yet learned to control their humanity. But think about this. Perhaps without you even knowing, they could be really trying to improve. They could be seeking therapy or other help as much as they can. This could be an opportunity for you to help them improve even more.

"Maybe they're an angel-on-earth on a much higher Platformation compared to you, yet still struggling sometimes to control their worst human faults. Perhaps their faults you see were even worse when they were lower down the Angelic Path, with less understanding. Unknown to you they may have fought and won battles against most of their demons. Enough fights may have been won to be allowed a Dispensation by their version of God to move to a higher Platformation. God will know if they deserve a fighting chance to move upward, even though a human fault could be so ingrained it might never be fully controlled.

"Maybe they're not an angel and are still learning non-LOve lessons. Perhaps they will not achieve the status of being in their final lifetime in this life. They could be in the type of lifetime you previously experienced, to learn enough lessons to reach the potential final lifetime you are in now. Whatever, maybe think that they probably need your help and LOve. They might need someone like you to point to a better direction, a way to achieve something that is currently not in their dreams.

"Maybe they're not an angel in their final lifetime yet. But they may have almost overcome enough lessons already, and are close to having a chance of being in the last lifetime and treading an Angelic Path. Perhaps they have studied or experienced spirituality adequately enough, and with just a little more help from someone like you to support them towards a more loving and LOving way of understanding life, they will be allowed to write another Contract, and join the community of angels-on-earth in their potential final lifetime.

"Maybe they have an illness you don't know of, that makes them feel grumpy, angry, miserable, backbiting or whatever. Perhaps this is an opportunity for you to share your LOve and knowledge, or to encourage them to seek support from a professional in medicine or therapy. It may be a wonderful service to help them back to a more healthy state, so they can feel happy again.

"Maybe they're not in their prospective final lifetime like you are, and they're not learning lessons about Godly LOve. But the point is you are.

"Your life is about LOve. Think about it. If your mission is to share the LOve you know inside you unconditionally with our world, you cannot possibly do that until you have unconditional LOve for everything in our world.

"How can you say, 'I'll do my soul purpose for everyone and everything,' until you have unconditional LOve for everyone and everything?

"So you can't share unconditional LOve on a higher Platformation as you don't show unconditional LOve yet. It's probably a universal Law.

"One of the soul's big secrets is that you won't be allowed to do your soul purpose on Earth and share your LOve with everyone unconditionally, until you have unconditional LOve for everyone. Do you realize? That is an essential point to understand and remember."

Clues on How To LOve Others' Imperfections

"To accept others' imperfections, you need to stop wanting from others the Godly LOve and perfection you know inside you.

"This is an important point, so I will repeat what I just said. Please stop wanting from others the LOve you know from inside you.

"You and others cannot be permanently perfect because everyone has faults of imperfect chemical combinations in the brain, hormonal or monthly cycle faults, or genetically inherited faults.

"Also, no human being knows everything. Do you know your own lessons for your soul path development? Probably not! So how can you be disapproving of others who, like you, may not know whether they have learned appropriate soul lessons, and who still portray human faults.

"This issue of LOving to not loving someone else's faults is something that every person and every angel will have, one way or another.

"It is impossible to avoid other people, so, unless of course you're in a damaging type of relationship, which you should leave as soon as possible, it's better to learn about and accept others' faults LOvingly and unconditionally in your heart and your mind and your soul.

"Other people may not value your kind heart, kind words, good deeds, but to share your LOve with people who are imperfect is 100% a good lesson for your future path. It may help the other person eventually understand your LOve too.

"You need to see everyone, not as a body, but as a soul. You need to look at every person, including yourself, only as souls on a path, learning individual lessons as they tread different pathways up their personal mountain of life. They are like you, trying to find their Destiny, in imperfect circumstances.

"In future, try to see them not as imperfect people. Imperfections in a person are just their flesh and blood. See them instead as perfect souls.

"Angelic souls always have perfection; the body, mind, and

emotions do not.

"Angelic souls are always Loving; the body, mind, and emotions will not be.

"Angelic souls always purvey goodness; the body, mind, and emotions cannot.

"Angelic souls are everlasting Light; the body, mind, and emotions are not.

"There is nothing that Godly souls cannot achieve given the right circumstances, if you can overcome the limitations of the human body.

"Remember that everyone has a soul inside their human body. The soul is on its path, inside that body, with a Contract to fulfill. See everyone with a soul. Do not deny those souls chances to serve in their way.

"People's human behavior may seem distasteful to you, and be repugnant in the eyes of most peaceful and LOving beings. But if a person's soul Contract detailed the need to learn through anger, revenge, guilt or any other issue, then that soul inside that human body needs to achieve that Contract, even if that way of life isn't considered perfect by others.

"Please try to see the Contracts of others in a different light. See others' Contracts for their soul to achieve, not the human being. See the soul's Contract as simply another way of sharing God's LOve, a way that you and all other humans can probably never fully understand.

"Apart from the Godliness in your soul, you're not God. You're not even close to God, because of the veils that shut across the visions of your mind's eye and your soul. So you can't ever understand why God might need the success of the issues and Contracts of the souls of others.

"Look after your Contract. Serve yourself with LOve so you can LOve others easier. Accept that your Contract may have made you meet that type of person who's not so nice. Because whether you stay with them or not, how else would you have learned that lesson?

"This is a good time to join or start a "Secrets of Angels on Earth" Group where you can practice LOving others' imperfections, and they can practice LOving yours.

"If you as an angel cannot easily LOve other people, maybe you could just focus on LOving their positives. Most people have positive aspects to themselves. You'll find if you love others' positives, their virtues will take on a different emphasis, and become stronger.

"Then, as you grow in ever more unconditionally LOving ways, you'll gather evidence from family, friends and people in your Angelic Group for Evolving Souls about how much you change, with an increasingly beautiful temperament."

On Having No Judgement

"By the time you reach higher Platformations, maybe you'll have earned the right to judge. Probably you'll have judged others inappropriately, and learned lessons to earn wisdom about judgement. With the wisdom gained from experience, you are more likely to make good, logical judgements. We'll consider this later.

"But on this Platformation what you can't consider about someone who is imperfect is something akin to judgement. You have not experienced enough life events. So you are not qualified through the University of Life to judge.

"How can you judge if you haven't had many life experiences to make a fair and reasonable assessment?

"You're a soul in a body and don't have the perfect Law Books of God to refer to, for good judgement. You only have imperfect law books of humans.

"So how can you judge others when you cannot access God's Laws that may need imperfections for a purpose that's higher than your dreams?

"How can you judge fellow human creatures when you don't

know their soul Contract? They may even have agreed to be a martyr to help the understanding of those around them. Maybe they agreed before coming to Earth that they must achieve the very things you do not like.

"How can you judge anyone when you can't even be perfect and therefore need to be judged yourself?

"Non-judgement of others' faults is about developing spiritual LOve. Life is about not judging, and instead enjoying the understanding that you can share the beauty of LOve inside your being, outside you with others, almost regardless of anyone's human faults.

"People who are sad do not need your sorrow, or your anger if they're angry. They need your LOve.

"When someone seems imperfect, develop non-judgmental positive outlooks.

"Even if their pre-birth Contract was not about how to become an angel, perhaps they will find their way and learn needed lessons, and progress onto the Angelic Path.

"You have probably already gone through many lifetimes, and if this is potentially your prospective final lifetime, you know many things, consciously or hazy unconsciously, about LOve and your purpose, about your need to help humankind somehow.

"But human pathways are slow in learning. Compared to the vast knowledge of the never-ending Supreme Soul, you know nothing. You know nothing even if compared to the relatively little knowledge available to the minds of all of humankind.

"Do you get what I'm saying here? If you don't have LOve, your judgement could be tinged with non-LOve ideas, and that may be unfair on someone.

"So on this Platformation try not to judge another person. Unless there is serious abuse, simply accept whatever behavior as part of being human. Accept misdemeanors. Accept that people are, like you, human, and will always think, say and do silly things. Try to LOve them all anyway.

"Be part of Earth's community called human beings. Let things develop in natural, smooth ways.

"Then you can move on."

Timing To LOve Others' Imperfections

"Part of the lesson of LOving yourself or others is in timing. When is the right time to resolve your or their crisis? When is the right time to fix your or others' learning curve on that part of the path? When is the right time to help you or them move on?

"Answers to these questions are complex for a mere mortal on an early Platformation who's not aware of God's plans for their path, who hasn't had enough life experiences yet to gain wisdom to discern about others' ways of life, and who doesn't possess adequate angelic insight of the reasons for their existence.

"Lessons have to be learned at the right time, when you've gone through enough conflicts and interactions of life to gain glimpses of what your lessons could be.

"Lessons are baffling to learn on the early and middle Platformations of the Angelic Path, when experiences may be too powerful to comprehend the lesson.

"Anyway, while you endure early Platformations your God and LOve connections are likely to be weaker, because it's not easy to still focus on highest possible LOve.

"In other words, because your early Platformation issues continuously bring you down to Earth, away from high frequency divine LOve, it may take time to learn the needed lessons.

"This is the same if you cannot muster the divine LOve that's inside you to help yourself, and support those in more need than you. You can LOve anyone, and anything, anywhere, including animals, the environment, peace projects, or whatever might make this little part of our solar system a better place to live.

"LOve, though, can eventually help you escape from your various bonds of torment. LOve can move you along your path when the timing is right for your angelic soul.

"You do not need to fear the timing. Do not worry about how long each Platformation takes to resolve through the learning of lessons. Just play your angelic role. Help those around you to accept your human faults. Then you can improve your LOving acceptance of the faults in others.

"The timing may be right when the pre-determined time comes for your Destiny. The timing can be right when your human Free Will makes the choices on your soul's path.

"The time is right when you justify your LOve by fulfilling the requirements of your heavenly Contract.

"Relax though.

"Maybe you will never recognize the subtle and effective resolutions of conflicts on your path. Some resolutions are so subtle, slowly resolving issues squabble by squabble, relationship by relationship, that movements up towards the next, happier Platformation are barely noticeable.

"It may be only one day in the future that you look back on your life events, and in retrospect think something like, 'Gosh, was I really like that? Thank God I'm better now!'"

LOving Animals, the Environment, etc.

"This Angel Story focuses on sharing your LOve with humanity, because that's how most angels-on-earth share LOve. A significant proportion of angels, though, feel they cannot accept other people. It almost breaks their gentle hearts that people can be so imperfect.

"So some angels turn away from sharing their LOve with people, and toward LOving and helping animals, the environment, a charity, anything that does not make them connect with imperfect people.

"Animals are classic as a project to help. Or just to have as a pet, sometimes instead of a partner. Pets can't answer back, can they? Pets will share LOve right back at you. Some pets cuddle, and seem appreciative of all you do. Pets mainly have no judgement. They seem to have unconditional LOve, exactly what your sweet heart desires.

"Maybe using pets, the environment or whatever to share your LOve with instead of humans is escapism from not-nice people. Perhaps it is acceptable to escape though, because it might not be what you do, but how you do it that matters.

"It might be that the environment, or animals as pets or a project, are easier to LOve. That may also mean that the karmic strings attached are stricter, that there is less room for the dispensations that will be discussed later, that you'll need to be a little more perfect to achieve the same credentials and respect from your guides and angels.

"Everything can be a route to prove your credentials of LOving worthiness. Tread whatever path you have chosen, with LOve."

On Positive, Negative and Instant Karma

"Karma is the Law of God that rewards or punishes you for good or bad words or deeds, or even thoughts, automatically.

"Hands up anyone who believes they received positive karma, a reward from your version of God for doing something good.

(Hands raised.)

"Yes, almost everyone believes they have been rewarded for goodness.

"Hands up if you believe you have been punished for doing something bad.

(Hands raised.)

"That's how it is, almost everyone.

"You see, if this is your last lifetime, when you gain rewards for doing good, that positive karma will have an effect after moving on from this life. Positive karma will affect you with rewards for a higher status in the next part of your existence. I will discuss more about this later.

"Whereas when you do bad, negative karma will drag you down the path, not up, until you understand better ways of behavior. Negative karma may give you an unexpected punishment. You need to learn from it fast.

"You see, you cannot, as an angelic being, as far as is possible under your individual circumstances, leave negativity behind you on Earth after you pass on. So karma gives you praising rewards and warning punishments, to give you a clear idea of how you are doing. And that gives excellent clues as to how you should perhaps progress.

"There is not only positive and negative karma. There is also instant karma. Instant karma means that, in response to your thought, word, or action, you receive an instant positive reward or punishment.

"Hands up if your reward or punishment was instant, within a day or two.

(Hands raised.)

"Exactly; most of you have experienced instant justice. That goes for me too!

(Laughter.)

"The point is, you cannot keep a secret from God. You need to learn your lessons.

"As an angel-to-be, you have a Godly, LOving soul. But your soul's host, your human body that is not perfect, needs to find ways to be as pure as possible in thoughts, words, and deeds.

"It won't always be easy, because you have deeply ingrained habits and health issues.

"Part of a lesson is to rise above obstacles on your pathway, towards achievement of your soul's Contract.

"Another part of a lesson is to respond to karma with optimistic and grateful manners, speedily, within your capabilities.

"Look out for karma. And take action. Instant karma helps you recognize and release any of your inappropriate behaviors.

"Then you can more readily develop LOve-Based Living, and a truly LOving God-consciousness."

Lessons from Clues of the Four Forces – Destiny, Free Will, Accident, Foolishness

"An angel-on-earth's lessons are created by the four seemingly chaotic and conflicting forces of Destiny, Free Will, Accident, and Foolishness.

"Those four are the power bases of life, the structure from which all karma is formed and relieved, and from which all Contracts are made and broken.

"Everything you ever think, speak, or do, falls into the judgement of the Gods, filed away under one of the four categories of Destiny, Free Will, Accident, and Foolishness.

"Some people think that everything is Destiny. Is dripping hot soup down your white top Destiny? Is it Destiny that you dropped your phone and it smashed? Maybe, but it's unlikely. Perhaps you could be skeptical that everything that ever happens is Destiny. That would make God a dictator. I doubt that's true.

"Within the chaos of human-made thunder and blunder, the four unseen forces help, lead, or hinder your path. So although there is Destiny, there are also three other forces that might shove people down pathways. I'll describe the four forces in brief.

"The first force, Destiny, can be defined as God's normally secret LOving plans for your life, the goal set by your pre-birth Contract. Destiny must be achieved by angels-on-earth so as not to return to Earth again, and to progress to higher realms. Destiny will always lead you forwards. Destiny will forge paths in your unconscious mind, for your conscious thoughts to follow. Destiny is the ultimate achievement, not just for you and your soul, but also for those above such as your angel guides, who constantly strive to guide you towards your life's final achievement. To achieve your Destiny is like winning a gold medal at the next Olympics.

"The second force, Free Will, can be defined as your normally secret LOving or non-LOving ideas of what you think you want or need for your life. It is your choice, literally, of anything, at any time, at any crossroad of life. Free Will, in the positive sense, is about good choices you make to satisfy the needs of your humanity, and especially the needs of your LOving soul, your Contract, and your Destiny. Free Will usually satisfies your wants, not your needs. You might want a holiday. You'll relish the fun. Instead, maybe you could have achieved something special for those less fortunate on your soul path? Sharing your LOve to create happiness might be more desirable for your soul's journey. I am not saying you shouldn't have a holiday. I am saying Free Will is about trying to decide the best ways forward for your soul path, every time you have a choice.

"The third force, Accident, is more chaotic. As God is not a dictator, Accidents can and do happen. Accidents cannot be prevented. If a plane lands on runway ice, and crashes, killing the 300 people on board, was it Destiny for them all to die? Maybe not… Maybe it was an accident, and the ice could not have been foreseen. It was not Destiny for them all to die. Maybe a traffic jam due to a car crash made you miss an important business conference. Maybe it was not Destiny for you to lose a contract that could have improved the lives of many. If you think about it, every day there are Accidents, tiny and big. Meeting someone in a street or store could be an Accident. Accidents create chaos in your life. If possible, try to discern the difference between Destiny and Accidents.

"The fourth and final force is Foolishness. Foolishness may be less easy to recognize, hard not to do, and impossible to rectify. The main Foolishness is when you know you should or should not do something, but you do the opposite. Maybe you are at a crossroads of life? You know taking one path could give you a happier, healthier, more successful and LOving life, and lead you closer to the top of your soul's mountain path. But you deliberately ignore the option, and choose a path that is more unhappy, not so healthy, less successful and LOving, and takes you away from your soul's needs. Foolishness is doing the opposite of what you know is right. Don't blame yourself for Foolishness. A good life is about learning from mistakes.

"As part of your learning curve towards wisdom, an angel-on-earth like you needs to accept these four forces of Destiny, Free Will, Accident, and Foolishness, not only for you, but also for every other person regardless of how they are or what they do. Accept them for every potential force they may possibly have, with your forgiveness and fullness of divinely wonderful LOve.

"Accepting the four forces, or trying to improve them, is a gift, a way of life, a path to the Supreme Soul, and greater good. It's a picture being painted for the blossoming of your being, the flowering of your human nature to spring your soul forward to its Destiny.

"See people as experiencing the Destiny, Free Will, Accident, and Foolishness of Godly glory, not human gory. See everyone as lovely beings placed here by their God, for goodly but unknown purposes.

"See everyone you meet as the most LOving brotherly or sisterly souls treading a path like you have done in a previous lifetime, or like you are treading now.

"Nobody, not even a therapist or an angel can change some of the more drastic aspects of Destiny, Free Will, Accident, and Foolishness. Forces can only be overcome by each individual themselves, if they persevere or are lucky enough to find acceptance or their own solution to improve their way of life.

"Some people may not be able to help their traits such as being too timid or brave. All traits could be affected by Destiny, Free Will, Accident, and Foolishness.

"But the point is, if you are a criticizing type of angel, you may not approve of others. Maybe they are too loving or not loving enough, too busy or not busy enough, or too quiet or too noisy. Can you discern whether their ways are due to Destiny, Free Will, Accident, or Foolishness?

"As shocking as the thought might be, because human beings cannot help inherited traits or learned responses, if someone can kill, rape, torture or maim, maybe only God could understand whether their actions were due to Destiny, Free Will, Accident, or Foolishness.

"But in the higher scheme of life and post-life, all may be well. All is simply another story, another way to reach the same result, maybe with additional lifetimes added for misbehavior.

"Angels-on-earth need to respect others treading a different path, or a different part of the path, or a different lifetime, and respect the chaos of Destiny, Free Will, Accident, or Foolishness thrown into the mix.

"Others' ways may be antisocial or of extreme abuse. You may read their stories in newspapers, and your heart churns. You wish the world were completely peaceful, without Earth's torments and horrors. And you wonder what to do, and realize there's little you can do because there's so much that's not ideal in the world.

"So you fret more. Your LOving heart flutters in reaction to events.

"One day you find the way to accept non-LOving deeds. You find the way to accept the Destiny of others, their Free Will, Accidents, or Foolishness.

"Maybe you can create an organization, even voluntary, that helps people you previously disliked or despised. Maybe you can start your own charity. Maybe you just develop naturally.

"When you can accept everyone regardless of what they have done, when you can accept all peoples everywhere with LOve in your every thought, that's when you are freed from the futile chains of wanting the whole world to be as LOving as you.

"Destiny, Free Will, Accident, and Foolishness are philosophies to understand. But for angels-on-earth, on this particular Platformation, if you can accept humankind and the faults of everyone close to you, then you will move further up the Angelic Path, and reach closer to your ultimate Destiny, your reason for being.

"There are many other issues to discuss before talking further about Free Will, Destiny, Accident, and Foolishness. It's enough to say at present that one of those four headings can be the creator of scenarios or the cause of clashes of every single thing that can ever happen to you. There is no other option.

"But within these four headings are many approaches to life. Some are easy, some tough.

"If you tread a confusing path, maybe you can't just waft through it. Perhaps you need to do a thesis."

Introducing the Thesis for the University of Life

"Have you been to university? If so, you probably achieved competently to get there. You probably achieved brilliantly to progress to write a thesis or dissertation and pass a master's or doctoral degree.

"Similarly, if you're to accept your and others' human faults, as well as tragedies and disasters, there will be much to be competent and brilliant at to pass through the University of Life.

"As at a traditional university, in the University of Life some people learn quickly and efficiently. They have a natural ability like Mozart learning how to play the piano. Other people though are not naturally gifted, and may need to study.

"Writing a thesis is not like when you were very young, and a school teacher asked you to write something about your family or something you did the previous weekend. How long did that take? An hour in a classroom maybe? No, it's unlikely you can achieve acceptance of all human faults within an hour. How could you possibly accept all faults of everyone close to you, and of those in international news, in an hour?

"A thesis is not like at junior school when you were asked to write a composition. A composition may have taken a weekend to write. Acceptance of humanity's faults will probably take more than just a weekend.

"And a thesis is not like writing an essay in senior school. An essay may have taken a few weeks. Acceptance of non-LOve is unlikely to be achieved fast.

"Finding true acceptance is more like writing a thesis. How long does it take for a thesis? A few years...

"That is a good analogy. You might need to attend the University of Life for a few years, and unconsciously write a thesis on acceptance through experiential decisions or information you have studied. Maybe your thesis could include information from the book of these two days.

"Most angels write a University of Life thesis instinctively, unconsciously, secretively. Conclusions come automatically, after experiences of interacting with people.

"It doesn't have to take long if you write your thesis more consciously. Perhaps you could literally write a thesis for your University of Life Platformation.

"A thesis may be needed for any Platformation, from the beginning to the end of your lives.

"If you believe you have an angelic child or teenager, help them write their thesis to find better ways forward. Then, when the child becomes an adult, you as an understanding parent can advise how to write a new thesis, to overcome new challenges.

"Adult angels can also write a thesis to help them find their way forward, and overcome their Platformation lessons.

"Daily study and practice are the twofold essentials of whatever you need to resolve or improve in your life. But maybe a more controlled way to study and practice and find the best way forward is needed for some.

"If you've not been to university and don't know the structure of a thesis, I'll explain."

How To Write a Thesis

"The University of Life is a real force. Within you are natural, university-like learning processes based on trial and error experiences, from which you consciously or unconsciously write a thesis, and come eventually to your conscious positive results and conclusions.

"But what is a thesis?

"A proper university thesis is a report on a research project and seeks solutions to a problem or series of issues in your field of research. It designs a title for the research, perhaps in the form of a question, and intends to discover relevant answers that were unexpected at the start. The topic, results, conclusion, and recommended ways forward may be previously unknown, or even controversial.

"So it is with University of Life theses. Via research, you seek potentially unique or controversial answers that you previously didn't know.

"Before starting to write, find your title, your thesis statement. A thesis statement isn't easy to find because it needs to be unique to you, and specific for the Platformation you are on. Your title should not be too simple, or too general. A title such as, 'How do I accept everything this week,' is far too broad and vague, and unrealistic in its deadline. 'How to accept myself and parents' is more specific, but still not unique to you.

"A thesis title like, 'How can I accept the nastiness of parents, and inherited nastiness within myself,' is more specific, but still not unique enough to you.

"After trying a few more titles, you may revise it to, 'Because my family line has genetically-inherited anger, have I chosen to be born into this family to learn a Contract lesson about anger, and if so, how can I accept or break the inherited chain through the use of pioneering complementary therapies within standard psychology?'

"This statement is now specifically unique to you, has

controversial elements, and identifies defined issues and possible ways forward. It needs to be briefer though.

(Laughter.)

"All Platformations, and your angelic-human conflicts on them, can be reduced to a single, specific statement or title, relevant to you and your need.

"When you've found your title, it's time to write the thesis. All theses have a structure. There's a beginning, middle, and end, with chapter headings and subheadings. The whole process leads to a conclusion, with recommendations on the best ways forward.

"Maybe you can try this to help overcome a feeling of being 'stuck' in your life?

"Open a computer or cardboard folder. Write fast or slow according to your available time. Write the following chapter headings.

"Chapter one is the 'Introduction'. State what the topic is, why the question in your title statement is essential to your life, and the solution you need to find in your human or soul development. Explain, non-judgmentally with an open mind, what you hope to achieve.

"Chapter two, the 'Literature Review', shows your Internet library-base. Bibliography research reveals how many others may have tried to solve issues like yours. You may find an easy answer has already been evidenced by someone else. When you try it, it might help you. You may not need to continue your thesis.

"Chapter three is about a 'Gap in the Knowledge Base'. It explains why others' answers, that may have helped them, do not seem relevant to you. Here you can include the various limitations of other people's methods and conclusions.

"Chapter four is a 'Proposition To Fill the Knowledge Gap'. It describes a general way forward where you might achieve your aims and objectives. This includes possible approaches, methods, and techniques; or relevant courses, books, Apps, or teachings.

"Chapter five, 'Methods', shows specific details on how you intend to find your solutions. Here, you'll be as detailed as needed, including the theories behind the methods.

"Chapter six, the 'Diary/Journal Records', is a record of what you do each day to try to achieve your aims and objectives of chapters four and five. Practice, practice, practice…

"Chapter seven is about 'Results' from chapter six. Include the aspects of results that seemed more constant, reliable and helpful, or the opposite. Discern if there are better approaches that may help you for life.

"Chapter eight, the 'Discussion', answers questions about what the results mean and why they help you or not.

"Chapter nine, the 'Conclusion', explains how your solutions worked or not, and suggests new ways forward. That could include starting a new thesis either because the previous one didn't provide adequate answers, or because the current one offers perfect answers and you need another thesis on a new subject.

"You may achieve these chapters unconsciously and naturally, without thinking or planning, over quite a longish period of time. For some angels, that natural way is adequate. For creative types of people, a logical approach like a thesis may seem like prison. They prefer the freedom creativity brings.

"But if you're stuck, if you haven't got a clue as to your way ahead, especially if you're a logical type, why not consciously write a thesis? Perhaps you'll achieve success and rise above a Platformation much faster? Your thesis could even become the basis for a self-help book, to support other angels' paths.

"I 'prescribed' a thesis for an angel patient. He had suffered relentlessly, and his logical thoughts loved the nine-chapter thesis approach. I suggested he write regularly for however long needed, until he resolved his Platformation dilemmas.

He returned the following month with his thesis solutions in a folder, cured of the what had been holding back his life.

"If you find a potential thesis solution you researched is inadequate, return to a previous chapter. Start again with a different possible solution. It's what you probably would have done unconsciously anyway. But now you are in conscious control of the hunt for potential solutions.

"If you structure something in your life that needs to be solved into a thesis, you'll be focused. You'll be less likely to 'run around in circles' repeating the same patterns.

"Be patient. Remember, a thesis takes time. Go forward with as much haste as your life permits, but relax. There is usually no great risk if you don't rush.

"Even so, a thesis is better than just hoping or praying things will improve. You may find solutions to life faster, with more ease.

"And in so doing, you'll earn your wings relatively effortlessly from the University of Life."

Clues To an Angel's Secret Grief Process

"When talking about how some angels-on-earth seek and find solutions for aspects of their lives, it's worth mentioning grief. There's potential for some angels-to-be to go through a grief or bereavement process. The word 'bereavement' is used in some cultures to mean 'grief'.

"Remember that, from before birth, you have a precise conscious or hazy unconscious memory of perfect LOve. You lost that connection to perfect LOve when you made your Contract, and, like any loss, there is potential for a grief or bereavement-type of mourning.

"A potential clue to why you react with life in the way you do is to see if you fit into one of the four phases of a grief process, shock, emotional, mental, and recovery. Each phase may include any of many possible symptoms.

"So in the shock phase of grief, you may feel bewildered, numb, be unable to take things in, or have a sense of unreality. Think about it. If you've lost the most perfect LOve in the universe, would it not feel unreal? Would you not feel numb and bewildered?

(Sounds of crying.)

"It's not nice, but that is how it is.

"One day you move on to the emotional phase of grief. Here you may have an intense longing for the perfect LOve you lost, emotion such as sadness or anger that you've had to experience that loss, or suicidal thoughts because you want to return to lost LOve, or fear that your human existence will hold non-LOving experiences. As mentioned earlier, you may also have substitutions for that LOve.

(Sounds of crying.)

"Yes, it's sad. Again, that is just life, it is just how it is.

"Eventually, you move to the mental phase of grief with possible acute loneliness due to being separated from perfect LOve, frustration at not being able to do a soul purpose, apathy because your life feels irrelevant to your path, or a lack of purpose and resultant disorganization in your life. These may lead to despair, hypochondria, stress, phobias, depression, or other conditions.

"There are also increasing mental realizations of the conflicting issues of imperfect human love compared to perfect Godly LOve. It might seem awfully impossible to resolve love versus LOve conflicts, especially if you're not consciously aware that the cause of the conflicts is because your LOving soul desires perfection.

"The final phase of grief is the recovery phase, when you show signs of taking up new roles for your soul's evolution. Now you can rebuild relationships, find new opportunities for fulfillment, start true forgiveness of yourself and others, and start to rebuild your life by sharing your LOve in substantial and satisfying ways. The final phase is also when you may start true acceptance of everything in life, and everything seems pleasant. Acceptance of the unacceptable is part of most angels' paths.

"A grief process may take weeks, months, or an average of a couple of years. Even when the grief process is ended, twinges will happen to everyone.

"Similar to when people have varying degrees of grief at the passing on of someone they loved, you may go through your version of grief at any speed, and with any combination or progression of symptoms. It's your unique process. It's a process that, if you get stuck in a particular phase, might need a thesis to find answers and methods for resolution.

"You may also seek professional help for any aspect of any of the four phases of your grief process. Either one of the shock, emotional, mental, or recovery phases might be dominant, and medical professionals might clinically diagnose you as going through a grief process. But they can only try to place you into one of their boxes, searching your human issue, or loss of close family or friends, or even the loss of a pet or something you loved. They search for something in your life that could have kick-started your grief. They cannot see your LOving soul yearning for the LOve it lost.

"So, unfortunately, adequate support is unlikely to come from orthodox counselors, psychologists, psychiatrists, or medical professionals, because your underlying angelic issues of grief for the loss of LOve perfection are not within their understanding. They have no appropriate working model.

"Hopefully, one day in the future when angels-to-be reach the higher echelons of psychology or other therapeutic models, they can introduce the angelic-bereavement concepts and help this sad category of angels-on-earth that is currently rarely helped.

"Until then know it's a University of Life process to overcome naturally and unconsciously in your own time, or for conscious action to take as needed, perhaps with a literally written thesis.

"Either way, you'll win in the end."

Clues on Rising from the Platformation of Having To LOve Humanity

"When is the right time to move on from the platform of having to LOve humanity? There are many clues.

"You can move up to a higher, more agreeably gratifying Platformation when you realize that every person in every country on Earth is imperfect because they cannot help their God-given nature.

"You can move on when you learn to accept the face value of sin, the deeper values of karma, and the potential for anything whatsoever to be in anyone's Contract. You cannot resolve someone's karma, or write another Contract for another person. They may receive a tougher Contract immediately, as payback for trying to cheat their previously agreed Contractual obligations.

"You can move on when you learn that a person's future isn't in your hands, it's not down to you to always save everyone. That's because the most important soul-oriented decisions about a person's soul pathway are made by God, not you.

"You need to share the highest LOve and only highest LOve. Lower forces of love will not suffice any more. They are in the slow lane. You now need to drive faster, speed up your life, overtake love with LOve progression, put your feet on the throttle of LOve, and enter the fast lane.

"When driving a car, the fastest lane is only for good, experienced drivers. Beginners who drive fast can be potentially dangerous, maybe causing accidents due to their lack of skill maneuvering around hazards, and lack of ability to discern when to accelerate and when to brake.

"And so it is with souls on their paths. If beginner souls on an Angelic Path were let off their learning, if they were allowed to relinquish the learning about their LOve L-plates too early, they could cause chaos on their road.

"So it is far better to have streamlined car driving tests, or for souls, Platformations to pass.

"For example if you pass the test of acceptance of the faults of everybody you know, and those you read or hear about, then you're qualified to move on to the advanced 'driving' test. You are enabled to learn extra skills to maneuver the hazards of the less perfect people you will meet regularly in life, and share your LOve with them all.

"All this is needed for acceptance because nothing in the non-beauty of humankind will contain more beauty than the beauty of not requiring your LOve L-plates, because you have learned to accept all things with LOve.

"So keep trying to accept the imperfect loves, sexual loves, jealous loves, possessive loves, friends' loves, fatherly or motherly loves, love for your work or hobby, love of food, love of whatever. Try to accept all the non-perfect human types of lowly love interactions. Try to accept all sorts of love that are nothing whatsoever to do with highest Godly LOve.

"That will not seem ideal to some LOving angels-to-be. But LOving acceptance of all things that are not as perfect as divine LOve is indeed a way to overcome the human imperfections on this part of the soul path. On another part of the path, you may need a different interaction, because you will understand different soul path needs.

"You need to find ways to LOve others and everything you know, under all circumstances; and nothing else except LOve.

"That is OK. Being on one of the early platforms is OK. That's what this life is about. It's about learning your lessons as you experience life. At the end of the life, it's only about human love or Godly LOve.

"When you first try unconditional LOve for those you dislike, you'll most likely fail. You'll fail because of the Platformation needs, that you initially have no idea how to overcome.

"It's OK to fail, for in failing comes learning, your thesis gets written literally or unconsciously, and you eventually overcome the Platformation exams.

"Because by then you'll have learned unconditional acceptance, and you'll be able to share LOve through your hands, heart, mind, soul, thoughts, actions, power, and might, in an amazingly adorable way that is right for everyone you meet, not just for those you love.

"If you can do all these things, if you can LOve everybody and everything, everywhere, under every circumstance, perhaps you can move on to the peak of the Platformation of acceptance of the faults of humanity. Maybe then you can start the next Platformation, which is about sharing your LOve unconditionally."

New Science on Diet and Vegetarianism

"Before talking through the issues of sharing your LOve unconditionally, let's mention diet. Of course, most human beings will experiment with diet at some point in life. Eating the best possible diet for optimum health may be deeply considered. But as with most things on the Angelic Path, the motivation for angels-on-earth to find a good diet to help their lives is different.

"As they grow older, from deep inside their souls most angels know it's important to care for their bodies and minds. Appropriate high quality, high variety, life-giving foods support their LOving souls' aims on Earth, by staying healthy with fullest vitality.

"Angels-to-be may try many diets. Perhaps they'll try the latest dietary fad; a local system that's being promoted heavily by friends; a nationally or internationally famous diet; or a doctor's or scientific suggestion. The important thing for angelic souls is to discover what type of diet gives the most energy, most vitality, most life-force.

"Just a little word of warning about medical diets that abound on the Internet. If you find something that seems appropriate for an illness or condition you have, always seek a doctor's professional opinion first. Then follow whatever advice is given according to the doctor's knowledge.

"A doctor's opinion about medical diets is needed because much research has been undertaken about diet and chronic or critical disease, and about diet and medication. It is a terribly complicated subject. Research shows that different illnesses or medications may need you to eat more, less, or totally avoid certain foods. A diet may create a potentially serious contraindication with a medication that may make the medicine less effective, or the illness worse.

"So seek a doctor's opinion before you start a diet. The doctor may suggest a diet that needs to be followed to support certain medications, illnesses and sick health conditions.

"Many angels-on-earth eventually decide to eat less meat, and more fruits and vegetables, and feel healthier for it. Their decision is backed with scientific research by Imperial College London. Research results suggest that the best health benefits can occur if you eat ten small handfuls, 80 gram (2.8 oz.) portions, of different fruit and vegetables every day. Compared to people who eat less than ten fruits and vegetables daily, you become healthier.

"Even a small daily intake of 2½ portions of fruit and veg showed a 16% reduced risk of heart disease, a 4% lower risk of cancer, and a 15% reduction in the risk of premature death. If you increase the consumption of fruits and vegetables to ten portions a day, the Imperial College research shows a 24% reduced risk of heart disease, 33% lower risk of stroke, 28% reduced risk of cardiovascular disease, 13% reduced risk of cancer, and a 31% reduction in the risk of premature death.

"So fruits and vegetables have super-charged health benefits in most cases, for most people. This is because fruits and vegetables consist of nutrients and substances that are good for health, but that cannot be found in other foods.

"For example, the antioxidants in fruits and vegetables can potentially reduce cholesterol levels and blood pressure, improve blood vessels and immune system, reduce DNA damage, and lead to cancer risk reduction.

"The journal, *Thorax,* found that five or more servings of different fruit and veg daily is linked to a 35% lower risk of chronic lung disease.

"A good case can be made to become a vegetarian. As the saying goes, you become what you eat. Eat healthily, you become healthy.

"Be aware though that, as it states in the acclaimed book, *Eat Right 4 Your Type,* although some people could need to eat vegetables to prevent illness, some others might need to eat meat to stop becoming ill.

"I know people who stopped eating meat to become vegetarian, and within two years became sick with specific conditions. After they read the *Eat Right 4 Your Type* book and reintroduced meat into their diet, they returned to good health.

"I'm not saying this would have happened to everyone. But it's a potential danger or solution to look out for. Diet is a very complicated subject.

"So always check with a doctor first if vegetarianism would suit your conditions and your medication.

"Spiritual organizations, though, often recommend a 100% fruit and vegetable diet.

"For example, the Brahma Kumaris promote the quality and variety of vegetarianism as a better, kinder, healthier, more spiritual way of life. They suggest that fear, for example, can be carried from a dead animal into your body. If you want spiritual enlightenment, maybe you do not want an animal's energies inside you, dragging you down and away from the LOving God-force.

"Brahma Kumaris and an increasing number of spiritual and green environment types of organizations go one stage further.

They recommend a raw fruit and vegetable diet, because less cooking means more nutrients, which can lead to even better health and spirituality.

"Anyway, if you hope to help the environment, research on global warming shows that animals used as food produce ten times the environmental concerns associated with plant food. The population of the planet is increasing at a rate of about seven million extra people every month. Eating millions of extra animals daily could become unviable. Within this century, available land and feeds, and the gasses and wastes animals produce, are likely to be environmentally unsustainable. It is even suggested that becoming mainly vegetarian could help save humanity from extinction.

"Every day, whatever else you eat, maybe you can also add different vegetables on your plate, and choose from a varied fruit bowl. This may give you the best chances of avoiding chronic diseases or early death. You might also more easily gain holistic health, and uncover inner peace.

"Angels-to-be may then, with the vitality of excellent energy and health inside them, have more potential to successfully achieve their souls' tasks and destinies."

Happiness and LOve-Based Living

"What do most people desire? Money in the bank? Maybe not! Research suggests that most people want happiness, maybe from basic food and shelter, or a vacation, meal out, cinema, watching a sunset, music, and so on. But temporary events create non-permanent happiness.

"How do angels find more stable, more permanent happiness? Assuming your basic needs are satisfied, happiness is progressed only by steadier, more secure, more permanent varieties of human love or Godly LOve.

"Some angels are lucky to enjoy relatively stable human love with a partner, friend, family, and so on. Or steady Godly LOve through a philosophy, an inner knowledge, or LOve practice such as prayer, yoga, meditation, or helping others.

"Myriad ways can achieve more stable happiness. And all can lead to LOve-Based Living.

"LOve-Based Living is an approach to life that seeks to put divine LOve into every thought you have, every word you speak, and every action you take.

"LOve-Based Living is an approach that tries to be kind and caring, with better, happier interactions with everyone and everything but with a particular motivation.

"LOve-Based Living has one motivation behind all your thoughts and actions. Godly LOve!

"Some angels think that everyone is an angel too, and if they give LOve, they'll get it back. It is not possible, though, that your LOve is always returned. Everyone has potential to become an angel, but most people will not overcome needed lessons until another lifetime. Until then, human faults may dominate. They may remain unLoving, unkind, and unresponsive to your LOve.

"That means that most people won't understand your LOve. It's for you to offer LOve, not to expect or want to receive LOve in return.

"LOve-Based Living is a role, like an actor in a play who wants their characterization of holy LOve to be believed. The actor will research, practice, and enhance the role of holy LOve. The intention is that the LOve role becomes reality in his mind, heart, and actions.

"If that is achieved, the actor can win the hearts and minds of audiences, who will believe the actor is not whatever different type of character he or she played in a previous role. Perhaps they played the role of a villain previously, but the actor truly is now playing the character of a benefactor. And because of the actor's research and practice, the audience will believe the new benefactor role. Maybe you can be an actor too, an actor acting out scenes of LOve on the stage of life.

"At the beginning your LOve-acting might feel awkward. It may seem as if people you are with will see through you as a fake. It might feel that your LOve cannot be viewed as real and true. You could think that the LOve you act out will never be taken seriously.

"Actually, some people may see you as fake, especially if they've seen your human faults. These people cannot see inside you, they cannot know the LOve glowing from your soul. Naturally, they may mainly recall your unfavorable ways, how you shouted, were unkind, or whatever.

"It will take practice to portray your new role on Earth as a gentle, kind, sweetly LOving human being, only wanting to help others as much as you can.

"It may take time to relieve past events or confrontational situations from others' minds.

"But eventually, if you act out your new LOving role well, they can bear witness to the latest version of you that is true and authentic LOve.

"It's like a famous actor who once played the role of an antihero and became a household memory. When the actor plays a new role, a role of a character with different heroic qualities, how can the audience believe the actor is then a completely different person?

"Audiences respond to a new character role because the actor researches how to behave in his new role, then practices the new role with conviction. You can also do this by researching LOve, then practicing your role as a LOving being with perfection.

"An actor uses the possession of new facts about the new role's needed character and personality, and becomes the new person as completely and as believably as possible. You can do this too. You can accept that you can change into a new person, with new and better attributes, for a new role of LOve-Based Living.

"You can act your LOve role daily. Be LOve permanently.

Walk and talk LOve. Portray LOve to all people, especially those who, because of your past words or deeds, thought you were unLOving.

"From now on, be LOve despite what others do or say. Be the sweetest act on Earth. Let others follow your LOve, like cinema goers follow a star.

"If you achieve even a part of all this, you have progressed on the Angelic Path.

"You will one day attain LOve-Based Living.

"Like an actor who becomes the role they play, you will be LOve.

"Then happiness can follow, automatically."

Chapter 7

Relationships, Partners

Finding a Partner – General Clues

"The search for a suitable partner is complex enough for many non-angelic people. But the same type of relationship search by angels-on-earth is worse. It is fraught with issues that more often than not make finding a suitable partner a near impossibility.

"There are two main clues to consider, before explaining about the types of relationship an angel-on-earth could have.

"First there is the clue of the feelings of divine LOve residing in your soul.

"Second is the clue of whether or not your partner has LOve in their soul.

"You know, your soul that is full of LOve makes you want everything to be LOvingly perfect. You might be extreme in wanting perfection, and want your partner to do perfect actions, say perfect words in a perfect tone of voice, express perfect LOve, and even think perfect thoughts that portray a perfect expression on the face.

"When this doesn't happen, when your partner does not talk, act or exist as perfectly as you'd hoped for, in the divine LOve ways you desire, perhaps you then change partners, hoping to find someone with more ideal, perfect LOve next time.

"For many angels-on-earth, the cycle may repeat. You one day wonder if you'll ever be able to find that perfect relationship because you can't accept that a perfect partner cannot be found. You somehow know that you were with everything that was LOving once, so why not experience that LOve again with a LOving partner?

"In fact, maybe it's you angels who don't make good partners. You are the ones seeking perfection, and when you don't find it, you get angry, sad, or frustrated and so on. Even though you are seeking perfection and hating not getting it, much of the time you'll think it's the other person who's the problem, not you.

"Hands up if you can relate to that.

(Hands raised.)

"Yes, almost everyone has thought the other person was the problem, that they are not LOving enough. Whereas it was your wanting the perfection of LOve that doesn't exist in humans that created your relationship issues.

"And so you may repeatedly split to find a new partner, all the time not understanding the conflict isn't between you and your partners, but between you and your soul.

"But, you believe that your relationship can improve, or you'll one day find that perfect twin-soul partner who deserves your LOve, because you have LOve inside you. You think your LOve can conquer your relationships, one way or another, and all will be well.

"It's a complicated situation, especially because most angels do not analyze the type of person they need to partner with, someone who is 'nice' and who could help them achieve their soul paths. That lack of analysis leads to angels repeatedly engaging in relationships that are not good for themselves as a human, or for their Destinies.

"There are five types of relationships for angels, including celibacy. And there's also sexuality. That's the next subject, to discern how your soul's LOve might affect your sexuality."

Search for LOve Through Sexuality

"Most angels-on-earth, mainly in Western countries, go through phases of trying different partners. Non-angels do too. But the motivating forces, the reasons behind an angel's different partners, sexual desires or promiscuous phases, are usually for one of two specific reasons.

"Either to enjoy lots of quick fixes of highest LOve that regular new relationships or sexual climaxes may bring.

"Or to have short 'relationships' that are so brief you do not have the experiences that go with understanding another person's faults.

"Hands up if you've been like this.

(Hands raised.)

"Hmmm, almost three-quarters of you. Indeed, your angelic search to try to find LOve, especially in the teens or early on in adult life, can potentially create phases of sexuality that some people would view as not to the standards of their society.

"When I tell this story, a few angels have come up afterwards, and privately said something like, 'Actually, I used sexuality to get lots of quick fixes of LOve.' Some enjoy tantric sex, others seem not to be embarrassed when they say they made a conscious choice to turn to prostitution. They explain that they felt the desire for numerous orgasms, because they knew orgasms could help provide them with regular highest LOve feelings. Or they say that during or just after orgasm their soul briefly leaves their body and joins the oneness of God's LOve and they want to repeat that experience again and again. Or they felt an intense need for nonstop relationships so they wouldn't experience a partner's not-so-positive side.

"It's just how it is. Some angelic people have many, many relationships. Others become more extreme and go deeper than just more and more relationships. Instead of meeting new partners in a bar, club, App, or Internet site, or through tantric sexuality classes, they turn to prostitution. It's a surefire way to get what they want, an exciting, sexual experience, or an orgasm that takes them to the heights of LOve feelings, or a quick way of sharing LOve with someone in need. Yet they experience these LOve feelings without having to know each person's faults. So they are never disappointed a partner is not perfect. After all, it's easy to join an 'escort agency' and say, hey I'm available, and get a quick fix when someone needs a 'date', and say goodbye after, knowing the agency will not release your confidential details to your escort.

"You all still have your eyes closed.

"Please raise your hands if you satisfied the craving for perfect LOve through quick fixes of prostitution, knowing you wouldn't have to go through the difficulties of a human relationship.

(Hands raised.)

"Yes, about 10% of you know you sought LOve through the quick fix of sexual prostitution. That's a high figure if you sampled the population. In fact, international statistics are that around 1% of women have worked as prostitutes.

"So angels-on-earth attract more people to prostitution, perhaps because their driving force is different to most non-angels who do not comprehend enjoying quick highs of LOve without having to deal with one partner's humanity every day.

"It certainly doesn't mean all prostitutes are angels. There are many other reasons why people turn to prostitution. Nor does it mean a prostitute stays a prostitute. For angels learning their lessons of Godly LOve and human love, it's usually only a phase to help understand LOve versus love issues, a lifestyle choice of LOve.

"But another factor weighs heavily on the sexual thoughts of some angels. Some angels-on-earth know that this could be their 'prospective final' lifetime, and that after 'passing on', they won't be able to enjoy sexuality anymore. Some people with angelic souls consciously choose lots of sex because they know they can't make love after their final lifetime. So they think they might as well make the most of sexual experiences now.

"Whichever way these aspects of angelic sexual experience are looked at, in one regard, it is all being motivated by the same underlying forces. It is using sexuality as a drug, a way to escape humanity, a way to feel at least temporarily as if they are with LOve.

"When they learn lessons of sexuality, that it's LOve inside them that drives them more than orgasms, more than any type of relationship, that's the time they can leave the drug of lovemaking behind them.

"Then they can move on without the sex-drug. They can make gentle and passionate love with a loving partner, instead of having sex just to achieve a high LOve sensation.

"Then they can begin to share LOve as nearby or as widespread as they choose, in more relevant and significant ways to their ultimate soul Contract."

Celibacy

"For many angels, sexuality seems too earthly, too lowly a force, and not always for good. That's because sexual relationships can unintentionally affect their own or other people's passions, in ways they would not have wished.

"Celibacy might therefore become, for some angels-on-earth, the best way forward. Logically they may think that being celibate could help lift them from the earthly to the heavenly, and prevent them being unLOving.

"Also, for some angels searching for LOve, not finding a divinely LOving relationship may become so unbearable, you may feel you have only one option left. Celibacy may offer a higher, happier, more perfectly LOving relationship and togetherness with God.

"Not all angels-to-be go through a celibacy phase. But for those that become celibate for life or for a while, it may be the path to peace, the highway to highest LOve, the road to relieve non-LOving relationships.

"Celibacy can also become a way to find yourself, to know your true nature, to realize who you are and what you can become.

"Celibacy provides freedom to learn more about God, to find your God-soul within.

"Abstinence can help uncover your true angelic soul. You'll

have space to realize that you are different because you have a need to achieve a soul purpose, a need that others don't have. Celibacy gives you room to feel what your soul purpose could be, a soul purpose that you might sense isn't far off.

"Of course, many people go through a celibacy phase, whether they're angels or not. But, as always on the Angelic Path, the motivation for an angel's celibacy is about LOve.

"A celibate may think a partner will drag you back to Earth too often, that you'll not be able to stay 'up there' with God.

"You might believe sexuality is not the best or most natural path to God, and that celibacy will help you reach God quicker and easier.

"And you could like to be alone. You feel good by yourself, without outside pressures to interfere with your soul search for LOve.

"Some angels become nuns or monks or such like, to leave the 'nasty world'. They prefer to focus on their journey towards the perfection of the Supreme Soul's LOve.

"Most angels at least contemplate a celibate way of life, without a partner. But most angels realize they can't shut themselves away from human life. Often they think relationships and sexuality are God-given gifts to be explored.

"Some people believe their soul's Contract must be achieved above all else. Even though a human relationship might be imperfect at times, it's maybe a better option, because their Contract's Destiny might be impossible to fulfill in a convent or monastery.

"Celibacy inside a marriage or relationship is another option. That means finding a partner who agrees with your celibate philosophies. But that could bring its own challenges if one person changes their views about making love.

"There is another alternative. The Brahma Kumaris were honored by the United Nations for their teachings about souls. Regardless of your race, religion, or anything else, global branches of the Brahma Kumaris try to support an angel-on earth's pathway toward their angelic Destiny. Other practices of Brahma Kumaris that can underpin your angelic evolution will be discussed later. For now, let's focus on how and why they advocate celibacy.

"Brahma Kumaris say that an angel-on-earth has the Free Will choice to be celibate as a single person, be celibate with a partner, or not be celibate at all.

"Celibacy is recommended as offering the best chance to seek God's LOve, away from human non-LOve.

"Celibacy is considered the most decent and accelerated way to learn about yourself because you won't have someone else telling you what you should or shouldn't do, or what type of person you should be now, or learn to become.

"And celibacy helps you grow without non-Godly sexual provocation that could hinder your soul path.

"But because the Brahma Kumaris do not dictate that you must be celibate, even if you are not celibate, you can still attend their helpful programs and courses about human, soul, and soul path development, to achieve your life's Destiny quicker, easier, and more effectively.

"There is another motivating factor I've found in angels-on-earth who become celibate. That is, some of you know this could be your prospective final lifetime. You realize you've had every chance to enjoy sexual experiences in previous lives. And you know you can't make love after death, because there's no sexuality then.

"So you might think something like, why not get used to a lack of sexuality now? Why bother with something that will soon become useless? So you abstain, and create space to learn about yourself, your higher inner LOve nature, the beauty you wish to become.

"For most angels who tread a celibate lifestyle, it's a temporary phase, a phase to unravel the LOve part of your soul, and connect it to the love part of your humanity.

"Perhaps the Gods above LOve people who go through a phase like this? It might make their job easier if you give yourself space to find your God.

"If you're not caught up in a live-together relationship, your heart, soul, and mind become free, and it's easier to discover who you were meant to be. You won't have to change yourself, albeit as a natural occurrence within a relationship, to become like a part of your partner. You become you, not a part of someone else.

"If you're by yourself, it might be more effortless to move along your path, because it's usually easier to see signs for progression put in your way by those above when you are not influenced by a partner.

"Signs will be considered later."

An Angel's Five Types of Partner – Basic Questions and Clues

"One of the most common questions angels-on-earth ask is about their relationship, their partner. There are two main basic questions.

"First, whether they should stay with their current partner for life, or should they divorce or leave them, and if so when.

"Second, whether soul mates exist, and if so, is it easy or possible to find their perfect partner, their soul mate.

"After innumerable such questions, it became apparent there were five simple answers, based upon five types of relationships.

"It also became apparent that there were specific angelic reasons as to what action an angel-on-earth may need to take about each of the five different types of relationship. Qualitative comments suggested that people with angelic souls had standard and profound LOve reasons that motivate their decisions about why they might choose a specific action to stay with or leave a partner.

"Most people have relationships that are not perfect. Even those people who will not be angels in this lifetime fall within most of the five categories. So some of the sections on relationships could help everyone.

"However, there are two main clues, angelic reasons that angels-on-earth should keep at the forefront of their mind when considering what decisive action to take about a relationship.

"First they should consider whether the decision to stay with someone or leave them will benefit their angelic soul purpose. Will staying or leaving help the most to achieve their Destiny?

"Secondly, any final relationship decision should be taken in the context of LOve. What is the most LOving way forward for everyone concerned? By staying with someone, is LOve reduced or enhanced? Will you be able to share LOve more if you stay, or more if you leave?

"These two reasons hold very different motivations to stay with or leave someone compared to non-angelic people who do not understand LOve. Whether to stay with someone or not has an underlying LOve context for potential angels-to-be.

"The five types of relationship partners for an angel-on-earth are:

1. A 'normal' human who is not yet in the prospective final lifetime, not an angel-to-be, at least not yet, who is non-LOving and genetically horrid.
2. A 'normal' human, who is not yet in the prospective final lifetime, not an angel-to-be, at least not yet, who is non-LOving and genetically nice.
3. An angel-on-earth in the prospective final lifetime who has a different ultimate Contract to you.
4. An angel-on-earth in the prospective final lifetime who has the same or similar ultimate Contract or Destiny as you.
5. The type of angel advocated by spiritual organizations

such as the Brahma Kumaris where you may agree to share celibacy within a relationship.

"I'll talk about each of these five types in turn. But as angels number only about one in every 300 to 400 people, you're much more likely to meet non-angelic partners. So the next topic is about having a non-angelic partner."

Relationship/Partner Type A – Genetically Horrid Non-Angels (General Issues of Interaction)

"If someone is not an angel-to-be, they will not be in their prospective final lifetime. The person must still learn many other non-LOve lessons. If they do well perhaps they could join the Angelic Path one day, in training to share LOve. In the meantime, their lessons could be about almost anything.

"The one thing non-angels don't yet understand with deep feeling is higher LOve. They might study or read about LOve, and have a logical appreciation of divine LOve. But they can't have a LOve feeling within them, because they won't have a conscious or unconscious memory of the LOving place their soul was before birth.

"Also, they probably won't feel as if they have an important role of LOve, a Destiny, to achieve. And they will probably interact accordingly in a non-LOve way with you, and everyone and everything around them.

"What they will have is a dominant force of some type of emotional or mental abusiveness. Usually this is drawn automatically from their genetic inheritance. They portray the worst traits of the family line. The thing for you is, they can't and won't control inappropriate behaviors. They don't want your or anyone else's help to improve.

"It's not always easy to discern the difference between a genetically horrid person, and an angel-on-earth on an early Platformation who is angry or whatever for not being with the

LOve they remember. Both could seem similarly unpleasant.

"But the clue as to whether they are or are not an angelic soul is whether they have a memory of LOve inside, and their answers to the Angelic Questions mentioned earlier. If they can't describe a feeling of LOve, and cannot answer the Angelic Questions appropriately, they are unlikely to have an angelic soul yet.

"If you determine the person is not an angel-on-earth, the likelihood is that, because of the non-LOve lessons they need to learn for their particular paths, they are not nice people. Often they may be tyrannical, abusive, or have countless problems.

"All you want is ideal LOve. But that's one thing you'll never get from a genetically horrid person. You may have sweet times, happy times, good times, especially if you say you've had enough of the person. Then they may do their best to win you back, to control you with alluring words, flowers, promises to reform, anything to stop you leaving. But the balance of life will be disagreeable. The non-angel person will almost certainly soon return to type, and the pattern could repeat.

"If this non-angel type of person is intimidating, you as a LOving angel may be easy to dominate. They'll tell you what to do, when to do it and how to do it. You could lose your Free Will, lose your way on your soul journey, and even lose your feeling of self-being or your mind.

"Of course, your inner LOve has hope. You'll hope the person will change, hope your LOve will change them, and hope they'll get to know LOve like you. But unless you ask the Angelic Questions, you probably won't realize these are unrealistic hopes that are not prompted by your knowledge of LOve but your lack of understanding of non-LOve, that not everyone can LOve like you.

"If the partner is abusive, many LOving angels will accept the abuse, thinking that this person will understand LOve one day, they can't stay abusive forever, and your LOve will conquer their abuse.

"But it's almost 100% certain you cannot win. Their power-seeking abuse is most probably stronger than your meek LOve.

"You become more abused, more downtrodden, more of a depressed broken spirit, not even realizing you've lost the battle to share your LOve to improve your partner.

"Another major factor with a genetically horrid non-angelic person is, because they don't know LOve inside them, and don't have a tug towards a special form of service, they can't understand you. They can't understand why you want to LOve everything, why you want everything to be perfect. They can't understand why you will, one day, want to help those in need.

"So you may end up keeping the thoughts on your future secret, because the non-LOving person will almost certainly try to talk you out of being so LOving or doing your soul purpose.

"Because they're genetically horrid, they may try to force their opinions on you. And you can feel devastated.

"So if you have a partner who isn't genetically nice, what's the way forward?"

Relationship/Partner Type A – Genetically Horrid Non-Angels (Clues To What Actions You Can Take and Why)

"The answer as to whether you should stay with a genetically horrid partner is simple. You almost certainly need to leave them to be able to achieve your real soul purpose on Earth.

"But though the solution to leave is simple, it usually isn't easy.

"You must choose whether to stay or leave. Initially, most angels decide to continue. An angel's heart is LOve, and they believe that if they keep trying, eventually their LOve can help the partner change for the better.

"So this type of angel passively accepts ill-treatment, in return for the hoped-for potential of bringing LOve into their partner.

"If they have children, they will want LOve for their children. Leaving the partner will not give the children the love of a father or mother. So angels continuously hope their partner will change, for the sake of the whole family's potential for happiness, while at the same time not realizing that the relationship could be having an even worse effect on the children than divorce.

"An angel may also continue with the relationship because their angelic heart is so delicate, they don't have a fortified attitude to bear trials of separation or divorce. For many, it's better the person you know, not the future you don't. Your kind angelic nature tells you to be harmless. You don't want to leave because you may want to be kind under almost any circumstance.

"One day, you may wake up to the simple fact that if you stay with a genetically horrid type of person, you have less chances to fulfill your Contract.

"That means you might have to reincarnate again, and maybe try to overcome a similar life next time. You may be given another chance to help improve something or someone, to prove your worth.

"So eventually, most angels take the unpredictable step to leave the partner, with the angst of knowing their LOve was limited and could not help, and the uncertainty of an unseen future.

"It's a period when the angel's LOving heart is pushed to bursting point. Sentimental reactions could last for a couple of years after the final separation or divorce.

"But for angels who are leaving a horrid partner, it's a vital period.

"They need the strength of mind to stick to their decision.

"They need clarity of thought to know that, without being held back, one day they'll have a superior chance to share their LOve, to fulfill their Contract, to achieve their soul purpose to be of use to a much-needed part of society.

"You may realize you should have left the partner behind

sooner, but at least you are now free to heal yourself, and achieve whatever is needed on your soul path."

Relationship/Partner Type B – Genetically Nice Non-Angels With or Without Health Problems (General Issues of Interaction)

"There are two types of genetically nice non-angelic people: those who have many health problems, and those that don't. Both types may still have to learn from at least one other lifetime.

"Healthy and non-healthy genetically nice non-angels do not understand LOve. It's not inside them. Due to the classic interaction types, there are classic reasons behind the decisions why angels could select a partner.

"First, let's talk about genetically nice persons with health problems to overcome. They could have issues that are physical, emotional, mental, attitudinal, anything. Some may have the lot.

"I call genetically nice but ill persons 'worst-case scenario partners'. They are deserving because probably their condition was not their fault. Because they are nice, they deserve love and happiness. Worst-case scenario partners are those you want to LOve and help because they are nice, but who, despite your best attempts and prolonged LOving efforts, may be impossible to help.

"You may think that Type A genetically horrid non-angels are worst-case scenario partners. But at least you know they are like that, and that knowledge means that you might know that one day you should leave them.

"Type B, genetically nice non-angels with many health problems are different. They are pleasant. They are so nice you want to help them from the bottom of your heart.

"Here is the crux. Due to their never-ending problems, you could waste your life, waste your whole soul purpose, trying to help them.

"You as an angel though, wishing to share your LOve, will

try. You will LOve them, care for them, and try to nurture them to health and happiness. But you find that their ill-health keeps returning.

"Or you find that when you help one condition, it seems another comes to the surface.

"It's a never-ending task, but your angelic LOve won't accept you cannot help.

"You continue, not understanding that though you may help some issues, you could spend a lifetime and still not achieve your Destiny. Which means you cannot do your real Angelic Service, your soul purpose that could help so many more people, not just one.

"And you eventually realize you may not be able to achieve your personal Destiny.

"Type B genetically nice persons with no health problems are the opposite. They may be physically fit, show warm feelings, be mentally strong in a balanced way, and seem to possess wonderful God-given gifts. They may not understand the highest feeling of divine LOve, but they're nice.

"They may know little, have little, or do little, but they're good. They may not be exciting, but they're genuine, their personality is gentle, and their character is sweet. Even though they will not understand LOve, or your desire to make the world a better place, everything about them is just nice, ideal to help and support your goals.

"But overriding niceness is sometimes not exciting enough for an angel. The partner may seem boring.

"So, despite that Type B person's niceness, you may seek thrills elsewhere."

Relationship/Partner Type B – Genetically Nice Non-Angels With or Without Health Problems (Clues To What Actions You Can Take and Why)

"What can you do about genetically nice persons, either those with many health issues or those who are just nice? What are the reasons you should take action?

"First, let's take the case of genetically nice persons with health problems.

"In a positive sense, someone like that provides great opportunities for lessons on how to share LOve, how to help with LOving perseverance. They provide perfect lessons to show that sharing LOve is important for you, and concentrated efforts are needed for best results.

"But, after you have helped the person for long enough and learned those lessons about sharing your LOve, there is another important lesson. This lesson is useful later in your life, when you are sharing your LOve within your soul's Destiny.

"The lesson is, even though you're an angel and think your LOve can help anything, and you want LOve to help everything, there are such things as lost causes. There are such things as worst-case scenario people who cannot be truly helped in the wholesome, complete way your angelic heart will always desire.

"Worst-case scenario partners, and other worst-case people, may not seem lost causes. When you are on an early Platformation, you have a different perspective, because you have not experienced sufficient life events to learn enough. They need your LOve, and you couldn't hurt them by leaving, could you? So you can stay?

"Accepting your limitations is a lesson for some angels. You truly think you can help anyone and anything, if only you achieve enough with your angelic heart and mind.

"But when you have had adequate experiences, you may realize that your partner's or a person's health problems can be a lost cause, impossible to help fully.

"The worst-case scenario partner may always take up so much of your time, you may never fulfill your calling on Earth. So you might, sadly, have to leave them and help the majority, not help just the one.

"The huge lesson, maybe a hurdle to overcome, is that, no matter how you try, there will always be cases you can't help. You are learning your limitations. I'm not saying carers, for example, should give up, only that your limitations need to be understood, and choices need to recognized.

"But you see, you may have an important role to help improve life on Earth. Maybe you have an even bigger Destiny than helping one worst-case scenario person.

"You might have to learn the lesson that even those all-powerful feelings of LOve inside you will not, sadly for you, help everyone.

"You may have to learn that to help the majority, sometimes you have to leave behind the minority. Unfortunately for them and you, for they're nice, unless you decide to be your partner's carer, one day you may have to leave this worst-case type of partner.

"You see, if your LOve cannot make a big difference to their life your natural angelic nature may feel too guilty about being with them every day and not making a big enough difference.

"If, or when, you leave that hopeless case type of person, you'll have learned two vast lessons: the beautiful lesson of how to persevere in sharing your LOve; and the sad lesson of when to stop sharing your LOve with a worst-case scenario so you can help the majority in need.

"So what about the type of partner you could meet who is just genetically nice? The type who has almost no problems at all, but is just nice? The type who is not an angel, they're an average human with other lifetimes to come.

"Their niceness does not mean they're angels. You can tell they're not angels by asking questions to determine their understanding on LOve, whether they feel LOve within them, and the Angelic Questions. If they can't provide adequate answers, they are just healthy and nice.

"They probably come from a non-angelic family, where their

family members have good health and genetically inherited niceness or tolerance. They and their family can tolerate your human-angelic conflicts. They can gently support whatever angelic soul path you choose, and maybe one day they'll help your contractual soul purpose.

"What is the lesson here with an angelically nice person?

"Actually, maybe there's no real lesson as such. Maybe this is your ideal partner.

"Maybe they're boring, but they're perfect. Maybe someone so nice will give you positive human love even though they can't understand the divinely perfect LOve you know.

"You can rant and rage or be depressed or sad because your human side is still learning about your soul LOve.

"And even though the nice partner can't understand your LOve or the reasons for your passions, they are likely to still give you nice human love.

"Genetically nice people with good health, from genetically nice, healthy families, will always care for you and want the best for you.

"They will allow you or help you to evolve. If you are upset, they will be passive until you calm down, and then show you ways forward. They will not mind, because they're nice. They will let you study or not study, allow you to be busy or lazy, while you wait for signs for your path. They may even let you go away by yourself when you need space to be alone.

"But most importantly of all, when they have been nice and consistently helped you through your Platformations, they will still be there for you when you start your happy ways of LOve-Based Living. They will be there for you when you begin your project to improve something that can use your skills.

"Their niceness will help you. They will be passive and let you evolve. And one day they may take part in your soul purpose to help you fulfill your Contract.

"Hang on to someone genetically nice but without health

problems. They may be boring, but they're one of your best options for a happy lifelong relationship."

Introducing Relationship/Partner Types C & D - Angelic Bands, Corporate Brands

"Before discussing the next two types of partners, angelic bands and brands need to be considered.

"In my 20s I started to write a book. It began with a car crash that killed a man who had earned the right to join the angelic realms. I knew the book would be about the missions of Angels on Earth, but stopped writing because I had zero ideas of what angels' missions were. Nowadays I understand much more.

"The clue is in imagining the analogy with the three large international organizations, Coca-Cola, Pepsi, and 7UP. There is a hierarchical personnel chart, a human resource structure, from the lowest to the highest persons in each organization.

"Large international companies hire basic but essential workforces of cleaners, storekeepers, drivers, IT personnel, secretaries, administrators, and maintenance staff. It may not matter if a cleaner, storekeeper or whoever worked for Coca-Cola, or Pepsi, or 7UP. They would all do more or less the same line of work for each company.

"As workers earn promotion in each organization, they may become lower-rung supervisors, inspectors, or managers, in charge of cleaners, storekeepers, and so on. Each lower-rung management personnel could easily do the same tasks in any soft drinks company. There is little that's unique about their careers.

"However, the higher an employee rises in each organization's personnel structure, the more specific their role becomes.

"Middle and higher management persons have increasingly different assignments for the brand of soft drink they joined. Their posts are less likely to be easily transferable to other companies because the branding is becoming unique. Slogans, colors, logos, advertising, websites, mission statements, social media campaigns, business philosophy, strategy, and so on, all begin to possess a branding uniqueness that may not be so relevant to the other companies.

"If someone is particularly brilliant, they may earn promotion to join the board of directors, or even become President, Chairperson, or CEO. At this level their roles are unique. They are true experts in their brand, possessing vast knowledge and wisdom about the special plans, aims, objectives, strengths, weaknesses, opportunities and threats of Coca-Cola, Pepsi, or 7UP.

"Personnel might rise to the highest secretarial level, the most senior security person, and so on. All occupations can ascend to their ultimate, where the person becomes a real expert in that field, someone who can be relied on to be as perfect as possible. The higher the person goes within the organization, the more likely it is that their professions become specific to that organization, and are not easily transferable.

"And so it is with the angels-on-earth. Corporate brands are a good analogy for angelic bands.

"For example, in the angelic realms it is normal for angels of a feather to flock together, and join a particular band of angels, relevant to their experience, knowledge, and wisdom. In other words, each angelic band will have its own different, ultimate, purpose that is completely different to that of every other band. And your accumulation of knowledge and wisdom will be needed for one particular band only.

"It is also normal that each band of angels has less specific vacancies available. Just like a secretary, or IT or maintenance person in a corporation, a lower level angel's potential task may be interchangeable with angels in other bands.

"It is OK, totally acceptable, for many angels-on-earth to stop at these lower positions, and not rise higher. Or to stop at any level in the band they've joined. All organizations need janitors as much as directors. Not everyone can be a President or on the board of directors. Not every person, not every angel, needs to strive for such high goals. All levels are needed to staff and run the company, or band of angels.

"When angels-on-earth start to tread their higher Angelic Path on the pathway towards their specific role and Destiny, they may feel a stream of energetic information emanating from their angelic band. The message of the band, portraying their reason for existence, their ultimate goal of being, is getting through to their unconscious minds.

"With this stream of branded and banded consciousness commonly comes a feeling of better morals and ethics on how to live your lives.

"There is potential for how joining a particular band of angels with a specific purpose might impact your relationships.

"Because if you are to meet and live with or marry another angel, happiness could depend on whether or not you both belong to the same angelic band, and have the same angelic calling. It depends on whether you are twin souls, or not.

"And happiness could depend on what level in a hierarchical angelic banded role you've reached compared to your partner."

Relationship/Partner Type C – Angels Not on Your Soul Path (Higher Platformation Issues)

"Many angels-on-earth at some point wonder if they could one day meet and marry another angel. The thing is, there are few angels around. Only about one in every three or four hundred people are angels treading their soul paths in their prospective final lifetime. So you might have to meet three to four hundred possible partners before you find an angel. That's why you feel alone, remember? You might be the only angel you know.

"Anyway, like there are so many drinks companies, large and tiny, all around the world, there are also so many angelic bands to join.

"So even if you are 'lucky' to meet a partner who's also an angel-on-earth, the first issue is that it's highly unlikely you'll be on the same Angelic Path, learning with the same band of angels, at the same level within that band.

"It might feel great to start with. On all levels of your Angelic Path, perhaps you'll both understand LOve inside you. It may feel blissful, as if you've found your true twin soul, and that both your feelings of LOve will last forever.

"However, your relationship may eventually depend on whether or not you both have a conscious memory of your Contracts.

"It's rare, but if you and your partner both have conscious memories of your Contracts, you know whether you are both angels learning lessons. You're aware of the love versus LOve issues and can sustain each other through parts of each Platformation. As you grow together, you may even develop at the same speed, and go through each Platformation at approximately the same time, helping each other evolve in LOve understanding. If this happens, it will be a beautiful life, mutually supportive and ultra-rewarding.

"Unfortunately, this is unlikely to happen. You or the other person, or both of you, are far more likely only to have a hazy unconscious memory of LOve. That means that, on the lower levels of the path, you may not know you're both angels, and only see each other's human faults. And you may split up, because at younger ages you are not so tolerant, and seek perfection.

"The probability is that if you meet an angelic partner they won't be on the same soul purpose path as you. They will veer towards their specific angelic band that is a different band to yours.

"Then the main relationship issues may come later in life, on the higher Platformations of your paths, on the sharing of LOve part of your paths when one or both of you is trying to resolve something you notice in the world that needs improving.

"You see, almost certainly you will have different projects. The analogy mentioned before is that one of you may have a duty with Coca-Cola, and the other with Pepsi. This different branding is highly likely to split you in different directions, even to different parts of the world.

"For example, to fulfill your Contracts, one partner may end up teaching at a local college, the other heading for Africa.

"Can you stay together under those circumstances? That could be your joint decision."

Relationship/Partner Type C – Angels Not on Your Soul Path (Clues To What Actions You Can Take and Why)

"Couples who are both angels-on-earth may have different Contracts, and therefore divergent Destinies to achieve.

"Remember, you are both still human beings, with your physical, emotional, and mental human faults. Those human faults could overshadow your angelic LOve so darkly, you may not grasp each other's needs of Light.

"You know your path is right, and might believe your partner is heading in the wrong direction, and should take a similar route to yours.

"You could want to join their path, when in reality you should be treading your own.

"Or one or both of you may be so busily consumed with your individually specific soul goals, you leave little room for anything else, including for caring and LOving each other.

"Of course, even if your partner is on a different busy path to you, you might stay together for various reasons.

"For example, when the Platformation of sharing LOve arrives, and one of you heads to countries that are irrelevant to your path, you may be able to maintain a long-distance relationship, and see each other at weekends or when possible.

"Or you could maintain a relationship where you'll mainly

do your soul projects separately. You could occasionally fly to various towns or countries with each other, where one of you has a LOving way to enhance others' lives. Assuming you can both schedule enough spare time on your individual busy paths, you could enjoy working holidays, supporting each other's LOving paths.

"These are good options to move forwards together. It will probably feel OK to be apart from each other, because you'll both have so many new, loving friends. Your new contacts made due to fulfilling your soul tasks mean that the partner type of togetherness relationship may not feel quite so important as before. You will not feel alone.

"Anyway, when you both share your LOve within your unique, considerable, and intensive schemes and projects, you'll receive so many invitations. New friends will naturally wish to honor and respect your LOving good works.

"As you both progress to your higher level soul Platformations, each of you might have so many friends and invitations to handle, it could seem like an invasion, an impossibility to ward off the leading of partially separate lives.

"So you may have little choice but to live apart at least part of the time.

"But there's little reason why you might not still have happy times together in your relationship, in between your schedules, providing you can both adjust. Consider public figures such as Presidents or Prime Ministers of different countries who are married to working partners. The very different busy lives mean they will spend much time apart.

"But they can still stay together happily, when their soul lives and human lives permit."

Relationship/Partner Type D – Twin Soul Angels on the Same Soul Path (Lower Platformation Issues)

"Finding an angel-on-earth partner who is on the same

angelic soul path as you is similarly fraught with relationship perils. Consider the scenario of one partner being on a higher Platformation, ready to share their LOve through their soul purpose, and the other person has not learned enough lessons yet to reach that level. How can you understand each other?

"Perhaps the person who is flying high on the pinnacle of their Destiny can look down their mountain path of lessons, at their well-trodden and successful steps, and recognize how the other partner may need to trudge. But how can the trudging person understand a partner who has already overcome those hurdles, and is flying free?

"Also, a potential relationship breakdown is possible if one partner is not ready for their angelic soul purpose and wants to hang on to old ways, to be together daily, and to do everything together. Whereas for the other person it's time to charge ahead and achieve their individual Destiny. Maybe the soul's route must be experienced by themselves because their partner has no inkling or even wish to understand what needs to be achieved.

"Maybe one partner has been comfortable with a particular way of life, and can't let go, whereas the other has to let go to help many in need.

"Maybe one partner has a fear for the future because it's unknown and scary, whereas for the other, the path has opened in exciting ways, with total clarity of exactly what new processes should be doing to achieve their goals.

"Maybe one person will be too consciously afraid they will lose their partner to the soul purpose, and rarely see them enough to enjoy a relationship, whereas the person sharing their LOve on their path may still LOve their partner dearly, they just need to fulfill the Contractual terms for their soul.

"Maybe one person is unconsciously afraid that such a vast and challenging soul purpose is looming for them too, and they see the workload of their partner, and become scared of such a workload for themselves, and it frightens them away from their path.

"In brief, if one partner can't let go for whatever reason, if they cling to old patterns and do not facilitate the new LOving ideals that can increase local, national, or international happiness, either the relationship or the soul purpose may be doomed to failure.

"Life on the other hand can be amazingly marvellous if you meet an angelic partner and both of you are on the same soul paths, with identical soul path Contracts and acts of LOve to achieve. Living together can be gorgeously warm and LOving, especially if you both reach ultimate soul goals you share, at the same time. Then life becomes excitingly rewarding, where you contribute LOve to each other, sharing the same calling to make a difference together, as twin souls.

"Unfortunately, most angels-on-earth do not grow with togetherness understanding of their souls' paths at the same speed. They learn about different human love and Godly LOve lessons at different times of life, especially if one partner is much older. More often than not, even if both angels-on-earth are on identical paths to join the same angelic band, one angelic partner will not understand the level the other angelic partner has reached.

"You see, as mentioned, if you reach a higher Platformation than your partner, you can look down the mountain of angelic life-lessons, and know what they can do.

"You can explain with every argument you can think of that you know what they can and should do to achieve the next Platformation of LOve.

"But will they listen? Probably they won't.

"They can't listen, because they're still learning through personal experiences in the University of Life. They hear your words, but can't understand. They feel your LOve, but they see your faults.

"They may still have to experience karmic lessons, interactions due to loss of LOve, and addictive desires for LOve. Until they learn their life lessons, and earn the right to move along the path to the next Platformation up, they will probably never understand your wisdom, or that you have already learned those lessons.

"Anyway, how one partner needs to learn their Platformation lessons may not be how the other person already learned their lessons. Each person's processes, methods or techniques of learning could be poles apart.

"And the same can happen in reverse. If your partner moves higher than you, you will rarely be able to understand their lives, motivations, and inspirations.

"Even if you move at the same speed through the Platformations, lower down you probably won't understand you're both angels-on-earth.

"Then you are likely to interact in human ways, seeing each other's human faults."

Relationship/Partner Type D – Twin Soul Angels on the Same Soul Path (Clues To What Actions You Can Take and Why)

"It's perhaps a sad framework for life that, if you have a partner who is an angel-on-earth with the same angelic soul purpose as you, it should be a fun, happy life. But because you're both learning your lessons, one person will probably be on a higher Platformation up the Angelic Path. Therefore one may see the other's faults, that they are not as perfect as they would wish. And you may then split up.

"But something may keep you together. Through all the ups and downs, you know that you love each other, that you both understand LOve, and you are destined to share your lives together.

"You know you can LOvingly support each other's paths, and reach out for the other's LOving help when in need.

"You may consciously realize you are creating a mutual bond of learning. Eventually, you might both join the same band of angels.

"When you've learned enough, and passed enough University of Life tests, the time will come to focus on sharing your LOve with the world. When you discover that you both have the same soul purpose, you will know you have found your twin soul.

"Working LOvingly as one with your twin soul will be an amazingly happy time. Your partnership can become even stronger, even more magnificent, because of the bonding you've built as you've passed through your Platformations together.

"The main quality needed is patience. You need patience to help the partner correct their mistakes and learn their lessons. Patience is needed to lay back and watch them make mistakes. Patience is needed not to react, and instead to regularly share unconditional LOve. Patience is needed just to let them learn their own lessons, in their way, and in their timing. You need patience to know the right time will come for each other to progress, and to harmoniously balance your lives together for the good of all.

"If you're both blessed with adequate patience, as you move through the Platformations, you'll both be blessed too. God and the angels above will notice your mistakes and errors. They will also recognize and record your noteworthy attempts to do what is right under sometimes exacting circumstances.

"It's rare for two partners to know they are angels-on-earth, especially on early Platformations. But if you both know this truth, stay together through thick and thin. Assist, and be of service to each other's development.

"When it is time to do your soul purpose, if it's the same soul purpose, have fun.

"It will be fun to share your LOve with the world with someone you love. To share human love and Godly LOve at the same times as each other, in the same ways, and the same places, will be as enriching an experience as you can ever dare hope.

"If you help each other throughout your twin soul Destinies you will both benefit greatly, and be inspired to achieve greater heights by being supported by two such LOving beings as you."

Relationship/Partner Type E – Celibacy (General Issues of Interaction)

"Although celibacy was mentioned before, it's an important option for many angels so we'll explore the subject a little more. Remember, it is a main concept of the Brahma Kumaris and other spiritual organizations that celibacy readily recreates Godliness within an angel-to-be's soul, and kindles a relationship of LOve with the Supreme soul.

"So the fifth and final type of relationship an angel often contemplates is celibacy, a loving relationship between themselves and God, with a partner alongside their LOving journey. Celibacy with a partner may seem to offer a safer path than other relationship types. Celibacy is how angels can live in purity of spirit. It is a way for angels to love themselves without confusing and confounding the pure LOve of God with the baggage sexual love or lust can bring.

"For some angels-to-be, celibacy means they will not be so distracted from their souls' destinies. They can more easily and more regularly focus on their search for God within themselves and a sharing of LOve to expand joy.

"Finding a partner who understands that sexuality does not have to be an essential force in a relationship, and who instead unconditionally accepts your passionate desire to share Godly LOve, may be a partner worth keeping.

"Confidence and bonding can then grow high, because they need not be concerned or distracted by a partner's potentially impure sexual whims, needs, and ways. To not be reliant on someone else for sex, to not have someone reliant on them for sex, to not have a partner who might regularly interfere with their lives sexually, facilitates freedom to achieve their LOving reasons for existence in any manner needed.

"Mental strength can then increase automatically, supported by their loving partner, until they overtake their Destiny with self-determining, self-sufficient, self-realized projects.

"As mentioned before, some angels-to-be know their past lives. And they know they previously experienced physical sexuality in at least some of those lives. So, they also know that the lesson of sexuality has probably already been learned; they need other lessons now. They sense it is now time to move on to a closer, celibate connection to God.

"The Gautama Buddha parted from his wife and child, to try to reach divine enlightenment, free of the impurity of wants and desires. I am not advocating leaving your family at all. But if family or partners are abusive, or if they try to prevent you achieving your soul's needs on Earth, perhaps dedicated angels-to-be can try a similar process to the Buddha, and share projects or schemes to help others with LOving, compassionate action?

"Celibacy also gives chances to learn self-control, to search without sexual hindrance for ways to overcome ungodly thoughts, to be in charge of bodily desires, and to be more LOving. If you learn to control your flesh, and your brain's neural pathways learn how to make other self-control decisions too, then you become naturally more likely to control your path, and succeed in your soul purpose ahead.

"Some people who become celibate feel it easier to connect to God, and gain spiritual benefits. It may seem that life becomes easier, quicker, more effective. It may even seem like God is rewarding you for controlling earthly sex desires. You would reward your children for solving lessons at school, wouldn't you? Maybe, as God's children, some of you may be rewarded too in the school of life, still able to bond in a loving relationship while solving inherently burdensome sexual lessons. Whatever that means to you as an individual.

"Understand that God wants to help you achieve your soul's mission. But perhaps for some people that's not so easy if your LOve thoughts are fogged, and jumbled with thoughts of sex or masturbation. This is especially true if you are with someone who might mainly want you as an object to control, or for sexual gratification.

"If you seek celibacy in a relationship, finding a concerned, caring partner to share a celibate life with is like winning the lottery. Not easy, but ecstatic if you win.

"A mind cleared and cleaned of sexuality issues leaves room for more important matters, such as unconscious conversations with God about the next important steps on your Angelic Path.

"Many people though, including angels, crave love from another person. They hope the right relationship will come soon. They hope they will find their twin soul, twin flame, the love they desire from so deeply within their souls, but cannot yet attain.

"Consider the reason for a relationship. Is it to find someone compatible, a twin soul to share a happy life together? That does not need to include sexuality. If you can find a partner with similar celibate thoughts as you, you may achieve your desired compatibility, relationship happiness, and a pathway to your LOving Destiny."

Chapter 8

Destiny, Free Will Issues

On Leaping Too High Too Soon

"Let's talk about angels who know they have a vocation to achieve, but who want to leap ahead quickly.

"Recently, I received an email that said, 'I'm a 30-year-old angel, and can't wait to do what I'm here for. If you have any clues how I can leap ahead, let me know!'

"Angels often want to leap. I replied, 'One word you wrote is not appropriate. It's the word, "Leap".'

"There are not many angelic leaps. The path is a slow growth of gentle pushes, of experiential knowledge. You find truth on a ladder's bottom rung, then feel in the dark the rung you can touch above, notice how that rung feels, and then when you are spiritually ready, softly tug yourself up.

"Few angels know what the next year has in store, because next year's goodies are usually hidden. Gifts that secretly await may be incredibly profound. But knowing that before you are ready to climb the next level may give such a surprise, you'll crash back down the ladder.

"Do not leap ahead too soon. You will progress naturally when you are ready to use your future gifts.

"If you persist in wanting to leap, please buy a 20-rung ladder, stand it against a wall, and try to leap to the top. Impossible? Some angels might not think so.

"But that's a good analogy for what you are trying to do. You are trying to leap without carefully climbing rung by rung, feeling and learning the sturdiness and safety of the footholds at each step.

"If you want to leap, may I suggest you have seven buzz-phrases? Back off. Calm down. Enjoy life. Love friends. LOve the world. Accept all. Create good.

"Let's talk more of climbing and leaping ahead."

Climbing Your Life's Mountain

"Although an analogy of climbing a mountain is not new, and it can help non-angels, it is more useful and pertinent for angels-on-earth with a Destiny to reach. To see life as a mountain to climb may let you view Platformation hurdles in a different and better light.

"There are many routes to the mountain's peak. Some will be easy, some not so. Some paths may be so straight you won't learn enough lessons, others so meandering you'll have too many lessons. A path may be so narrow you won't have enough choice to find your real soul purpose, or so broad your soul purpose will be lost within too many options. The route might be so long you'll never reach the end, or so short there might not be enough time to achieve almost anything.

"On your soul's mountain, there may be symbolic rivers or ravines to cross. You will need to build bridges.

"There may be crossroads, T-junctions, twin-forks, and spaghetti junctions. Your Free Will should to decide which route to take.

"And there may be metaphorical boulders blocking your way, holes in the path you might fall through, dead ends to turn back from, mudslides that cover or hide your path, and overhangs to overcome.

"One thing is certain. Climbing the soul path up your mountain of life needs a great deal of time. All those of you who want to do it now, to get to the mountaintop now, to do your soul purpose on Earth now, remember this for the rest of your lives. It's near impossible to get to the top without choosing a route from your Free Will, and overcoming that route's hurdles along the way.

"You'll need perseverance. You'll need to learn special skills.

You'll need reservoirs of love, and fountains of LOve.

"Whether you reach the mountaintop might not depend upon your choice of route. Many routes could lead to the summit. Any route could be important. It's equally important what parts you decide to climb, why you chose to climb those parts, and how you tread them.

"Enjoy the routes. Do not glance back with regret, for all you can ever do is live, love and LOve according to your Free Will, and what you know at the time.

"Become a master of your Destiny, with or without support from others with more wisdom about the path than you. Resolving mountain paths is part of the innate beauty of angelic mastership development.

"Benefits of finding support from a True Angelic Master will be described later, but if you're lucky enough to have one as your guide, take advice about each obstacle on your path. Masters are like a gateway to knowledge you need to understand your life. Or instead, attend courses of the Brahma Kumaris, or start a supportive Angelic Group for Evolving Souls to share "Secrets of Angels on Earth" so you can discuss life's successes and mishaps with other angels-on-earth, and ease yourself up that mountain.

"If in doubt, take any route that seems to lead towards sharing your highest LOve. It may not matter which route. If you take a route that seems unreasonable for your Destiny, your angelic guides might soon take you off that path, and guide you onto one that's more relevant.

"At best, you may be lucky and choose a way that is your destined soul path.

"At worst, the way may be too long or confusing, and guides may have to plot a new route, especially if you haven't followed their signs. So signs are the next topic."

Signposts on Your Soul Route

"If you were driving in a strange foreign country, without any form of satellite navigation, you would use a map and watch for signposts to point the right way.

"Similarly there are maps and signposts on your life's roads, albeit substantially secret, to point the right way to your soul purpose.

"If the maps and signposts are produced and used by you, it's called Free Will. Sometimes Free Will can lead you to your Destiny.

"If maps and signposts are produced and used by your angels, your God, it's called Destiny.

"Free Will and Destiny live closely together. Issues about having too much of one or the other is a separate topic, because chaos can result.

"Apart from Free Will and Destiny, there are also Accidents and Foolishness. Accidents you have little control over, whereas Foolishness is a human trait we all suffer from occasionally.

(Laughter.)

"Destiny and Free Will are the two main forces to understand. They help you achieve soul goals, and find happiness on Earth joined to the pleasure of Heaven.

"Destiny and Free Will are the bringers of LOve and good fortune, or barriers of your human or soul life if you take no notice.

"Getting the balance right between Destiny and Free Will can make or break your human and soul paths.

"So the keyword is 'balance'. A balance between Destiny and Free Will is so important for angels.

"Many angelic angles need to be understood. Let's look at Free Will first."

Your Three States of Free Will

"Free Will means your human nature can make choices that may or may not be relevant to your soul. Some choices will be awful and take you down an inappropriate track. Other choices may be brilliant and guide you to a route you had signed for in your Contract.

"How do you make better decisions from your Free Will? The answer depends on your type of person.

"There are three primary states of Free Will. Most angels have all three at different points on their paths.

"A clue to how you tread your life's path is, which of these options are you like the most?

"Option one is, do you get anxious, depressed, sad or fearful knowing your soul has a role to play? Do you try to force your human and soul paths to merge, to seek and achieve your ultimate reasons for existence? Do you worry that you're not on the right path, that you must find why you're here, and find it now, before it's too late?

"Option two is, are you mainly passive? Do you let your human and soul paths drift wherever life flows? Do you let gut feelings guide you with no analysis? Do you release decisions to those above, with no responsibility for your own actions? Do you hope all is well, that you'll find the right path soon, but rarely do much about it?

"Option three is, do you become rebellious and deny your path? Are you so fearful that Destiny may force you down a route, you often take a different way? Do you dislike the thought that unseen forces can guide you? Are you afraid of losing control of your Destiny?

"These three states of Free Will are common behaviors for most angels at different points in their lives.

"So it's necessary to know issues of the three states of Free Will in more depth."

Clues To Free Will 1 – Being Too Anxious To Find or Achieve Your Soul Purpose

"Angels-on-earth know they need to fulfill a soul purpose. But some take their role too seriously. They want to do their mission, and do it now. They don't want to wait even a day. Many of you in this room are like that. We have spoken about it.

"Hands up if you've been like this and have felt this state of Free Will. Perhaps you've sometimes felt anxiety to do your soul purpose as quickly as possible?

(Hands raised.)

"Hmm, about half of you...

"That is not good. Your anxiousness won't open your path, it blocks it. You have so many thoughts about how, why, where, and when you will get there and achieve your Destiny, that you create blocks against it. You can't see the woods for the trees.

"Issues around how to find why you're here, what you need to do, may take up most of your thoughts most days. You could become completely unfocused, and end up confused. Then you might be unable to find what you seek, unable even to notice signs from your angelic guides trying to help your search.

"But you have something else to consider which you may disregard in your rush to fulfil what you are here for, now. You may not be able to find your soul purpose if you try to reach your mountain's peak too soon.

"You know, you can't possibly fulfill your Contract, do your soul purpose, your reason for existence, and make a positive change in a bigger way until you've put all the relevant building blocks in position. You can't build a solid house without solid foundations. You can't do brain surgery without learning about the brain. You can't jump from rung two on a ladder to rung 30.

"You need appropriate foundations first, then learn what is needed, then climb the ladder to your goal.

"To help, maybe start a "Secrets of Angels on Earth" Group, to support evolving angelic souls, or join an organization like the Brahma Kumaris. Build foundations, learn about soul needs, and climb the rungs of your path one at a time.

"As a final analogy, if twelve stepping-stones are placed to help you cross a fast-flowing river, you would not try to jump quickly from the closest stone to the last. You could slip, fall in, be ripped by the current, and never reach the other side. You should take each step slowly but surely, ensuring you have a firm footing before moving on. So it should be with your soul path.

"If you release your desire to cross the river of life quickly, if you accept you may need to seek additional stepping-stones to fulfill your role, perhaps you'll not block the signs from your angelic guides.

"Then you're more likely to get to where you so desire to be, in quicker and more manageable steps.

"So if you're feeling anxious and so on to find or achieve your soul purpose, maybe try to back off. Allow the appropriate way to unfold in its own time, in its own way. In the meantime, maybe you can relax and enjoy anything or everything a happy life has to offer.

"Also, an angel-on-earth, who is too much wanting to find the right path, may seek advice from clairvoyants, spirit guides or angels or whatever to help them too often, and seek numerous readings and predictions.

"That may be OK for some angels, if not taken to extremes. But I've known people who, wanting to find and do what they're here for, rely on clairvoyants, and lose their Free Will almost entirely.

"Balance should be in all things. Part of the reason for your existence is to understand LOve, and the beauty of your path through Free Will. Where's your lesson if you flee from living, and delegate your life and soul path decisions to a clairvoyant? There is no experiential lesson there.

"If you did not cross the stepping-stones one-by-one correctly and firmly, maybe you'll not achieve your dream.

"Seek help from all sources, but if you seek support too much, discard it and learn your lessons through personal experiences and balanced Free Will.

"The one exception is support from sources who know the Angelic Path. For example, True Angelic Masters won't need to be clairvoyant. They logically know which Platformation you are on, and which stepping-stone or rung on the ladder you might need to take next. If you're lucky enough to find one, they can help you grow.

"If you are too anxious and your anxiety means you might not achieve your Contract's Destiny in this lifetime, it's far better to lay back and let your Free Will become more passive, more balanced, more aware.

"Then you can just wait.

"Wait for the unasked-for signs, the unrequested big event, the unexpected greater understanding. Time is needed to achieve adequate learning on all Platformations, including this.

"Wait passively and contentedly, please."

Clues To Free Will 2 – Being Too Passive To Seek or Achieve Your Soul Purpose

"The second state of Free Will is being too passive to seek your soul purpose. It's the opposite of the first state of Free Will, when you are too anxious, and desire to achieve your soul purpose fast, and the anxiety blocks your pathway to success.

"Being too passive to seek or achieve your soul purpose occurs sometimes. Especially this occurs when you are on the Platformation of acceptance, and have integrated acceptance deeply within your consciousness. You now truly accept everything with LOve in your heart, soul, and mind.

"Maybe though, you can almost not open your mouth to speak, for fear of not accepting something enough.

"In this case, you've done well learning your lesson of LOving acceptance of humanity. You LOve everything you previously hated or disliked. But now you're way too accepting. You've become far too passive. You are so passive you are unable to create an action that could help you to find and accomplish your

Contract.

"Hands up if at some time, or sometimes, you've been like this.

(Hands raised.)

"About three-quarters of you have been passively too accepting.

"Some of you will have been through patches where you deliberately decided to be passive. Perhaps somehow you knew that it wasn't the right time to perform on your path anyway, so you might as well be passive. You might as well do nothing and wait for something that feels more right for your soul's LOve.

"If you choose to be too passive, to use too little Free Will, you need to claw a bit of action back. Try to share your LOve, somehow, anyhow, any type, anywhere. Otherwise your passivity may mean it's less likely you'll learn the lessons of love and LOve, and achieve your ultimate Destiny in this lifetime.

"However, you may have achieved what was needed on the Platformation of acceptance, appropriately, with balance. You can now deliberately choose to let your human and soul paths drift passively. You can let your unconscious thoughts take you where they will.

"Then you may be more likely to notice that your God or angelic guides are trying to contact you, trying to give you signs of what, where, who, why and how you should be.

"The important question is then whether you're being too passive to do anything about their signs. Being too passive when you've seen signs is Foolishness. Nothing is always for goodness.

"When you let go of Free Will just enough to allow in the angelic forces above, they can unveil your Destiny easier. But you may be so passive your Foolishness rejects the signs.

"When you let go of Free Will, you allow Destiny or Foolishness to reign supreme."

Clues To Free Will 3 – Being Too Rebellious or in Denial of Your Soul Purpose

"The third state of Free Will is when some angels-on-earth deny or rebel against their soul path. They do not want unseen forces to secretly shove them down a route they didn't ask for. They are unconsciously or consciously aware of their future Destiny. They somehow realize that they must have made a Contract, and they don't like the thought of being out of control. They don't like the idea that they must keep to Contractual terms and conditions, for the rest of their life.

"They're rebelling against being held to a Contract, against being advised what to do, or what not to do. They seek anything in their lives that does not seem like they are being dictated to, because they desire independence. They seek the ability to control their choices of life.

"Hands up if you've felt like this.

(Hands raised.)

"Yes, most of you... That's a standard way for an angel-on-earth to interact.

"If you sense inklings that Destiny has guided your fate, you may rebel and consciously take a different route.

"The best-laid plans of your Contract, the best-laid plans of your angelic guides, all will pale into insignificance compared to your rebellious Free Will strength of mind, yes?

"Funnily enough, your soul purpose may still be of significant importance to you, but in a way that **you** want to do it, not how other people, or unseen forces want you to do it.

"Perhaps you may even know deep down that you can't do your soul path yet anyway. If you feel like that, you are probably correct.

"It might not be relevant to tread your soul path yet because you still have to learn much more, and you still have to experience much more. You need to live a human life to achieve your soul life, in later life. So you deny your path now, so that you can bask in the glory of enjoying Free Will.

"I'll tell you a little story about someone I know well. This person always knew his daughter would share her angelic LOve by doing what he was doing, a particular soul path that helped many thousands of people around the world. When she was in her 20s, the friend said to her, 'You know, you should be doing what I'm doing.'

"She replied, 'No I shouldn't. I'll be doing what you're doing in my 50s.'

"It's good to know your path…

(Laughter.)

"Her father continued, and said, 'It may be a good idea to come on some courses.'

"She replied, 'No thank you, it's not relevant to me yet, I'm doing different things.'

"He tried a third time. 'If you come on the next batch of courses, you'll learn much about what you'll do in your 50s.'

"She was emphatic in her response. 'No thanks. I'll read your books.' Her father hadn't written books then, but he has now.

(Laughter.)

"The probability is that his daughter's current path isn't the path that was laid out for her. She has chosen Free Will. Rebelliousness runs in that family. But maybe it's not rebelliousness. Maybe she knows her path genuinely?

"Can I tell you another little story? These are good examples of rebellious Free Will. A friend's daughter phoned her family after being at University for two weeks. 'I don't like it here,' she said. 'Come and get me.'

"'You've only been there for two weeks,' her parents replied. 'You can't leave already.'

"'Yes, I can,' she said. 'I've already phoned a different university, and they've accepted me.'

(Laughter.)

"She was there for about three weeks when she phoned

her family again. 'I don't like it here either. I'm applying for Cambridge University.'

"'But you can't keep changing universities,' her parents said.

"She replied, 'It's OK. I knew I'd go to Cambridge when I was three.'

(Laughter.)

"Eventually, she was accepted into Cambridge University.

"She had exercised Free Will, denied her Contract, and rebelled against the knowledge that her path included Cambridge.

"But more importantly, she had the inner drive, the spiritual vision, and the human humility to realize she had to back down from the denial of her path, her rebellion, before it was too late.

"Think about this for yourselves. If rebellion against your soul purpose continues for too long, you may deny your Contract.

"Then there are only a few options left, all of which are down to your angelic guides."

Guides and Guardian Angels

"I've met many people who say they have seen a very strange thing. They are never able to describe it fully or properly. They struggle for words. Usually they end up saying something like, 'I've seen a sort of gigantic Tower Block (apartment building) 'Tower Block' is the phrase commonly used, and is perhaps more 'catchy' than 'apartment building'. Are you suggesting 'Tower Block' is not 'American' language? If so, perhaps use 'Block of Apartments' and change the four times 'Tower Block' is used. Or a phrase that captures the massive scale of what some people see in the sky, but it's too vast to even understand a small part properly. It's so big, I can't describe the size.' They often gesticulate with their hands, opening their arms wide in the air, trying to show how impossible it is to recount the dimensions.

"You know the saying, 'There are more things in Heaven and Earth than you can even dream about?'

"Well, this is one of those things that most people will never dream about, but which, for those that can dream or daydream, seems to be real.

"If they can find adequate words to describe a part of the Tower Block in more detail, they commonly say there's a room in the tower for every person on Earth, with immense space to enable expansion as the population grows. In each room is one table, and around the table are typically three, or occasionally four, guides.

"They go on to say that it seems one guide may be a person's main angelic guide, the Guardian Angel. They might call the guide by different names, like Chief, Life Guide, Doorkeeper, or Gatekeeper. Their role is to allow people and events into and out of human beings' lives. They will plot ways to help the person they have the responsibility to guide, down relevant paths. Their responsibility may also include letting the two other guides into and out of your life.

"The other two guides are usually not the two who were at your Contract, not your mother and father. They probably are guides for specific needs.

"For example, if you take up dentistry for four years, you may have a dentistry guide for four years, and if you are a soldier for ten years, you may have a soldier guide for ten years.

"The point is, the three guides have different roles and responsibilities. They are trying to help dissimilar aspects of your human and soul life, yet combine with each other. That may lead to differences, where one guide may need you to do something, be somewhere, or meet someone, but their aims are incompatible with the objectives of the other two.

"People who see this often notice that the guides are studying what seems to be a large map spread across a table. It appears that they are trying to plot a route for the next part of your human or soul life. They wish to ensure that their differing goals can be compatible with each other's, so you can overcome a hurdle, or so you can be guided towards your next Platformation. They are attempting to help your Free Will choose your Destiny.

"If you see the Tower Block, and angels or guides are in your room in the tower, they may be at a pivotal point of planning for your life.

"You might be one of the few lucky angels-on-earth who is allowed to see your guides plotting your route carefully. Then you can know consciously all is well, that there'll be an Angelic Path arriving soon to help you on toward implementing your soul calling.

"This can take the pressure off you, and you can relax, knowing that even if you don't understand, all is well in the higher scheme of life."

The Map of Destinies of Your Life

"The best way to describe the map of the destinies of your life is to imagine a map of the country you live in.

"Then imagine you need to travel from north to south. There are many routes and many ways to move along each route.

"Maybe you could fly quickly, directly, or go fast by train with a few stops on the way.

"Perhaps you could drive along a highway, dual carriageway, or main road.

"Or you could catch a bus, or choose the scenic route, traveling through villages, taking your time in a leisurely manner.

"You could pedal by bike, or walk on foot, and amble along, not worrying about how long it will take to arrive.

"And of course, you may decide to stop off on the way to visit a good friend, to absorb knowledge from a famous museum, or experience the thrills of an amusement park.

"But whichever way you decide to travel from the northern to southern parts of your country, you are unlikely to choose dirt tracks unless you have no choice.

"You are angelically guided in the same way because your

angelic guides in the Tower Block are poring over a map.

"The map of your life looks remarkably similar to a large-scale road map of your country, except there are lines relevant not just to places you need to go, but also to people you need to meet, and experiences you need to have.

"It's a very complicated map because each of your three guides is trying to achieve their objectives for you. That means, relevant to the needs of each guide, there are three sets of places you need to go, three lots of people you need to meet, and three types of experiences to enjoy or endure.

"So guides pore over the map. Your every thought, word, or action may need them to plot another route, to fulfill all three of their different aims on the same road, or at the same junctures.

"The guides plan potential destinies, secreting them away from your conscious mind, leaving it to your unconsciousness, your Free Will, to decide which route you will take.

"You, at one point or another, can use Free Will. You might choose your own, incompatible choices of routes. You may even think you will never, ever accept any guidance or any Destiny.

"If you use Free Will to turn away from your angelic guides' plotted courses, they will need to plot a distinctly different course again, and maybe again and again, hoping your Free Will can eventually choose the right path. They cannot force you to take a route. That would be dictatorial. They are not allowed to dictate your life, only to guide it.

"As a last resort, your guides will have little choice but to let you achieve your Destiny in the next lifetime. You do not have to complete your Destiny in this lifetime. You can break your Contract.

"But be assured you will probably return to Earth again, and again until you fulfill your Contract.

"So you might as well accept some guidance, and travel along your soul path now."

Plotting the Destiny Routes

"Let's suppose you need to travel from a city in one country, to a city in another. You need to decide which route is the best choice to take, considering your reasons for traveling. You also should check which method is most appropriate to get you to your destination on time, and whether any stopovers are needed.

"Your angelic guides try to do the same. Their aims and objectives are to agree on a meeting point or points on your soul path at which you need to arrive, because there, all of their three contrasting aims will be met.

"By the time you reach a meeting point, they will have previously helped and guided you to build adequate foundation knowledge for your next steps on your soul pathway. If you recognize their signs, or make excellent choices of your own, you will be able to achieve the next rung on climbing the ladder towards the attainment of your Contract.

"They're guiding your Destiny, placing thoughts in your way to guide you on a path, without ever dictating, never telling you or forcing you to do it. Always the guides allow for your Free Will. They continuously re-plot your way, and re-plot again and again if needed.

"The speed and ease of the route may depend on your Contract. I have met angels with strong memories of making their Contract. When being asked what they'd like to do, some say a sentence like, 'Give me your toughest task, I can handle it.' Most people I've met who remember saying, 'Give me your toughest task,' have regretted it ever since. Some, though, may have special soul callings, and become exceptionally gifted leaders, game-changers, teachers or role models for a better world.

"After you move on from this world, if you want to return back down to Earth for another go at life even when you've achieved your Destiny and it's against all the advice of those above, I suggest you don't say, 'Give me your toughest task.' The guides have authority over plotting your path. They might have to plot dirt tracks for you, even if you have a dazzling potential to make a difference for a better existence. Well, you asked for the toughest task.

"Hands up if you know this.

(Hands raised.)

"Yes, there are a lot of you. Even if you don't remember your Contract, you know this to be true. Most of the time, the guides will try to get you onto aircraft, a train, or a cruise ship, to get you to your destination quicker, easier, or with more enjoyment. They hope to help you find a fun life of LOve-Based Living.

"But you have Free Will, and if you deny the route, they may try a motorway.

"If that doesn't help, and you refuse to travel along a faster motorway, they'll plot smaller, not so easy, but good roads.

"If you deny that option, they might try to guide you to travel along the narrow, winding, bumpier, potholed routes.

"As a last resort, when your Free Will rejects every positive opportunity placed in your path, they will have little choice but to plan dirt tracks."

Lessons for Destiny on Dirt Tracks

"Your guides can easily recognize if you're blocking your soul path by being too anxious, too passive or too rebellious to do your soul purpose. Depending on your Contract, they might need to plot a new route, and plot and plot again until you get it, and choose a better way forward for your soul.

"Eventually, they may determine that they tried their best efforts to guide you. But they also realize that your Free Will is led too much by your anxious, passive, or rebellious nature, and never in this entire lifetime will you be able to fulfill your Contract. Then they may, as a last resort, try to plot dirt tracks to help you get back on course.

"In other words, after trying to get you onto the right track in positive ways enough times, if you are disregarding their signs and seem likely to never achieve your Destiny, they may arrange a type of dirt track experience, to help you back to the right vision of your path.

"Then you might find your life changes. You may enter a period of illness, bankruptcy, shock, or loss of someone or something, have an accident, near-death experience, or awful career. Anything might happen that could make you sit up and reevaluate what you are doing and how you do it, to give you another chance to tread your path properly.

"In the whole scheme of how the universe works, though, all might be well. The most vital aspects to judge at the end of a lifetime are whether or not you achieved your Destiny, and how you did it.

"But please do not consider everything that happens is a lesson. That's not how it is. Try to discern whether life events comply with the universal Laws of Karma and Destiny. Is there something you are doing with your life that maybe is not the best option for your soul?

"I repeat, it's important to discern that not all illnesses and events are Destiny. Illnesses could be genetic or acquired from the community. Accidents could be exactly that, Accidents. Losses or awful careers could be due to Accidents or Foolishness.

"I've met many people who think that even the tiniest most simple thing that happens to them must be due to Destiny. That is not how human lives or divine forces manifest. Please don't believe that everything that ever happens is determined in your Contract, or by those above. Learn discernment. How to discern will be mentioned later.

"Some angels don't like to hear the potential for guides to help them become ill, or steer them toward a not-so-perfect situation or relationship and the like.

"That is because angels-on-earth know perfect LOve. It doesn't seem as if an illness, accident or near-death experience can possibly be LOve. And of course, angels are also human beings, brought up to respect the values of society where only good should ever come to anyone.

"Angels-to-be who need adverse lessons on dirt tracks often haven't evolved enough in a specific way. They don't yet perceive the contrasts between Godly Unconditional LOve, and Godly Conditional LOve. They can't grasp that kindness and highest LOve motives can be compatible with conditional lessons. More about Godly Unconditional LOve and Godly Conditional LOve will be considered later. They are seemingly conflicting concepts for some people to understand, so for now, perhaps it is better to tell a story to demonstrate some of the issues involved?

"I remember when, for over ten years, I'd achieved so many miracles on people or animals who were supposed to be sick forever, or die from whatever, and yet were cured in one session in my clinic, at their home, or even when meeting in the street.

"But I never dreamed of telling about those cures. I didn't want ego, didn't want to boast about possible miracles. I was so passive, not even my parents and friends knew.

"One day, my adrenals collapsed to 17 nanomils on a synacthen test. Steroids prevented early death.

"Doctors predicted two years to live. Steroids extract calcium from bones. Nothing at that time could rebuild bones, so a prognosis was a painful death when bones fractured and punctured the lungs as I breathed.

"While dying, I had a cataclysmic thought. Curing through healing was my soul purpose to help the world. Unexpectedly I realized that I'd been too passive, that I had no intention of ever doing my soul purpose.

"At that moment came a flash of enlightenment. If I would never manifest Contract and Destiny, then God, guides, and angels were entitled to warn that accomplishments could come in the next lifetime.

"It felt like a good decision was made, that sharing soul LOve was more important than this particular, wasted, human lifetime.

"I'd been too humble. I should have told family, friends and others about patients' cures. Maybe I should have advertised, been on TV and radio, anything to show there were ways to potentially improve health and well-being.

"Spontaneously, I promised my soul that if I had another chance, even in the next lifetime, I would do it properly next time around. I felt the promise go deep inside the soul.

"A few nights later a dream stated that on Sunday at 10am I must visit a specific church where I'd never been before and ask, 'Who is your best healer?'

"It felt silly to obey a dream, but I did precisely as told. A born-again Christian service was in full swing. As people danced in the aisles to Jesus, I said, 'Hello, who is your best healer?'

"The wife of the pastor, a medical doctor, placed her hands on my back. That area, near the adrenal glands, felt like a block of ice for an hour and a half.

"Later, when I swallowed steroids, it felt like I'd overdosed. Feeling amazing natural energy, I requested another synacthen test. Doctors refused, saying adrenal collapse can't be cured, and tests are expensive, so I had to accept I would die. But vitality had returned. I persuaded them to one last test.

"Adrenal function had returned to 285 nanomils, enough natural adrenalin to survive. Doctors couldn't believe it, and wrote on hospital notes, 'Cured by a healer.'

"I felt embarrassed that because I hadn't healed openly, many had suffered needlessly. Yet that lady in the church had selflessly cured something doctors had said was incurable.

"I kept the profound, heartfelt promise to my soul, and dedicated this life to a soul purpose of healing, 16 hours a day, seven days a week. Within a few years, so many wonderfully positive things happened. It could only have been guides setting up a pathway through their maps of life. I was guided in extraordinary ways.

"A man stopped to chat outside a Mind, Body, Spirit Festival in London. After discussing patients' cures and near-death experiences, he offered an invitation to appear on Danish TV, and to join the Danish royalty Knights of Malta. It didn't seem strange. It somehow felt natural.

"'Sorry,' I said. 'I don't feel strong enough.'

"'You're coming to Denmark,' he replied. 'If you think you can't fly, I'll send an air ambulance!'

(Laughter.)

"In busy Oxford Street, in London, a lady fell, and held her ankle in agony, unable to stand. I didn't speak, just placed hands on her ankle until the pain went and she could stand again. I tried to walk away, but she stopped me. 'What did you do?' she asked.

"'Nothing much,' I said, and walked away again.

"'Come back!' she called. 'I sprained my ankle, and you healed it in a two minutes. What did you do?'

"So I mentioned about being cured.

"'I'd like you to work for me,' she said. 'I'm a director of complementary medical services in prisons. You can help prisoners and train other therapists.'

"Working in Her Majesty's Prisons, Feltham and Coldingley, was wonderful. Our research presented at the House of Commons showed prisoners and warders relieved from stress, depression, anger, and so on. All from helping a lady who had fallen in the street.

"Suffice to say, mystically unexpected meetings pushed toward Destiny as if it was urgent. Within five years I was offered honorary degrees and a visiting professorship. Invitations came from doctors to work in their prestigious Harley Street, London clinics, from Japanese Reiki Masters to be their Honorary President of Reiki in Japan, from A-list Beverly Hills film stars, from the UK's Doctor Healer Network, from the House of Commons Committee for Complementary Medicine, from a

Native American tribe to be their shaman, from Tuaregs in the Sahara Desert to be their medicine man, and in unlikely ways to become a therapist or advisor to four royal families in three continents.

"Not wanting to deny a soul path again I accepted every invitation, just saying, 'Yes,' to everything.

"It was an astonishing time. But I also felt terribly ashamed because I realized that, if I had been less humble and more open ten years before, I could have helped to improve so many more lives.

"I tell this story because it's relevant for many people. Think... Are you wasting your life, not doing anything special enough to enhance society?

"Do you have a gift to help society but aren't using it entirely and never intend to use it?

"Be warned. Your guides will try to hop you on a plane or along a motorway, or whichever fast track they can. They will try, try, and try again. But if you continuously deny your path, they may need to try dirt tracks to give you an awakening.

"Don't be scared, please. Dirt tracks are your angelic guides' final resort. Before that, you have many options on routes up your mountain.

"How to notice Destiny Signposts is important for many angels, so that's the next topic for your soul's path."

Clues To Notice Destiny Signposts

"If you're aware enough, eight options let you view Destiny Signposts along your pathway. All can lead to positive LOve and soul path outcomes.

"Option number one is, watch for synchronicities that occur three times in quick succession.

"But, if something happens once, say, 'So what. Anything can happen once. It can probably be ignored.'

"If something happens twice quite quickly one after the other, maybe view the events as coincidence, but keep your senses on high alert for a third sign.

"If something happens a third time soon after the first two, see this as a potential sign that may point to a brighter future. Inspect that aspect of your life, and make appropriate decisions or action.

"Carl Jung, the Swiss psychologist and psychiatrist who founded analytic psychology, wrote a book entitled, *Synchronicity: An Acausal Connecting Principle*. He showed how something occurring three times may be Destiny.

"Here's an example... The first synchronicities that occurred in my life were before I joined the Samaritans to answer phone calls from suicidal persons.

"One day, I switched the radio on, and the first word spoken was 'Samaritan'. But I could not only hear the word. It was as if I could feel it as well.

"Later, I opened a magazine. The first word I saw was 'Samaritan'. Strong feelings came again.

"The next day, the third synchronicity occurred. In the street, two people chatted. The first word I heard was 'Samaritan'. The word struck like a lightning bolt as if it held a deeper meaning.

"If you're on a path, you have no choice. During the next week, I heard the word 'Samaritan' perhaps twice a day, in unusual circumstances. Once, I switched the TV on, and the first word spoken was 'Samaritan'.

"By the weekend, it was apparent that I had to apply to join the Samaritans, and learn how to help depressed and suicidal people.

"The interview was held by a man and a woman. The man asked, 'Why do you want to be a Samaritan?'

"I shrugged one shoulder, and said, 'I don't know.'

"He said, 'You have to have a good reason to join.'

"So I told him about the synchronicities.

"'That's no reason to be a Samaritan,' he replied.

"The woman spoke. 'It does happen like that, you know.' She looked like an angel compared to him.

(Laughter.)

"Joining the Samaritans was a most valuable learning experience. So please follow synchronicity. It won't occur often, but when it does, it could be of vital importance to your Angelic Path.

"Option two is to follow your intuition, gut, soul feeling, or senses with visions, hearing advice, or feeling the way forward. Rarely, some people can smell or even taste what they should be doing next on their paths.

"Sometimes you'll just know the right path to take. Maybe a thought, words, or picture will pop into your head with a sudden deep knowing to take action. Analyze if your senses, insights, instinct, thoughts, and feelings are correct, and take action accordingly.

"A third way to see signs is to view them as logic, to make logical decisions based on coherent knowledge of your nature, your gifts. You have the potential to use rationale, to judge your abilities and how to use them in the best and most LOving ways to change things for the better.

"Sit down occasionally, and logically consider what to do on the next phase of your path. Make or change plans regularly, according to your logical judgement, at any moment of your path.

"A fourth option is to ask what you should do from three people you trust. If all three suggest that you take the same path, especially if they are also angelic souls, take that path. It may be right for you.

"The fifth option is to contact angelic guides and ask for a sign. Responses come via automatic writing or conscious asking. Be aware, guides may seem to know everything, but they don't. They are learning lessons too! So you might get conflicting answers because guides all have their own purpose, their own goals to guide you.

"If guides know your needs because you asked, they can help on your behalf, better. Your life can become a two-way mirror where they reflect your wishes in Heaven, and you reflect their wishes on Earth.

"The sixth option is to ask a True Angelic Master, which will be discussed as a separate issue later. For now, know that a True Angelic Master should always fully answer any question about your Angelic Path, and advise based on wide and deep knowledge of conscious angelic experiences.

"A True Angelic Master will not say things that do not help you such as, 'You're not ready to know yet,' or 'The answer will come to you one day.' Unless, of course, you are trying to climb your ladder of soul life from the bottom to the top in one gigantic step instead of properly learning lessons on each rung one at a time.

"The seventh way to obtain signs is to pray for answers or clues. Pray to your spiritual, religious, or Godly belief. Then watch for relevant happenings that seem to be a synchronistic response to your prayers, and act.

"The eighth way signs can occur is via regular reviews. For example, every autumn I consider the soul path in the year ahead. Decisions on which projects need to be achieved in the following year are based on signs from strong feelings or logical thoughts that are more emphatic closer to New Year. By the time friends or family discuss New Year's Resolutions, resolutions can already be set, and ready to take off.

"All eight options may help you to your Destiny, soul pathway, and fulfilment of your Contract. Double-check signs by how you feel about them, what your logic tells you, and whether you can move ahead with LOve.

"Destiny Signposts may not, though, be there because there may be no dramatic change of direction needed for months or even years. If there are no Destiny Signposts, please don't get anxious. A soul within a human being has no defined timelines of when something must be achieved. A soul's life is not a set of strictly timed rules.

"Never try to lead your life through seeking constant signs. Perhaps you're already treading the right path, and need to stay on it for some time yet.

"Seek signs frugally. Don't seek constant streams of signs because you are of course human. You would be superhuman to always be right. Seek only when needed.

"Sometimes, when you are going through a rough patch, thoughts may emanate from your lowest consciousness. You may think it's a sign, but the thought may not lead toward the highest LOve outcome for your soul. The lowest consciousness can provide almost the opposite 'solutions' of what your higher consciousness and soul would hope for. So discernment is needed.

"If in doubt, do the eighth option. Or do anything, or nothing. I'll explain anything or nothing.

"If you do anything, choose anything that may be your gift to soften something that's non-LOve; anything you've always wanted to try; anything you've not yet explored to its fullest potential; anything that's LOve. And then go for it. An option you've never tried before may be your Destiny.

"If you do nothing, stay away from all decisions. Lay back. Continue what you're doing.

"If you postpone decisions, also stay alert. Watch for signs of what to do. Stay aware. Look for new Destiny Signposts. If it's not your soul path, you'll soon receive signs to do something else.

"Do not be overly concerned whether your life-path choice is right. Angelic guides are with you using maps of your life to help you find your way. They watch you seeking Destiny Signposts, help you find your right path, support you on it, and then help you over the hurdles. They are underestimated friends on the journey.

"If your Contract has been achieved, guides can help you make another Contract, one that is too subtle to be aware of, or one that you may literally have to sign to heighten your awareness on your new path.

"Destiny Signposts let you share your life with your guides, and let them share signs with you. Destiny Signposts release you from the concern of not knowing your future and show you hope. Destiny Signposts connect your nature of Free Will or Foolishness to the Destiny needed to fulfill your Contract.

"Enjoy freedom of mind. Search without judgement. How can you know it's the right path until it's trodden?

"You will be puzzled by crossroads on your path. How will you know which to choose? Does it matter? Maybe the search down a path to find your Destiny is a dead end, and is merely a part of your path of learning.

"A method to double-check the fork to take at a crossroads is time-lining, an attempt to see the future.

"First, visualize the crossroads. Feel or sense which of your future routes seem the two best options.

"Then imagine you've taken one fork, and are three months ahead of now. Look around you at the type of situation you may find yourself in, and the potential people and interactions you might have. How does it feel inside you? Good? Not-good? Brilliant? Sad? Happy?

"Repeat the process, projecting your thoughts one year ahead of now, and then five years ahead of now. At each timeline point, assess the situations, people and interactions that could happen, and check the feelings you might have.

"Next, try to imagine that you took the other fork, and repeat. Project three months, one year, and five years ahead in turn. Each time try to see the types of situations, people and interactions you may experience. How does each timeline point make you feel? What type of reactions might you have? What could your life be like if you took that path instead?

"Finally, which path contained the best situations, best people, best interactions, best feelings? Choose the path that seems happier, more positive, more LOving, or of more help to those in need around you.

"Ways to choose which path to take are not new. They have always existed to progress your soul.

"If you know this you may perhaps walk a path more peacefully and explore its potential to enhance your life, and move on with LOve in your heart for all humankind."

Secret Dispensations

"Eventually, on the Angelic Path, after angels-on-earth have adequately learned their early lessons, they can automatically progress to the next Platformation, and attempt to share their soul ways of LOve. That is, unless they have human frailties and limitations.

"For example, there is a potential that an angel-on-earth has a severe enough disability from birth, or has had an accident that impairs their physical or mental faculties.

"Or maybe an angel-on-earth was born into a family line with genetically inherited anger, depression, or whatever.

"Or perhaps the angel was born into a war-torn or disaster area of the world, where some of their friends or family are killed and they have few opportunities to enjoy sweet LOve.

"Maybe those scenarios are threats that might lead to barriers being erected on a soul path that could prevent the attainment of Destiny goals.

"Well, wouldn't it be a waste that an angel-on-earth could not try to achieve their Destiny, just because of a disability, accident, genetics, or living in a particular area of their country? It would be a waste if it wasn't their fault they could not achieve their purpose for existence.

"Dispensations can be made by those above for someone

disabled. That does not mean being disabled in the normal sense of the word. It means being disabled in ways that inhibit or prevent the achievement of the pre-birth Contract.

"In such cases, there's a secret held by those above. An angel's Contract may be altered. A new clause may be agreed to allow for the potential to achieve the original Contract, but with allowances for impaired physical, emotional, or mental capabilities.

"Dispensations can then support the angel's entire soul path. They can still become fully-fledged angels-on-earth fulfilling valid and valuable duties, because, taking the disability into account, energetically the Dispensation will allow them to provide a new and more relevant potential for accomplishments.

"Suppose you couldn't see the signposts, or your Destiny route, because your brain is not 'wired' to receive knowledge, or perceive in the way needed. Again, maybe there's a Dispensation to allow a new clause to be added to your Contract so you can achieve your soul Destiny in a more appropriate way, with allowances for your condition.

"It's like playing golf with someone who is a golf professional and you are not. You are given free shots to even up the odds.

"You often hear stories of people who've been ill or almost died, and who suddenly discover they have a soul purpose to achieve, or a way to ease similar ailments.

"It's as if they've been woken up, or been able to change their perspective on their path. One way or another, they've been able to receive a new clause or Contract to achieve.

"The Dispensation often facilitates an excellent new way forward, that allows them abilities to create amazing soul works of LOve."

Chapter 9

Angelic Ways

Angels' Early Platformations and Angelic Service

"Angels know they have a mission to achieve before they move on from this world, a Destiny to fulfill, specific aims that will help to complete their soul's Contract.

"Some angels find their soul purpose immediately, in their teens or 20s. They may start on the bottom rung of a ladder in an organization where they can rise to higher positions, sharing their LOve along the way.

"One day they'll take their organization in an improved direction, guided by their higher LOve and soul Destiny. They are lucky or guided enough to find the right career early enough in life.

"Most such people know they've chosen the right way forward. They know they'll rise through the organization to share their LOve within their company's hierarchy, to change the way it operates, to help society.

"Along the way, they learn lessons on love and LOve from imperfections within their family, friends, colleagues or bosses, or from international news, and eventually achieve their soul's goals.

"That isn't normal. Many angels in their teens and 20s do not find their soul purpose immediately. They drift from trade to trade, or are unhappy in their career, or wonder if they took the right college or university course. All the time wondering what their soul needs to do.

"They might not waste this unproductive time. It's a testing period for inner contemplation, with an underlying drive to find the right vocation.

"You know, it isn't important to find your right occupation

early on in adulthood. In your 20s and 30s, and even 40s, if you can't decide, take time out.

"Take a gap year from university or your profession. Travel the world. Learn about inter-cultural LOve differences.

"Or take a job you might love. Hire surfboards in the Caribbean, or help the aged near you. Learn about love and LOve from interactions with new environments.

"Or do something to make money and put it to goodly use.

"Choose anything. It isn't important what you do. You do not usually find a soul purpose till mid-40s to mid-50s.

"Hands up if you know you'll be doing something important in your 40s or 50s.

(Hands raised.)

"About three-quarters of you know the time to achieve your soul purpose is in your 40s or 50s. That's an important clue to take pressure off younger angels, who want to achieve a soul purpose now, too fast. Before your 40s or 50s, you normally first learn love and LOve lessons.

"Many Angels are specially gifted. They can be highly competent, even brilliant, in multiple fields. They have the potential to be local, national, or international champions in many sports. They could excel in many roles. They can be brilliant parents. Angels can reach peaks of achievement in almost anything they choose, family, hobby, sport, arts, music, or sciences.

"An angel may move on when they've reached the limits of their potential in a specific subject, when they've satisfied their curiosity, or when they feel they cannot improve without so much extra effort, it's not worthwhile.

"Angels-on-earth may know it's not right, not what they need to fulfill their role on Earth, to complete their Contract. It's just something at which they excel.

"It's not ethical to name famous people, but I've met world champions who knew they were angels, and moved on to another sport just because they knew their angelic nature would help them be good at that too.

"As personal examples, I could have played high level cricket, but knew cricket wasn't the soul path, so stopped. I played chess internationally until feeling chess was not the path. Potential in saxophone, bowls, singing, table tennis, and piano weren't the paths. A civil service manager kept offering a position at the Foreign Office. It didn't feel like Destiny. I was offered photography manager in Germany, but left. As a business consultant, I was offered directorships, but they didn't seem to be Destiny.

"I only realized the soul purpose was as a healer and spiritual teacher when those doctors predicted two years to live. When I accepted the Destiny enterprise, a cure came unexpectedly, and life changed dramatically for the better, and for most people I met.

"What this means is, trades during the early Platformations of an angel may not be important. The roles are usually human roles, filling time and space in human lives while you learn lessons to eventually support your Destiny.

"Within all of this is the calling named Angelic Service, your soul purpose on all Platformations. Any position that offers Angelic Service, no matter how concrete or loosely the quality of LOve service is, could be of excellent value when you attempt what you are really here for.

"Choose anything that takes your fancy to serve LOvingly. Serve angelically well to your partner, parent, friend, colleagues, boss, or in a hobby or sport.

"Learn additional skills to achieve your soul goals. Learn, then practice the lessons you learned. Train to offer your best Angelic Service to help others. Be ready when you need to share LOve. Experiment. Accept new roles and enjoy the learning curve.

"Later there's a topic how two or three lower level posts can build a foundation for a soul purpose, to be Destiny."

The Secrets of Money

"Money is a big issue, because conflicts scurry and flurry around between love and LOve natures.

"Many angels have been close to, or were, bankrupt, lost property, money, shares, whatever. They believe their loss was a monetary lesson, that money shouldn't be stockpiled or used only for pleasure. They realize that losses had forced them to a better pathway to advance contentment, and tread a more caring and LOving route.

"Of course, angels need to cover basic needs. And for some it may be OK to enjoy luxuries of life too.

"But the clue for some angels, the lesson to be accepted, is money is acceptable to have, and better used for the soul's path, or to help others achieve their soul's life purposes, good health, and happiness.

"Some angels go bankrupt two or even three times before realizing they should use money not on wants, but on human needs and angelic purposes.

"It's as if money for some angels is a secret lesson to be drained away. When at last they realize money can fund good works, they are allowed to earn more and more, so they can give more and more. When the person values money as a way to satisfy others' needs, monetary riches often come relatively easily.

"Some angels, rich or poor, achieve monetary lessons by serving humanity. For example, the Knights of Malta, mainly European aristocracy, offer part of their lives for free annually, to help the less well off. European royalty introduced free service over a thousand years ago. They had wisdom to use their inherited fortunes at least partly to help the needy. Maybe they understood monetary lessons of service for angelic souls.

"The Knights of Malta invite even poor people to join them

if they're dedicated to help others. Maybe a thousand years ago, they saw values in Angelic Service?

"Financially poor angels-on-earth learn monetary lessons by giving their time freely to help others in need. Time is merely another monetary lesson to understand.

"Angelic Service means taking action to LOve others. Voluntary service, supporting a sick family member, fundraising for charity, low-paid caring professions, working in the developing world all provide options to progress understanding that helping others is more important to Destiny than stockpiling money.

"Some angels know that they'll one day be rich. But they don't realize that riches may need to support their soul purpose, or that riches may come from the soul purpose. So they try to get rich in ill-judged ways.

"Angels often try affirmations for monetary abundance from 'above'. A word of warning though... If God, or your angels or guides do not agree with your demand, you may experience instant karma.

"A long time ago, I met a beautifully angelic young lady. Her affirmation requested £40,000 to pay off a mortgage and enjoy a holiday. She had no idea her husband had death insurance for £40,000. The next week he was killed on his motorbike. She received the money but had no husband to enjoy it with. Can you imagine how she felt?

"There are many similar stories. An angelic lady on a course in Denmark told how she said a prayer to God that she'd like to live by water. She did, that night, when the water pipes burst in her loft.

(Laughter.)

"Hands up if you had an unfavorable response after asking for abundance through affirmation or a prayer.

(Hands raised.)

"Yes, there are quite a lot of you.

"Raise hands if you believe an unfavorable response was a sign to show that money may be used in LOving ways for family and others in need, not just for yourself.

(Hands raised.)

"That's it, isn't it? Almost all who raised hands to the first question believe it was a lesson, that motivations to gain and use money were selfish, not LOving.

"The secret is, do not ask God for money before doing your Angelic Service. Do the opposite. Achieve Angelic Service and God's needs first. Then unasked-for riches may pour on you, because they will be deserved.

"For most of you, the motivation behind having money is the precarious point. With the right motivation, with thoughts to use money in LOving ways, that's when money flows. That's when you can be financially stable.

"So maybe make money your second priority to Angelic Service? Consolidate your life with LOve. Take any position, even voluntary, for opportunities to share LOve. Whatever you choose do your best, with LOve. Strengthen your LOve attitude ready for soul progression. A positive, focused, LOving attitude will help when it's time to achieve your Destiny. Surrender to Angelic Service showing divine LOve, the highest thing you can do this side of heaven. Then money may flow.

"Balance needs to be in all things. That includes the need for a balance in attitude about money.

"Some people have a positive attitude toward money, knowing that the better they serve, the more money they have. If you have a spiritual attitude that money can support your family to increase their contentment with life, and then help improve others' lives, money is a wholly positive force for goodness.

"Some spiritual people's attitude is that they should not have much money, not accepting that the more money they have, the more they can prevent monetary crises for loved ones, and the more they can donate to worthy causes.

"If you deliberately stay poor and spurn money at every God-given opportunity, that may not be your best soul path. Money may be being guided to you to support your future project on Earth, and you are turning it away.

"In the 1990s, a friend attended a two-day spiritual course about money. The teachings were that money was the root of all evil, and not good for a soul's purity. After, the spiritual leader asked what they thought of money now. The first few agreed that money was evil, they should never have lots of money so their souls can be pure. The friend responded, 'Everyone on this course is spiritual. If they had lots of money, they'd use it for good purposes. So I wouldn't like you here to be millionaires. I'd love you to be billionaires. It's better than money being used by bad people for bad purposes.'

"Apparently everyone clapped.

"There are though, as the spiritual teacher said, some types of angels who need to stay monetarily poor. This includes those dedicating their lives in Angelic Service to a charitable or Godly institution. Nuns and monks may fall into this category of not needing much money, like two angelic friends in the Philippines.

"One man was a monk for ten years. His role was fundraising enough money for all his monastery's costs. He knew that one day he'd leave to be a businessman, and earn lots of money to give to poor communities. The other man trained as an architect. He aimed to earn millions of US dollars, to donate to worthy causes. After that is achieved, his ultimate dream is to be a poor monk. Both men have similar monetary roles and goals as poor spiritual persons and rich benefactors.

"Spiritual beings such as the Brahma Kumaris advocate releasing desire of money. They then encourage Angelic Service within their organizations, charities, or NGOs, to support global needs in creative and LOving voluntary ways.

"Realistically though, most angels without money cannot help much, short of volunteering.

"Unless you've joined an organization, you'll need money to achieve a bigger soul purpose. The bigger the purpose, the more money you'll need.

"Some angels combine a business, academic or other career with a second, spiritual career. They earn well, and then donate part of their income to their personal spiritual ideals and goals.

"Angels-on-earth may feel a spiritual tug towards an underdog, and support charitable causes that get little help from anywhere else. They use money in spiritual ways to make a bigger difference that can lead to their Destinies. To find a good cause that no one else helped, but you can, even against all the odds, is Angelic Service, a goal you may support for the rest of your life.

"Do not be scared. If you have a great idea to help society, borrow from a bank, or request donations from friends or family. Crowdfunding is worth looking at. See if there's a crowdfunding platform in tune with your aims.

"If a heartfelt project grows, angels often start a charity or foundation, hire a professional fund-raiser, and raise funds from various types of funding organizations.

"Keep spiritual soul needs, not human greeds, in mind. "Secrets of Angels on Earth" Groups help members earn enough for their families, soul paths, and good causes. Help angels to increase happiness around them."

Clues To the Possibility of Failure

"Like all else in life, nothing is certain on the Angelic Path. Failure can occur at any time. You could fall off the ladder, whether you're on the bottom rung, halfway up, or at the penultimate rung about to climb to the peak. Reasons for failure are many.

"Maybe an angel-on-earth will lack ambition, motivation or determination, or focuses on love, not LOve.

"Possibly they cannot seek and implement proper solutions, or they might possess so much humility they think they're unworthy, that it's best to stay humble and not be noticed for good works.

"Perhaps there's a fear of success, of what may feel to be too big a task ahead.

"Some angels have detrimental attitudes to their teacher, master, or spiritual organization, even though they haven't reached their heights, and do not know their paths or Contracts. Everyone needs LOve, support, and respect, rich, poor, an aristocrat, a beggar, your teacher or a co-student. Respect LOve, and gain respect from those above, by respecting everyone, everywhere, under every circumstance.

"If you feel you're failing, find the courage to reevaluate your life's interaction. Change course. Pick yourself up with a new plan of constructive action.

"When the book of this Angel Party is published, read and reread it. Regularly check which Platformation you are on and what action you could take next. Maybe reread the section on the University of Life, and redo your thesis for the level on which you are stuck.

"You could start a "Secrets of Angels on Earth" Group and discuss failure issues with angelic members.

"You may seek help from the Brahma Kumaris, or a True Angelic Master, to find the new way ahead.

"Whatever you do, realize failure is just part of the human lesson. Accept failure with the LOve it deserves. Within failure, you might find the best possible route ahead.

"Discern why you are failing, then find a new, more positive way ahead, like a baby learning from experiences when it fails. How else does a baby become an adult?

"If you still fail, maybe that's OK too. Maybe you're still destined to be an angel.

"But if you can't stop making unfitting Free Will choices, well, that's OK. There are plenty of other options in this life and the next. You'll have a greater chance of success next time, and the next. Never worry. It is simply a part of universal life that most people will never be aware of. Life and evolution just happen. All will be well.

"So please give LOving thanks for your many blessings. All is well in the higher scheme of LOve in the universe."

Changing Toward Pleasant Platformations

"Angelic Paths usually become more enjoyable and fun as they progress. You are heading to a happier way of life that's more balanced spiritually, energetically, and monetarily. You've learned to be positive, relaxed, and LOving to others. You are heading towards a splendidly beautiful life of LOve-Based Living.

"But as you move through the Platformations, even if you may have done well, a few issues may still hold you back from a more pleasant path.

"For example, maybe you haven't found the best relationship, or you're still plodding along a human life. Perhaps conflicts between love and LOve need resolution, or you haven't found adequate ways to share LOve.

"Sometimes angels learn something intellectual or theoretical, then think they know all about it, and do not put their intellectual or theoretical knowledge into practice.

"Maybe these two days can help you realize potential clues on ways to move on.

"You can then practice, practice, and practice and truly overcome your Platformations.

"Maybe you can do this practice alone, by yourself. But maybe it's easier to move toward pleasant Platformations with others who understand?

"That's when it's of great value to start or join a "Secrets of Angels on Earth" Group, to practice and share relationship, monetary, LOve, and other lessons.

"You will have an amazingly beautiful life. Enjoy how the

University of Life is modeling your human love via your soul's LOve. Eventually you can be made of total LOve, able to give total LOve, under any LOve-need circumstance, and lead a pleasant life.

"When you have achieved all that LOve, when you've vowed to commit yourself to tread the Angelic Path with a dedication to improving your soul and the souls of others, when you're healed and are positive in attitude, I promise you, life can change wonderfully, pleasantly for the better.

"When you've started to shine your Light to become at one with the All, that's when your life on higher Platformations can provide an incredibly fabulous experience.

"A minor detail in all this is, do you have support from a friend you can trust under all circumstances?

"Raise your hands please.

"No? Not many angels have friends they can trust under all circumstances. Only a few hands were raised to that question.

"You see, most angels don't have such good friends, because the nature of the Angelic Path means you probably can't find an angel like you. So you can't talk about human love conflicts, soul LOve urges, or what you need to fulfill your Contract. You have to keep your thoughts and feelings and even the reasons for your soul path actions secret.

"You can't talk about these things very easily, for fear of being labeled mentally ill.

"What you may need above all else is a good friend you can trust, another angel or group of angels on the path.

"Maybe you can start a "Secrets of Angels on Earth" Group made up only of evolving angels like you, in your area of the world? You can help your members enjoy a more pleasant life by supporting each other through thickness of beauty, and thinness of danger. Wouldn't it be LOvely to grow with other angels?

"And, an even more pleasant experience can come if you can network with other angels around the world. You will feel connected, at one, in togetherness."

"Secrets of Angels on Earth" Groups

"You at this Angel Party have arrived from many countries around the world. Angels from other countries would also have loved to attend if they'd been available. After this, you will all return to your parts of the world.

"But do you have support there? Do you know angels in your area to share your Platformations with, and evolve happily together, in easier ways than if you were travelling your pathway alone? Probably not...

"Very few of you are lucky enough to have friends with angelic souls, close friends who are angels-on-earth like you, friends who understand divine LOve from deep within their souls, that you can talk to and discuss angelic matters in depth. Wouldn't it be LOvely to have friends who understand you?

"That is why it might be a good idea to start a Group of like-minded angels near you, to continue the sharing and caring support, and understanding and knowledge, started here.

"Our Facebook Group is called 'Secrets of Angels on Earth'. The aim is to develop soul wisdom faster and easier, into the angel you were born to become. An angel who learns effectively through each Platformation of life is an effective angel.

"You might be scared to start a Group, and feel unqualified. But you do not have to be a teacher of angels to start a sharing Group for angelic souls like you. Each member simply shares information about their path that could help other members. Members help them overcome hurdles on the path, and achieve their goals. In other words, members support each other's individual angelic paths and Platformations. No one is a leader. Everyone simply gives and receives help.

"Remember also that, after this Angel Party, when the book about our gathering is published, you will have the book of these two days as a reference for members. When a topic is shared or discussed, members can refer to the relevant chapter in their book for guidance. A Group huddle over a passage in the book that may help a member's path may sometimes be better than a cuddle.

"In these ways, you can in future receive and offer all the support and guidance needed for yourself, and other angels on their paths.

"I truly hope that many of you can start or join a "Secrets of Angels on Earth" Group near, or in, your home, because you will not feel alone anymore.

"Groups are normally free, unless you need money to cover room hire. It is your choice, and the choice of Group members whether there are membership fees or not. Perhaps your Group could collect donations for a worthwhile charitable cause. Or you could raise funds for members' soul Destiny projects.

"Groups' many benefits include meeting other LOving angelic friends.

"Think about it. In the past you have felt alone, felt different. You've been unable to find many other people, if any at all, who feel and know the highest Godly LOve like you. If you have friends who understand similar LOve and pathway issues as you, and who live close by, that is a rare blessing indeed.

"In an angelic Group, other members may have knowledge to help you, and your knowledge may help them. People, even in an angelically LOving Group, have lives that need solutions. You will be mirrors for each other, reflecting back needs, hopes and desires, and learning to treat everyone with LOve. This mutual support from people who are treading similar energetic LOve paths could become an invaluable asset in your lives.

"Groups go through stages, including stages where members' personalities or beliefs may clash. That is normal human behavior, and part of LOving each other unconditionally.

"It is easier to study how to feel and share thoughts on how different loves and LOves affect your life with those who can truly understand what you are going through, with unconditional LOve.

"Happiness is shaped by the sharing and caring of friends with angelic souls, and mutual support of LOve, soul, and Destiny achievements.

"A book, titled *The Way*, by a Master, Juan Sgolastra, describes how important it is to join a Group of like-minded individuals. He says that without joining a Group, individuals are much more likely to fail. A Group gives strength. Energy and power to achieve grows with the support of similar friends.

"Ultimately, if you can help yourself and others achieve soul goals faster and more easily, you will be doing great service. That's because each angel is destined to make a change for the better, to make a positive difference.

"Imagine 20 angels join your Group. Even if only a few make a big difference to local, national, or international societies, your Group will have facilitated beautifully pleasant changes to improve lives around the world.

"Your "Secrets of Angels on Earth" Group can become one of your greatest opportunities for LOving Angelic Service."

The True Angelic Master

"You've reached a Platformation where traditional sources that help you develop like websites, courses, books, and Apps don't help much, because they mainly help people's early Platformations. The main use now of such media is to study extra skills, like marketing, business, listening, or sharing love, anything that can help you use existing knowledge to attain your Destiny.

"To progress and immerse more fully on your soul path, you may now need a specialist with knowledge of soul paths and ultimate Destinies on an Angelic Path, which is yet to exist in adequate depth in any media.

"This is where a True Master comes in, a being who is at one with all, a halfway house between humanity on Earth, and angels above. Each segment of history has its own True Masters helping diverse geographical areas, for different facets of human life. Due to oneness with everything, all True Masters know what practical knowledge each person needs to achieve their Destiny, and, more crucially, the timing when the person needs specific instruction. The Master may help with anything: relationships, business, esoteric, family, monetary, health, all and any need or opportunity. The Master can recognize on which Platformation you may be stuck or lost, and help to guide you home, to your Destiny.

"I am not discussing a clairvoyant who answers questions psychically. I do not mean someone who teaches on, or channels from, angels above us, and not someone who is a spiritual guru. Although some of those types might genuinely understand parts of the Angelic Path, and all have their place, few would logically know how to help angels-on-earth adequately, especially on the higher Platformations of their paths.

"In the context of you being an angel learning lessons, you need someone with abilities to guide your angelic soul, regardless of what manifests on your Platformations, because he or she has already walked the Angelic Path to a high level. So I am discussing a True Angelic Master, not any other type of True Master.

"This angelic type of Master has researched, trod, and succeeded on all early and higher Platformations. Consequently, he or she logically knows about love and LOve differences, the many types of angelic callings and angel bands, and the paths to Angelic Service.

"This Angelic type of Master will never glue you to a life position, or force you to a route from which you can't escape, or trap you in their ways for the rest of your life. The Master, though, may seem at times to push a little too much, or not enough, for wise reasons you cannot be aware of. Wisdom causes the Master to interact automatically, like a dancing between different dances.

"This Angelic type of Master will help you achieve human and soul development, especially when sometimes your human desires and soul needs may contradict and conflict with each other.

"This Angelic type of Master has insight and wisdom to see inside your soul, to improve your human weaknesses and build on your angelic aspects of being, of which you may not even be aware.

"This Angelic type of Master can become a real friend whenever you are in need, even if you live in another country and rarely communicate.

"A True Angelic Master may be needed at all stages of life for angels.

"On early Platformations, if you follow such a True Angelic Master's advice, maybe some potential suffering can be prevented, because Masters possess the knowledge to understand your love and LOve conflicts. Masters know how to stop you procrastinating, or being too fearful or too desiring. Masters know your needs and how capable you are, that you must try to be perfect, but that you cannot be perfect. Masters can show how to release self-blame or self-criticism, how to prevent you creating your own defeat, and how to help you relax and have the courage to move on.

"The one thing you need to do is follow the Master's advice. I do not mean become a disciple, following every word blindly. I mean that, because a True Angelic Master has 'been there, done that', the advice is almost certainly worth following, even if you are not advanced enough yet to fully understand the reasoning behind the advice. You see, a Master has so much knowledge, it's impossible to explain every reason behind every comment. There will be reasons though, so follow with an open mind and open heart.

"For example, starting a Group for like-minded angelic people may not seem a good idea, especially if you don't always get on with people, or if you lead a busy life. A Master though may encourage you, knowing the benefits will outweigh anything else. For example, Groups are needed to help you not feel alone, and to achieve your goals without feeling isolated. One person by themselves may find it beyond them, because they cannot give themselves adequate critique. A Group generates and expands passion and ideas, inspiration and motivation. A Group can unite members towards the attainment of common goals. A Group helps you overcome interaction challenges, and shows how to LOve each other during differences of opinion and remain true friends.

"You don't know what you don't know. So if you find a True Angelic Master, accept the advice if possible. Life should then expand more happily in a faster, more relevant, and more beautiful direction. One day you will understand the reasons for the advice.

"Even if you gain good advice from a Master, if you are not participating in a supportive Group you may still feel alone. You're searching in the dark for your path ahead, seeking how to share LOve, feeling ever stronger that you're on the right path, but unsure of where to go and how to do it. An angel support Group will back up the wisdom of a Master.

"It's not easy to find a True Angelic Master because there are not many around. The book about Mastership, *The Way*, describes in depth the relationship between a student and a Master. It states, 'Out of every 1,000 people, only a few...' Only about one in every three or four hundred people are angels-on-earth, so far less grow to become True Angelic Masters. More may develop, perhaps some based on the book about this Angel Party.

"With the corporation analogy, your Contract may require you to, for example, reach the level of a janitor, lower level manager, or President. And if you don't make the right decisions, you could fail. That is where this special type of Angelic Master can step in to help.

"If you're ready to meet a Master, you may be guided, maybe in unusual circumstances, to who can help exactly with what you need. Perhaps by joining Brahma Kumaris, or starting a "Secrets of Angels on Earth" Group, you may find a True Angelic Master. You may even become one yourself, and help angels progress with joy.

"One man I know runs wonderfully successful Angel Groups. But he has no wish to be ridiculed by those who don't know the reality of angels. So he keeps his angelic knowledge a secret, until he meets another angel. Another person is so humble that she doesn't want to be known openly for her angelic Groups, even though she's a catalyst for positive change. And so on…

"Do you understand? Most True Angelic Masters keep their knowledge a closely-guarded secret, away from the prying eyes of non-angels. Their Groups are valuable to angels. They do not want their supportive network to be devalued by non-angels who can never understand.

"Most Masters sensibly help angels grow secretly. They don't wish to be trolled on social media by non-angels damaging and blackening their Light reputation. Sadly, some people damage another's expertise or social position, because it's different to their own views.

"I hope one day True Angelic Masters won't have to hide, and that their Angel Groups and advice won't be secret. I hope they'll be taken seriously as a force to help a segment of humanity, angels-on-earth, progress to share LOve and good works in bigger, better, and more open ways.

"And I hope and pray that one day there'll be many such True Angelic Masters in traditional therapeutic and psychological professions, to help and support angelic souls to an easier, happier, fulfilling pathway of LOve."

The Brahma Kumaris

"Many years ago I studied for two years with the Brahma Kumaris in England. I loved their approach. Courses and lectures included how to improve relationships, family, money, spirituality, love, anything that could help create a better human life.

"But underpinning every session was the emphasis on who some people really are, LOving souls inside imperfect human flesh and blood. Teachings freed each person's soul toward its Destiny, and released thoughts and actions from the confines of lack of understanding.

"The great thing, when I had very little, was that courses and lectures were free. There was even free vegetarian food, healthy, and deliciously home-made.

"For someone poor, the Brahma Kumaris were heaven-sent. To gain the riches of soul knowledge, without having to pay with riches I did not own, was like the eighth wonder of the world. Especially as all Brahma Kumaris seemed so perfectly LOving.

"But the Brahma Kumaris never taught about angels above or on earth. Maybe angel topics were on higher course levels. Or maybe they thought I was not ready to know about angelic nature. Perhaps they were guiding people through levels of understanding. Or maybe I did not study with them for long enough.

"Certainly they taught nothing about angels-on-earth. Years later it came as a surprise to discover that they are all, on the higher levels of their organization, angels.

"The Brahma Kumaris though had laid solid roots within of how to be a loving human, to accept the human faults of others, and to achieve the soul's Destiny.

"If you attend their courses, you might agree with some teachings, and disagree with other teachings. That is normal with anything you study. Just make your own Free Will choices on your path. Their teachings are recommendations, not dogma to be followed at all costs.

"You don't have to wear white, which Brahma Kumaris wear to symbolize purity, cleanliness, and honesty. Even if you don't join the Brahma Kumaris, as you tread higher up the angelic Platformations, you may find yourself naturally wearing paler, more pastel colors like pale violet, lemon, or creams, as your vibration automatically seeks the higher frequencies of God.

"Brahma Kumaris' ways and manners are relatively easy to accept. They have no religious message. They accept angels and seekers from all philosophies or religions, regardless of different beliefs.

"So although Brahma Kumaris have guidelines, angels-on-earth who feel alone, lost, separated, detached, or in whatever need, all might find help and support along their personal soul paths, to their individual destinies.

"That is why I recommend checking the Brahma Kumaris' website, buying their books, CDs, posters and other materials, or downloading their App, and checking if there's a Group near you.

"Hopefully you will find your True Angelic Master, one way or another, to help guide your various human versus soul conflicts down a loving path towards a fruitful and happy existence.

"Brahma Kumaris are all human beings of course, so may show human faults. But they are more often gentle, kind, sweet, caring, and experienced in human and angelic soul development. It would feel gorgeous if they share their LOve with you. You may not feel so alone."

The Soul Purpose Seeker

"There comes a time when you've developed enough. You've studied what you needed, and sought and succeeded with numerous techniques, methods, or advice on early Platformations.

"You may have studied with a True Angelic Master, or the

Brahma Kumaris. Or you may have started a "Secrets of Angels on Earth" Group on Facebook.

"Or maybe you found other game-changing ways to progress your path, consciously or unconsciously, and discovered your own personalized way forward toward your Destiny.

"You've used everything you studied and learned to excellent effect, and you've overcome most of your early Platformation hurdles that were preventing you from moving on.

"Now it's time to seek your soul's Destiny, to give yourself to LOve, and to be available for Angelic Service.

"Your thoughts, conversations, reading, courses, everything takes on a different, less secretive perspective, as you try to explore new ways to openly share your deep feelings of LOve.

"On the early Platformations, you were developing your understanding of human love and Godly LOve. If you learned the lessons well, you've integrated the two types of love and LOve. At last, it's time to do something positive with them, to seek a position that will be a practice for the real reason your soul is here.

"If you don't know what to do, there are three clues to help you find out.

"Clue one is that maybe you'll find the line of work you've done all your life is your true soul Destiny, but you'll seek a new angle to it.

"Clue two is that perhaps you'll have what used to be called a midlife crisis, and seek new pastures, an entirely new option, that feels more relevant to your soul path's future.

"Clue three is to start reviewing a number of different jobs you've done in your life, and begin to retread the paths. Check whether one of those jobs can be altered or improved with LOve, to facilitate better lives. Or check if two or three jobs can be combined into a new, pioneering system.

"Whichever way it is, the job you're seeking now is likely to be a new outlet that is a new way forward to share your LOve.

"There are a further two clues that help you find your calling.

"The first clue is, whatever you try should help your soul, or others' souls, develop or share love, LOve, health, or happiness.

"The second clue is, ensure that the mission you choose encapsulates your main gift, or an innate ability that historically makes you happy. Every other venture might be a waste of time as far as your soul goal and Destiny are concerned.

"On this part of the Angelic Path even though you don't need to seek in the previous ways anymore, you may feel like you should still seek.

"This is one of those periods when some people get stuck, continuously seeking and getting excited when they think they've found something 'better'. They don't realize that there is a potential scenario where, if they continue seeking, they cannot achieve their reason for existence.

"Accumulation of knowledge is useless by itself. I often hear people say something like, 'You'll never stop learning.' Or, 'There are always new things to learn.' But this is only ever true for your human side of life.

"Eventually, as far as the soul is concerned, there is a limit to the knowledge you need to do your soul purpose.

"I'll repeat that, as it's important. As far as your soul is concerned, there is a limit to the information that you need to learn, because there comes a time when you can simply share your LOve with the knowledge you already have. Gaining extra knowledge is probably a waste of your time.

"Of course, you could make an excuse from your Free Will, and think that such and such is essential to add to your repertoire, because maybe it will provide extra LOve or a better way to help others. When really, your existing knowledge could have helped many while you wasted your time learning something extra that won't add much benefit.

"Try to discern when you've learned enough to share your LOve. Everything else someone might offer you is a temptation, an illusion, and may confuse you and your soul purpose.

"In a worst-case scenario, if you become a constant student, acquiring nonstop knowledge, you'll never move on to sharing your LOve correctly and achieving your angelic goals. You'll never reach the summit of the mountain you've been climbing, never fulfill your Destiny.

"Seek information in order to use it to help your soul, not for the sake of possessing new knowledge."

Sharing Angelic LOve – Clues To Your Practice Run

"Please put your hands up if you know or think you know what real LOve is all about.

(Hands raised.)

"I think everybody put their hands up to that. But if you ask someone who is not on this path, they won't put their hands up. They won't know what you're talking about.

"But somebody like you, you remember LOve and don't have to search for it. You're not like other people. You don't have to start learning religions or other things to try to find LOve.

"Some angelic love subjects you learn might help you overcome certain early Platformations. But you don't have to study LOve, because you already know LOve inside you, it's already there from before you were born. You don't have to develop LOve in an outer way, from lessons. In the past it was easier said than done, but LOve is within you, you can feel it, and it's now time to share it with the world.

"Hands up if you've come to this realization.

(Hands raised.)

"Good, probably about two-thirds of you are like this. That's what this LOve is about. It's about sharing the LOve you know is inside you.

"On this Platformation, it doesn't matter how you share your LOve. You could share it in any way right for you, any way at all. As examples, maybe you could join a charity that already does good LOving works; study to be a psychologist or psychiatrist and try to change their professions with LOve; do a PhD or take an exam on something you hope will help improve lives; learn and teach a system of therapy, Reiki, counseling, or search for the best caring career. Complementary or alternative therapies are wonderful ways to share LOve, and improve lives. So many angels end up on that path.

"Or you could study marketing, management, or business models, thinking that perhaps these could be useful to your future, higher soul Platformation, where you could use your LOve for non-greedy business purposes. And you can share LOve with students, tutors, and janitors.

"Or you could move to a beach area and sell ice creams in the summer, and there you are sharing your LOve with all the little kids that come up, and they'll remember your LOve for the rest of their lives.

"One angel-on-earth I know is a painter and decorator and adds LOve into the paint as he pops it on the walls, so people feel a LOving atmosphere in their homes.

"Another angel is a diplomatic interpreter at the United Nations and sends clouds of LOve with her interpretations.

"Another angel takes in ironing and pours LOve into everything as she irons, so customers get their clothes back with LOve filled into every stitch.

"And three angels I know are scientists, working in different university laboratories, sending LOve to atheistic and skeptical colleagues.

"Choose any post.

"Don't think is this right, is there something better? Don't think is this what I'm supposed to do, is this my real purpose?

"It's not the time for analysis, because, for now, it's completely unimportant in the higher scheme of things what you do. Just choose something and do it. It's just a practice run, using your LOve in something, for your real Angelic Service to come, on a higher Platformation.

"You see, most angels need a practice run. However you attempt that practice run, share your LOve in whatever way you choose. When you eventually break through to your real purpose, it will mean you will have a head start on understanding how to share Godly Conditional LOve. That is another topic to discuss later.

"You'll start to understand, even more deeply than before, that you're here to share your LOve. It won't be so unconditional anymore though. Now it's more focused. You are practicing how to challenge the status quo to improve.

"On this Platformation, it isn't important whether you find your real angelic purpose straight away or not. It's about practice, because practice makes perfect. The more you practice, the more perfect the sharing of your LOve becomes.

"The more you help people or something in ideal, perfect, sweet and kind ways, the more you will share the God nature within you with your chosen part of the world, the more you will learn what is needed to achieve your real purpose of existence.

"You might even realize you can't share your LOve with everyone or everything, everywhere, because there's a limit to who, what, or how you can achieve a LOving outcome.

"So eventually, when you do your soul purpose, it will be more natural and more effective to share your LOve in perfect, conditional ways that help the majority of your targets in need."

Secrets of Sensations in Shoulder Blades – Clues for Seeing, Feeling and Hearing

"Eventually, while you are practicing your LOve, when you start to share your LOve in a more full-time, fulsome way, you develop deeper, more apparent feelings of unconditional and conditional LOve within you. That's also the time when you might feel pains in between, or in each of, the shoulder blades.

"Of course, a physical condition or stressed breathing could cause pain. But ask yourself these two questions.

"Firstly, are you experiencing a real physical issue for which you need to see a doctor or therapist to relieve or cure the pain?

"Secondly, is it not a diagnosable physical condition, and are you instead experiencing an energy movement?

"Please raise your hands if you had pains in between, or in each of, your shoulder blades, and you visited the doctor, and the doctor couldn't find anything, and then you realized it's an energy movement.

(Hands raised.)

"Maybe about a quarter of you…

"If it's a physical condition, medical advice and therapy should always be sought. Doctors are expert at diagnostics, and you never know what might be causing the pain. If there is a physical diagnosis, it's best to discover the cause and treat it early. The earlier the better!

"But if doctors can find no medical cause, and if it seems to be an energy movement, ask yourself this question. Did pain start when you started to share your LOve?

"Think about this. How long ago did you start to share unconditional LOve properly, one way or another?

"Was this when you felt the energy movement in your shoulder blades?

"Please raise your hands if you know pains in your shoulder blades began when you started to share your LOve.

(Hands raised.)

"Yes, the same quarter of you that realized the pains were an energy movement felt the pains at about the time you began to share LOve.

"And that is simply how it is. Pains are felt in or between the shoulder blades by a high proportion of angels-on-earth like you, when you begin to share your LOve properly.

"Physical sensations of wings are not common early in adulthood. For a few people it does happen earlier, you know.

Maybe, even though the angels-in-the-making are still going through challenges, they are allowed a Dispensation by those above to rise to the higher Platformation of flourishing their angelic wings.

"Or maybe they were climbing different parts of their mountain of soul life at similar times. And despite not yet overcoming the early Platformation fully, they had achieved the higher Platformation of sharing their LOve so well, they earned the right to develop their wings.

"But for most developing angels, wing experiences start when they have dealt adequately with early Platformations, and they have begun to accept humanity's faults, to develop unconditional LOve, and to share inner LOve. They will never forget when they first felt their wings, or the first times their wings were seen by others. But it's a subject they will rarely discuss with friends or family. Most angels don't wish to be laughed at, scorned, or trolled.

"Certainly for many years I felt unable to mention the first times my wings were seen, especially because at one time I would never have believed I had wings, or even that angels existed on earth.

"In the late 1990s, I had started sharing my LOve by offering alternative therapies unconditionally, free, to everyone in need. One day, a clairvoyant friend stared at me with a surprised expression and exclaimed, 'What are those wings doing growing out of your back?'

(Laughter.)

"I didn't tell her, but I thought she was hallucinating.

(More laughter.)

"I continued thinking she was hallucinating until the next day when three clairvoyants on one of my courses all saw the wings. The thing is, they had just arrived, and didn't know and had not spoken to each other. I was shocked, and didn't want to believe them. I have many human faults. 'How could I possibly be an angel,' I thought. I hadn't ever considered myself worthy enough to have wings. So without each of them knowing, I asked them all to write down the size, color, texture, movement, and shape they could see. They all wrote identical descriptions. I was shocked, puzzled, dumb-founded. But four people in two days seeing identical things meant there was a potential reality of the existence of wings, and that had to be thought about seriously.

"For me, the clincher that personally helped me understand that some people have wings was discovering that innocent young children could see wings on some people, and draw them.

"A child of about five years old who sat at the back of one of my classes drew a picture of me, and of another person on the course, complete with wings and halos, and smilingly showed the drawings around. His mother laughed, 'Aren't children's imaginations amazing?' I just nodded.

"And a boy of six years old said to his Uruguayan grandmother, Graciela, 'Please ask Allan to help me. He's got wings. He can help anything.' I vividly remember the help he needed, and the smile on his face after I resolved his problems.

"I began to realise that even though we have human faults and cannot possibly be perfect, we can rise above our human problems by sharing LOve, and doing good.

"For many years, clairvoyants on classes taught by a teacher of psychic subjects saw and identically described his large, bright, pure white wings, and similarly pure white halo.

"In another case, a spiritual teacher taught how to see auras. Some beginner students were shocked to see more than just the teacher's aura. Out of every class of about 30 students, about eight could see and describe exactly the same large, bright white wings and halo. It was unbelievable for them, and for him.

"However strange it seemed, however much that teacher didn't want to see himself as an angel, and certainly didn't want others to think he was an angel, he said he eventually had no choice. So many hundreds of people saw his wings, what else could he do, but accept that wings are a strange but true reality of life.

"It was and still is the same for me. It took a long time to feel ok about standing in front of people and saying, 'I am an angel.' Even though I say that on spiritual and angelic courses and lectures, it's still a difficult concept to impart, even with humility. If I am an angel though, I am an angel of peace despite my human faults that sometimes are not peaceful. I am an angel of healing and helping others, even though I cannot heal or help as much as I would wish. And I am an angel of LOve, even though my human faults do not always portray LOve. It is likely to be similar for you. Despite your human faults, one day you may have little choice except to accept your true inner nature that is yearning to escape the trappings of the body.

"So for you one day, when your wings start to develop you may either see or feel them.

"Some angels-on-earth can see their wings precisely, the size, color, texture, movement, shape, density, and whether they're furled or open, or go in and out.

"Some angels may feel their wings as a fluttering movement, a breeze behind them, a tingling, pain, or even a wind.

"And this might sound strange to angels-on-earth who haven't reached this Platformation yet, but a few people can hear their wings flapping.

"Hands up if you've actually felt your wings flapping or spreading or moving or something like that.

(Hands raised.)

"Maybe about a third of you have felt your wings.

"Hands up if, one way or another, you've seen your own wings. Maybe you saw your wings in a mirror? Like one lady I know who, when she was halfway down her stairs at home, she looked in a mirror, and saw her wings for the first time. She almost fell down the rest of the stairs.

(Laughter.)

"Please raise your hands if you've somehow seen your wings.

(Hands raised.)

"Hmm, a few less… And that's how it usually is, not so many. About 10% of you have seen your wings.

"Hands up if someone you know has seen wings on you.

(Hands raised.)

"There are about 20% of you. There's a strange reality here, isn't there? If someone else says they can see your wings, that's validation for you as an angel-on-earth. Especially if more than one or two people who don't know each other say they can see exactly the same type of wings.

"And what about, has anyone heard your wings flapping?

(Hands raised.)

"Not so many; but I'll bet hearing those percentages of angels here who have felt or seen or heard their wings has surprised some of you here, especially if you haven't yet experienced your own wings.

"It's OK, because maybe you're probably still on an early Platformation, and you've got the rest of your life ahead to develop the sharing of your LOve and the sprouting of your wings.

"Or maybe your wings are there already, but you're just not made in the way needed to consciously experience your wings.

"It can be scary when you experience your wings. For although you may know you've developed wings, who can you talk to? Who would believe you? It has to be kept a secret. Wings and halos are not subjects taught at school, or in the University of Life.

"In fact, when you were a teenager or in your 20s, and someone said they had wings, what would you have replied? Probably, if you'd said anything, it would have been not-so-polite. Or maybe you'd have been angelically kind, and just given a gentle, noncommittal remark to make them go away.

"People who develop, feel, see, or hear their wings know deep within them that they are angels. And when I meet some angels for the first time, and see they are angelic, I don't have to broach the angelic subject gently. I can ask outright, 'Are you an angel?' If a person has experienced their wings, they will almost always nod matter-of-factly in agreement. Because they know that is just how it is, a simple fact of life that, sadly, non-angels who make up the majority of the population will never understand.

"Some people ask why they should experience pain when the wings of an angel should be beauteous. Well, remember that you haven't found your ultimate soul Destiny yet. Probably you are still developing proper unconditional LOve for everybody and everything. Until that LOve has developed adequately, there will be a pain in or between the shoulder blades as the wings force their way in and out.

"Eventually, when interacting with LOve and you cannot feel pain, it means you have developed adequate unconditional LOve for everybody, everywhere, under every circumstance.

"In other words, when your wings have become fully oiled with LOve, they can slide in and out smoothly as you evolve up to an even higher plane.

"One strange fact of life is that one side, one shoulder blade, may feel stronger energy, or be more painful than the other.

"Those of you who have felt your wings, put your hands up if you've felt that.

(Hands raised.)

"There are maybe a quarter of you, most of the quarter of you who can feel your wings, that feel one stronger than the other.

"The side where you feel stronger sensations is where unconditional LOve still has not developed properly. You need to share LOve more deeply. But how do you know what to do? How do you share LOve in better ways? How can you help the wings slide in and out more easily, so well-oiled by LOve you cannot sense them at all?

"Here are some clues. The first clue is for those angels who can feel their wings. The second clue is for angels who see them.

"It is well-known that the left side of the brain is for logic and creates logical solutions, and the right side of the brain is more for creative aspects of life, and that the left or right brain affects the opposite sides of the body.

"It's interesting that the logical left side of the brain seems to affect the right wing, and the creative right brain seems to affect the left wing.

"So, if you feel the wing more on the right, the clue is that your logical sharing of LOve needs to be developed.

"Or if you feel the left wing more, your clue is that you need to be more creative in the sharing of your LOve.

"So, if you feel pain or stronger sensations in one wing, look at how you are starting to share LOve. Is it in a logical way, but you still have logical doubts or misinterpretations? Or are you sharing LOve creatively, but you may need to be less, or more, creative to achieve the best LOve results?

"The clue for those who see their wings is different. If you see the left wing smaller or darker in color than the right, your clue is to develop your creative approach to sharing your LOve. If the right wing is smaller or darker, the clue is to analyze how to evolve your logical aspects of LOve.

"Platformations, as with anything in life, tend to overlap. They are not entirely cut and dried stories, where one plus six, or two plus five, or three plus four equals seven.

"In general terms, this Platformation can be overcome when you share your LOve in deeper and more beautifully divine ways, and when you've developed your logical and creative aspects of LOve equally. That's when the pains start to go. That's when the wings can flip in and out without any pain because you've oiled them with adequate amounts of perfect, divine LOve.

"Now is the time when you can truly start to share genuine LOve with the world."

The Secrets of Bi-Location

"A most peculiar thing may happen when angels evolve higher on their pathway, when they've risen close to the ranks of their angelic band. It's called bi-location. Bi-location means being in two or more places at the same time.

"It's such a strange concept, that perhaps there's a need to explain that there are documented cases of bi-location throughout history.

"One person with recorded bi-location abilities is Ranieri, who was born in 1304. He was revered because his spirit body could be in an energetic duplicate form and create miracles, while his physical body was in another place, doing something different. Two recordings of his bi-location events still exist in the form of paintings.

"The first painting, entitled, *The Blessed Ranieri Frees the Poor from a Jail in Florence,* is in the French art gallery, the Louvre, in Paris. It shows Ranieri flying like a rocket as he helps poor people escape from unjust imprisonment.

"The second painting depicts Ranieri's appearance to a Catholic cardinal in a dream. It's in the Staatliche Museen in Berlin, and shows Ranieri in mid-air above a sleeping cardinal, pointing out a healing ointment the cardinal had to find and take to cure himself.

"Other religious figures such as St. Anthony of Padua, Úrsula Micaela Morata, and Padre Pio are also said to have bi-located.

"However weird it may seem, bi-location is a historical phenomenon that exists from early Greek philosophy to shamanism, spiritualism, and Hindu and Jewish mysticism. In Christianity, bi-location has long been recognized as a sign of being holy.

"'Holy' is the important buzzword here. It is strangely mystical that holiness seems to occur when someone has accepted the faults of humanity with LOve, and is sharing divine LOve from their soul with everybody, everywhere, under every circumstance. It seems that becoming at LOving oneness with everything creates an automatic connection to being 'holy'. Bi-location may be a natural side effect of holiness. xxx

"In other words, bi-location may be a sign of when spiritual dimensions have been discovered and implemented, and the LOving wholeness of body, mind, spirit and soul is connected to God and the universal spirit of LOve.

"Oneness with divine LOve may create the ability to reach out to help anyone, anywhere by unconsciously using a blueprint of your spirit bodies.

"When angels-on-earth develop LOve adequately, universal Law can allow the potential for their spirit bodies to automatically bi-locate around the world to help with whatever is needed, in an instant. Then you can appear to one or more than one person at a time, and help numerous people in need in increasingly special ways.

"I know some people find bi-location strange and weird. I also know many of you have experienced this phenomenon.

"Please raise your hands if a spiritual teacher or religious leader has appeared to you in one way or another.

(Hands raised.)

"About a quarter of you... Sometimes a leading spiritual or religious or other person appears in your dreams to help you, but normally it's as a physical presence when you're wide awake.

"Some of you have told me stories of seeing someone appear to help you in positive ways. Some, like a young girl in Malaysia, can smell the presence of her mother's spiritual teacher as a sweet, flowery honey fragrance. Intriguingly, it's the same smell reported by others.

"Spiritual teachers or religious leaders can be 'dead' or alive. In Catholicism for example, St. Jude is the patron saint of hopeless cases. I've heard of many cures attributed to his appearances. Some Indian mystics are available to be called on, to help with any circumstance you might experience, regardless of what country you're in.

"But I expect you don't tell most friends or family? You won't want to be considered strange by skeptics, or maybe even crazy. Bi-location is another secret in the life of an angel-on-earth. It's not a subject we talk about openly, is it, whether we do it or receive it?

"Astral travel is not the same as bi-location. Astral travel is when you deliberately choose to make your mind, spirit, or soul leave your body and travel to inspect something somewhere else in the world. Unless it's done with LOve, could the deliberate choice potentially be considered spying? For example, a person could spy on their partner, to check where they are, or spy on a safe, to note the unlocking code.

"Unfortunately, people can use astral travel for egotistical or selfish purposes. Stories abound of governments' secret services using astral travel experts to spy on other countries.

"Bi-location, however, is different. It is 100% unconscious. You can be in two places at the same time and not be aware of it at all.

"Harmlessness of bi-location must be considered. An angel should only do good for anyone or anything, anywhere. As you bi-locate unconsciously, your unconscious thoughts should be as pure as possible.

"Luckily, because bi-location normally occurs only when your non-LOving human flesh and blood and your LOving soul have developed and joined in LOving oneness, you will, by the time you bi-locate, have almost all perfect thoughts. You will still be an imperfect human being, with imperfect thoughts, words, and deeds, but importantly, during bi-location, your LOve has increased your potential to unconsciously help someone positively.

"You can now automatically bi-locate naturally and unconsciously to help others in need. Being spiritually connected to all types of need, you unconsciously know everything in need. So you have a special task, a dedicated soul purpose, to LOvingly help others with your spirit body.

"That is the purpose of bi-location. To help others in need, at anytime, anywhere, whether you know them or not.

"There are five reasons for bi-location. To comfort, to help a person or situation, to teach, to heal, and to gently discipline.

"Discipline is when someone is about to do something that's not, let's say, as LOving as it should be. The spiritual teacher or religious leader may appear to them with, for example, a stern look on his face, wagging a finger.

(Laughter.)

"Numerous persons in need have described spirit appearances, that helped, comforted, supported, cured, or taught them answers that changed their lives for the better.

"You won't need to have met a person in order to bi-locate to help. Even though I now accept the reality of bi-location, it is still not comfortable for me to openly say that people have seen me appear as if in a physical body, before I ever met them. Apparently, I appear in dreams to some, asking them to come to my teachings at a particular time and place, to help their lives in beautiful and fascinating ways. Things always worked out exceptionally well, except when this phenomenon originally occurred. A lady came early to a course, and said simply, 'I'm here.' I had no idea who she was. 'You must remember me,' she replied, looking astonished that I didn't know her. 'We were at the market in north London yesterday, and you said it would benefit my life to attend your course today.'

"I had never seen that market, and told her, saying I'd never seen her before. So she left, looking downcast.

"I felt so guilty when others arrived at courses with similar stories. Eventually there was little choice but to accept the strange reality of unconscious bi-location.

"Bi-location could become part of your LOving life on Earth. So, may I give you a few more examples, from people I know, and from personal experiences, so you know the types of events you might expect?

"A lay priest in Australia phoned me in England to say she felt sad. Later that day, I apparently appeared next to her, and physically placed my arm around her. She felt heat, and immense comfort.

"On another occasion I taught a class in Adelaide. Two ladies who had never met each other said I'd appeared to them about two years previously to help and teach them.

"A queen in exile from an ancient African tribe with a 700-year-old dynasty said she'd seen me appear before her son was born, while she and her son made his Contract for his soul journey on Earth. When her son turned 21 years old, she attended my Reiki and spiritual courses, and asked me to help him with counseling and advisory sessions. He eventually assumed the throne as rightful heir and king.

"There are many other strange but real stories that could be examples for what may happen to you one day.

"A clairvoyant said how she watched her spiritual trainer's energies as he taught her. She saw his energy body suddenly leave his physical body and zip away to a house fire to help a trapped child escape.

"When I exhibited about angels-on-earth in Mexico City, three elderly Mexican ladies who were friends walking past suddenly stopped and stared. They explained in astonished voices that I had appeared in their dreams to help their lives. They'd never discussed their dreams before, and stared at each other in complete disbelief that I'd appeared at night during their sleep to help them all.

"A lady I know in the north of the UK, Norma, was in hospital. She said that her spiritual advisor had no idea that doctors had said she'd die of cancer that night. Apparently the energy body of the advisor appeared to her during the night saying not to worry, she wouldn't die, and then gave her healing. She said she felt hands on her, hot, and she suddenly felt alive, cured. She said that the following year she brought her family to attend his courses.

"As a final example of unconscious bi-location, I heard of a Japanese Reiki student who had 40 patients a week. During every session, her Reiki master's energy body sat in an armchair, watching her giving hands-on healing.

"If she did something awry, apparently his smile would drop.

"If she didn't understand what to do better, he would walk over and show her what to do, and where to place her hands.

"And if she still didn't get it, he would place his hands on her patient as well, and do the technique for her instead.

"Strangely, she said when that happened, always her patients said they could feel two sets of hands on them. By the end of the session, they'd feel cured.

"Countless people I've met on courses say bi-location has helped them, so there are probably countless more who haven't said so.

"If your waking life is busy helping others eight or more hours a day, it's best to have no bi-location awareness. If you knew of every bi-location event, you'd be on overload. It would be impossible to function normally.

"I'm explaining these stories to help you see your developing potential. Bi-location is nothing special. It is simply a natural phenomenon that all angels-to-be might progress to and attain when they reach higher Platformations of divine LOve.

"Imagine you're on an early Platformation, and you bi-locate when you haven't learned divine LOve lessons adequately. You could bi-locate in 'naughty' ways. That could create karma for your life that you'll need to resolve.

"So, the warning is, although you may never bi-locate, if someone one day says you appeared to them, check your spirituality. Double up your intention to have a LOve motivation behind every thought, word, and deed.

"You're human and will never be perfect. But you now have a responsibility to be as LOve-perfect as possible. You need to program your conscious and unconscious minds to 24 hour a day LOve, so you can always, even unconsciously, interact with LOve.

"Then, when you fully practice LOve-Based Living, when you bi-locate to help others in need, it should only be for LOving goodness.

"Though the next level on your path is to come, you could be on your way to becoming a True Angelic Master, helping others 24 hours a day.

"All this may seem strange, especially as it's not common knowledge. But when so many people throughout history tell similar stories, every word may be true. It's just how it is.

"I hope and pray all of you reach this stage of unconscious ability to help anyone find happy solutions, at anytime, anywhere."

The Secrets of Permeation

"There's another strange but true point to be mentioned at this higher Platformation level of unconditional LOve.

"The waves, the frequencies of your LOve energies can permeate all things with incredible healing outcomes. Permeation with your LOve energies includes for photographs, writings, rings, books, clothing, and rooms. Anything that is personal to someone can be connected to and infused by your LOving energies to help their lives.

"Postcards, posters, photos, paintings, prints, anything that can portray the image of someone from a spiritual or religious hierarchy can potentially help cure or solve the recipient's needs. I couldn't believe it at first, truly I couldn't. But I've now lost count of how many times someone has said that they were cured or helped just by holding or looking at a picture of a spiritual teacher, or me.

"People have told me that, when holding for example a postcard of an image of me healing a child, they could feel unusual energies like electric, heat, tingling, or a sort of magnetic pushing or pulling and so on, entering their hand, and rippling up their arm and into their body, healing them.

"Some people naturally wonder if the feelings came from their own hand. I did too.

(Laughter.)

"But on putting down the photo and checking, they said they found different sensations in their hand, compared to when they held the photo.

"Some people would then place the picture on a table, and hold their hand over the photo without touching it. They still felt the same electric, heat, tingling, magnetic, or whatever feelings as if they were holding the photo. But no such feelings could be felt from the table without the photo on it.

"It's still amazing that people meditating on or holding a photo or image have been cured of a variety of physical conditions, and become happier, more confident, free of pain, and so on.

"Permeation also occurs with posters. Some passersby who saw the poster of my face at exhibitions burst into tears of release. The first time someone said they were sobbing because they'd seen my poster, I felt terrible.

(Laughter.)

"That was until they said their lifelong issues were cured, suddenly, unexpectedly. The passersby gave profuse thanks.

"It may be beyond your current understanding, as once I could not understand. But I have learned to accept that when your energies develop, when the force of LOve emanates from your being, all angel-on-earth souls, like every one of you here, can help others, even through permeating photos, posters and other materials, in Godly LOving and healing ways.

"At Mind, Body, Spirit festivals, my exhibition stand was manned by about 40 of my angelically-souled healers.

Permeation of the exhibition stand with their LOve energies always took place. Regardless of how big the exhibition was, or how many other stands there were, visitors often said our stand had the most LOving and healing vibrations. Clairvoyants saw that ours was the only stand with dazzingly bright, angelic silver coming from every healer, without exception. It was always the busiest stand, permeated with LOve. I was fortunate to have had so many highly spiritual students as helpers.

"Another strange but true way angelically LOve-developed energies can penetrate everything for positive benefits is in places where you live, work, or spend much time.

"Have you ever been house-hunting, and entered different buildings and experienced contrasting feelings? Even two different rooms in a house can feel unalike in their energetic feelings. That's because whatever mainly occurred in that house or room leaves a frequency imprint behind.

"If angelic unconditional LOve permeates the structure of the building and the fabric of the furnishings, visitors will feel better just being in the room.

"As an example, in the residential therapy center of someone I know, many people have been cured in the healing room before the healing session started. It became so common he would watch patients' faces as they entered. If they showed any sign whatsoever that healing could be happening, he'd ask them to take a seat, and then excuse himself for a few minutes.

"On his return, cures would often have taken place. Visitors would cry or laugh with relief at feeling so good.

"It is similar in his teaching room. Visitors often cried with tears of release within minutes of entering. After, they felt better than they'd felt for years.

"The additionally strange thing, he said, was that in the healing room, people's emotions were cured. Whereas in the teaching room, their physical condition was usually helped. It seems different frequencies had permeated and worked in those rooms.

"Remember this is nothing to do with anyone being anything special. You are just angels-on-earth, evolving your paths unconditionally, trying to achieve Angelic Service, with LOve. I hope that within all of you, there is a beautiful force for angelically LOving goodness waiting to permeate all you touch. That's if you don't glow beautiful LOve already.

"Isn't it wonderful that people can be cured just by feeling your angelic LOve vibrations.

"This is something you as an angel-on-earth need to be aware of on your journey, even though not all of you will have gifts of bi-location and permeation, for LOve and healing.

"Some of you may have bi-location and permeation gifts, but never be aware of it because it is likely that few people would tell you.

"However it is, it is fine. It's OK, perfect, just the way life works for you.

"Or you might become aware of your unconscious bi-location and permeation gifts that help others, because some people tell you what happened.

"If you hear of such cases, you have a great angelic responsibility to seek and keep as much purity as you can in your conscious thoughts. This should have an automatic knock-on effect to program your unconscious thoughts to LOving purity too.

"Don't be shy. Don't hide your Light. Share LOve, not only when you are perfect enough, on the higher Platformations, or when your wings are recognizable, or when you can bi-locate or permeate.

"Shine the Light of your LOve at every step you tread, and in every word you speak, always. Then your path may open easily, without you really noticing, or even without you particularly trying."

Three Clues to Success

"Some angels are lucky and find their soul purpose early on in life. They tread the mill within a singular company, or a singular profession, grinding their way as far to the top as they can. One day they will see how their LOve and Light can make a bigger, special difference to their organization or profession.

"Most angels-on-earth, though, will have dithered and dallied about what soul purpose to do. But they will usually have spent their waiting time wisely, searching for what else they can learn, what else could become one of their gifts they could use to share their LOve.

"Many angels continuously study new skills, maybe even for the whole of this particular lifetime. But there should come a time for action, to use learned skills fully, and to choose to use some of those skills for an angel's highest soul purpose on Earth.

"It's not always easy to see what to do. You might sense a direction, or be guided as mentioned earlier. Don't worry whether you'll tread the right path. Never blame yourself for not finding your path, because apart from Foolishness, nothing is your fault. You may have intense feelings of a big soul purpose to achieve. But almost certainly you won't know what to do, or how to do it.

"Your highest calling may be kept secret by those above, until you are ready to move up to highest Platformations to offer your life in Angelic Service.

"Some angels regularly focus on previous experiences, or learn new subjects. But they can't decide what to do as a soul purpose. It's like a secretive ship just beyond the horizon, slightly out of sight, but waiting to come into focus.

"I often get asked by angels what project they should do. But I've learned not to reply fully. I don't like to say their exact purpose because explaining too early is like taking a fish from water. The fish will soon die. The fish needs to swim around by itself, in its own environment, to achieve its Destiny.

"So I can't say your precise soul venture, because it's better not to risk putting you into an environment that is inappropriate for your soul's profession or lessons.

"But perhaps I can give a few clues, so eventually, when at last the time is right for you to attempt your highest reason for existence on Earth, you may progress more smoothly.

"There are three main clues to look at that may give options on how to succeed on the future peak of your soul path.

"The first clue is to look at your life, and inspect your expertise.

"Probably you've been good in diverse roles. Look at the roles you enjoyed more, that gave the most comfort. Inspect the two to three that shared more LOve, or that gave most satisfaction.

"If you can find two or three different roles you LOved, could you find a way to combine aspects of them into a never-before-achieved new system? The new system may entail a new method, new technique, new shop, new patent, new process, new product, new service, new whatever. The point is, it's new and different and has the potential to expand with your LOve, to make a positive difference to help many in need.

"That creates a unique angelic way to help your version of need. Search for your own pioneering way to serve humanity within LOve-Based Living. Seek something game-changing, that makes a difference because it's never before been successfully administered.

"The second clue is to know your working comfort zone. Ask yourself, do you prefer to be an entrepreneur, working as an individual, setting up something and running a project on your own, with you as the boss?

"Or are you more the corporate type, preferring to be in a corporation, or under someone's command?

"Let's discuss the potential if you're more an entrepreneur by nature, a sort of working maverick.

"Have you usually wanted to do things your way or no way?

Do you usually gain knowledge, experience, and self-confidence to achieve your dreams by yourself? Do you prefer to be a boss, controlling your self-employed business? Do you enjoy entrepreneurship to manage business startups, running, and expansion?

"If you answer 'Yes' to this type of question, and are a maverick entrepreneur by nature, you will probably start your own company or entity that will do some sort of good in the world.

"Your entrepreneurial spirit will likely be to start something new, by yourself, as a lone wolf. You might struggle alone, but it will feel right, like your perfect path.

"Some entrepreneurs are lucky. Their life has given access to quality people to help them, or money, or both. Knowing how to find quality people or money to grow a project to help enhance something that is not good enough will facilitate the entrepreneurs' aims and objectives immensely. It's quicker and easier usually to be interdependent, collaborating with or hiring experts that can fill specific and important roles, to create a core team in your LOving project.

"One thing when collaborating or hiring staff is to accept that people are not perfect. Remember that Platformation, where people have their human faults? Where their brain chemicals, hormones, or genetic inheritances might make them say or do silly things? Think about it. Would you like that type of person working for you?

"Be careful as an entrepreneur hiring staff. It will not be just skills you need, or the usual business criteria of being self-motivated, efficient, honest and so on. You will also need staff to be as caring, sweet and LOving as you can find, so your LOve project can manifest even more LOve.

"You may need money for your project, perhaps just a little that you already have, or can easily borrow or crowdfund. Or maybe your project is huge and you'll need millions of dollars.

Whatever money you need may not matter, because money might be part of your path. At the highest level money might come in strangely synchronistic, almost miraculous ways.

"Some angels start a game-changing charity, a pioneering business, a unique franchise, an exclusive Internet site, or train people to improve their lives or skills. Do anything to bring LOve into people's hearts. It is not relevant what you do. It is how you do it.

"If your life was enterprising, it is probably more comfortable to achieve your highest function on Earth based on entrepreneurial knowledge, skills and abilities.

"The third clue is, in most of your life, have you usually preferred to be within the safety and security of a corporate structure, under a boss who gives advice, or with someone experienced who can direct you to achieve your tasks in the best way?

"If this was usually the case, your highest position on Earth will more likely be achieved under a corporate umbrella, within an existing company. That means you'll be comfortable setting something up new within the boundaries of an organization. Perhaps you can suggest a new way forward for the company that is kinder to staff or customers, or more profitable in more LOving ways. Or maybe you'll be the instigator of great ideas to benefit the world, but leave it for the organization to develop.

"One of these three clues, to inspect your life's expertise, to use entrepreneurial skills, or to be under the security of a corporation or boss, almost certainly gives answers to where you'll find your soul purpose.

"It may not be relevant exactly what you choose, because there will be another higher Platformation level to discuss later to make sense of your life in a very different way. For now, you can manifest LOve under the umbrella heading of one of those three clues.

"You then have additional choices. You can share LOve in

your highest post on Earth by manifesting projects that are local, regional, national, or international.

"The clue here is to look at your working comfort zones. What have you usually preferred? What way of life has felt most comfortable to you?

"Maybe you've often been drawn to local charities or groups helping local people. Perhaps helping a local need is your comfort zone, and your knowledge of local affairs will light the way to your highest soul purpose.

"Or have you felt more comfortable working on a regional or national scale, and your knowledge in those areas might provide clues for your highest soul purpose.

"Maybe you prefer international travel. Then your comfort zone is global. You may be a global tutor, helper or promoter of a new system.

"The bottom line for the clues here is that one of these four previously experienced comfort zones, local, regional, national, or international, could provide your ultimate LOving soul purpose on Earth. Particularly, when one of those four clues are combined with one of the three clues mentioned just now, which are combining two or three of your expertises you've learned and enjoyed into a new entrepreneurial system, or under a corporation.

"Sounds complicated? It's just life. Most angels-on-earth attain success naturally, without guidance. They can succeed immensely, locally, regionally, nationally, or internationally. That's because something that usually takes a month or two to complete for a normal human being can be very easy for an angel to complete brilliantly in a remarkably short space of time.

"Angels-on-earth eventually reach Godly beauty, the highest state of oneness with everything. They join the ways of LOving angels, where everything is easy. They enjoy longer hours sharing LOve than ever, but it won't feel like it. It will feel heavenly, wonderfully satisfying. They are dedicating their human lives to their soul purpose.

"Previous Platformation experiences have connected relevant neural pathways in their brains, and gathered innate courage, ability, and motivation to just go for it, just do it, unconditionally, with LOve.

"When you reach your soul's ultimate goal in this lifetime, when you reach the peak of the toughest mountain you've climbed, there's only one way to share your LOve. And it's so obvious what you should do.

"It's so clearly evident there's only one task for your soul, one purpose for your life. You know precisely what your role is. You know, because the position is suddenly unique, an ultra-special way to share your LOve. And you do the mission and share your LOve automatically, almost without a second thought, because it's natural and comfortable.

"And you know it's right."

Godly Conditional LOve

"By now, it's natural and easy to do your soul purpose. You've learned many lessons on LOve and how to share it. For example, as a teenager, what was your interaction with love? For most teens, it's a matter of, 'I'll love such and such, providing something is given in return.'

"Teenagers have HCL, Human Conditional Love. Human Conditional Love is often demanding, based on personal human wants and desires. They place selfish conditions on giving love and often judge others harshly.

"For many teenagers, unless they get what they want in return for their love, they won't offer love. HCL has zero whatsoever to do with divine, selfless, Godly LOve. HCL is egotistical, and certainly not divine.

"Later on the learning Platformations of life, comes HUL, Human Unconditional Love. The angel-on-earth is learning they can't demand things they want.

"With HUL, realizations of love and LOve begin. There's acceptance that all people have individual ways and needs. They should be appreciated and accepted for who they are, in their own right, on their own path.

"But HUL is viewed only from the person's human perspective. HUL has little to do with Godly divine LOve, and is not about the soul. It's only about human love.

"Next, higher up the Platformation levels, is GUL, Godly Unconditional LOve. You can now LOve others using higher motivation. You've begun to understand Godly lessons, karmic wisdom, and paths of different types of souls who are trudging up their mountains.

"Even if you don't fully understand, you somehow know that the higher divine plan needs you to have Godly Unconditional LOve for everyone, and everything, everywhere, under every circumstance. You might see that GUL is very different to HUL. GUL is now your path.

"It is one thing to know about Godly Unconditional LOve because you hear or read about it. It is quite another to put GUL knowledge into daily practice.

"GCL, which stands for Godly Conditional LOve, is the most beautiful and satisfying Platformation, where you can feel as if you are at home, at one with your God. But it is also a Platformation that's not so easy to understand unless you're on it. In brief, it means that you have the highest possible LOve for everyone and everything, everywhere. But LOve is conditional, not unconditional.

"GCL means you will start to judge by placing conditions on the sharing of your LOve. You will judge when to use tough LOve to try to help something. The source of your GCL will be from the LOve of God emanating from within your soul, and by now embracing and emblazoning your human flesh and blood.

"If you understand the Bible, think of Jesus when he entered a temple and found it full of market traders. He did not use HUL or GUL, human or Godly unconditional love for the traders. He turned their tables over. There was nothing unconditionally LOving about spilling their goods across the temple floor. There must have been many angry people that day.

"But Christians assume that Jesus did not act in anger, and acted out of Godliness and LOve because the temple should be a divine place of worship.

"Jesus had probably learned HCL, HUL, and GUL lessons about lowly conditional, and unconditional, love and LOve. He maybe chose to use GCL passion, Godly Conditional LOve, to change his world for the better.

"It's an intricate concept. Unless you're on the GCL Platformation, it's too easy to think that Jesus had a teen-type tantrum, or should have acted differently, and accepted the traders with unconditional love.

"GCL is a big subject, understood mainly on higher Platformation levels, when angels have passed lessons to possess the level of comprehension needed for values of Godly spirituality, morals of humankind, and ethics of harmlessness. And angels have followed laws of humanity's love, and Law Books of God's LOve.

"Only then are you karmically allowed to use GUL to hold the future of a person fully in your hands. You can at that time judge, from a more valid, beautiful, and gloriously Godly viewpoint, whether to use tough conditional LOve. Perhaps you can be like Jesus, making conscious decisions to judge whether something should be changed for highest goodness.

"Can you judge from the purity of your LOve, with no human ideas attached to make your judgement more like a conditional love teenager? If you can judge others from your highest Godly LOve ability, everything will be said and done with LOve motivations.

"Your friends and family may believe in the new GUL you. Or maybe they won't, because they'll still remember the you that placed teen-type conditions on your love.

"The clue is to do everything as harmlessly as possible. The temple traders for example, after being thrown out, maybe opened stalls outside the temple in a more appropriate place. They did not lose out. Everybody gained. The temple could return to a place of peace.

"Angels-on-earth should also nurture good out of evil, so that everyone gains.

"I hope that when the book about this Angel Party is published, it helps readers to find GCL quicker, and to seek and know contrasting Godly Conditional LOve. I hope that angels try to overcome their HCL, HUL, and GUL Platformations faster so that they can relieve and achieve even more.

"I also hope you don't think you understand Godly Conditional LOve too soon, and try to judge others, and be tough, when you're still on early Platformations. If you have a lack of GCL understanding, you could damage others, and create karma for yourself.

"Life is a natural progression. I hope that you'll take responsibility to develop LOve, and overcome early Platformations as wholly as possible first.

"When you can achieve the status of Godly Conditional LOve, only then can you truly comprehend how to accept and LOve everyone within human love laws and God's LOve Law.

"Only with GCL will you have no personal prejudices, only the prejudices for God.

"Then the forces above can trust you almost 100%, and start to guide those in need into your path in increasingly specific ways.

"The start of your destined path will begin to unfold, like wings spreading across the Earth, a shadow made of Light."

Chapter 10

The Secret Angelic Word

The Secret Angelic Word Introduction

"Finally, you've passed successfully through many lifetimes, and through many Platformations in this life. You've probably gone through numerous repeats at learning lessons adequately, and at last you've got everything right.

"You've learned to LOve yourself, learned to LOve others, learned to share your LOve, and learned tough Godly LOve. You've passed many tests of LOve. You have even accomplished the needed LOve lessons of your final soul purpose.

"Then something may happen. It might become apparent that even the Platformation of performing your soul purpose well, at the highest level, was not really what this lifetime was all about. It becomes clearer to the angel-on-earth that there's something that could be even more important.

"You want to know this little secret, yes? The mystery of what can be more important than completing your soul purpose?

"OK, I'll explain. All your lifetimes have been leading to this singular issue.

"It's a very specific and rarely discussed issue of human and angelic nature, an issue that may have nothing to do with the human being's or soul's undertaking on Earth, that's obvious. It's an undercover issue, hidden behind all of the thoughts, words and actions you've ever had.

"The issue is about the individual angel-on-earth's deepest human personality or character gift. The issue is about the angel's gift as a human being, a gift that can be used angelically to help while on Earth as a human, and to give help from above after this life as an angel.

"This gift is deeply ingrained into the human persona and

soul memories of the angel-on-earth. It's about each person's exceptional quality, a quality suited for a unique achievement.

"It's a quality to enhance the soul's objective, regardless of what the objective is. It provides sustenance to all in need. It's part of the absolute purity of nature and oneness of Creation.

"This is nothing whatsoever to do with LOve. All angels-on-earth have LOve inside them. So at the highest peak of the path, it has to be something else, a quality to distinguish them from other LOving angelic brands and bands.

"Because eventually, with the sharing of your HCL, HUL, GUL and GCL, comes a realization of your singular purpose to be here, your one soul reason to be on this planet.

"Yes, it's to share love and LOve in all their forms with yourself, family, friends and society, locally, nationally and internationally.

"Yes, it's to achieve your Contract and Destiny.

"But it's much more than all that. There's one other reason behind all of this.

"And it all depends on which band of angels you'll belong to."

The Secret Angelic Word Soul Goals and Four Clues

"During this Angel Party, there have been clues that unveil the secret lives of angels-on-earth, of your LOving soul, and of your angelic reasons for existence.

"But another angelically secretive subject has not yet been mentioned. There are other clues to spot. So here is another subject, and a few more clues.

"May I ask you a question? How do you find which of the many bands of angels you might join?

"Any ideas anyone? No? I will give some clues.

"I've already said that you won't find clues from just sharing your LOve. All angels-on-earth share LOve throughout their lives. I've also hinted that you won't find your true purpose even from your best actions.

"Even after achieving all Platformations, angels might not see what they're seeking, to find something so well hidden. Usually you can't be consciously aware of what you know unconsciously.

"Unknown to your conscious mind, you have been unconsciously searching for something you may not have even dreamed of before.

"The secret to your ultimate Destiny is a very special word, a word that resonates with your being and with a certain band of angels.

"The secret to your Destiny is your one and only, true, Secret Angelic Word, your SAW. You came, you SAW, you conquered.

"To understand this final aspect of your Angelic Path better, perhaps you can think about angels differently, in this specific way?

"Think about this. Isn't there a name for every angel that exists?

"I don't mean names like Archangels Michael, Gabriel, and Raphael.

"I mean names like the Angel of Mercy, Angel of Justice, Angel of Abundance, Angel of Clarity, Angel of Truth, or the Angel of 'whatever'. I don't mean the angel of whatever. I think I had better clarify that.

(Laughter.)

"Actually, I think the Supreme Soul is the Angel of Whatever.

"So angels-on-earth eventually become angels of something, an angel of one Secret Angelic Word, one SAW only, to join with other angelic friends of that SAW.

"The next question. How do you find out what your Secret Angelic Word is? Well, I'll share some clues.

"First though, may I suggest a warning. Be careful in thinking about whether you know your word or not.

"This morning, somebody said that during the session they spontaneously knew the Secret Angelic Word for their soul purpose, their reason to be here.

"I replied that may be correct and wonderful, and very beautiful indeed. I also explained that if she has achieved her soul Destiny, perhaps, just perhaps, the word that came to her mind is correct.

"But that if she's still on an early Platformation, which actually she was, although the Secret Angelic Word might be correct, it is much more likely to be untrue. The word that came to her mind is just a word relevant to the Platformation she's on, not to the highest Platformation's ultimate SAW.

"Somebody else said that three words came to her mind last month. I replied that an angel does not have three words. An angel becomes the angel of one word only, the Secret Angelic Word that denotes their particular band of angels.

"It is most unlikely that she has reached her final Platformation, because her ultimate soul path will be the angel of one Secret Angelic Word. Three words could, perhaps, mean three things she might have to achieve before attaining her one, true, SAW.

"Yes, it will only be one SAW at the very, very top of the mountain, when you've passed all your lessons and achieved your Contract, and earned the right to use your Secret Angelic Word for the glory of God.

"Someone else last year said they knew their Secret Angelic Word. It was 'LOve'. I explained that LOve is almost 100% certainly not her SAW because every angel has LOve. LOve is a normal part of the path of being an angel. LOve isn't the Secret Angelic Word at the path's end. Angels-on-earth always share LOve, but almost never know their Secret Angelic Word.

"So, similarly, words like LOve, sharing, caring, supporting, helping, and so on are words that would apply to all angels-on-earth. They are not your relatively unique Secret Angelic Word. Any word that could apply to all angels-on-earth will almost certainly not be your Secret Angelic Word. Your Secret Angelic Word will almost surely not apply to anyone else you know.

"Don't make finding your Secret Angelic Word an obsession.

You are unlikely to find it, even if you think you can. Most of you will be on an early Platformation, where your Secret Angelic Word is not relevant, and not useful, for that part of your learning journey.

"It's better to focus on lessons you need to learn on the rung of the ladder, the Platformation you are on. Then you can eventually climb to the next, then the next Platformation until you reach the topmost peak of your mountain pathway. Then your Secret Angelic Word might make more sense.

"As with the three angels here today, the likelihood is that, if you consciously try to discover your word, whatever word you think might be your Secret Angelic Word will only be relevant to the Platformation you're on, not to your highest angelic nature.

"It's simple how it works, really. While doing your unique task of LOve, in the background of your enterprise, unknown to your conscious mind, you'll also be developing the final stages of your soul evolution for your one Secret Angelic Word.

"Your true Secret Angelic Word will evolve naturally. It is rare that your SAW will evolve through seeking. Your SAW is probably developing within you anyway, little by little. Unconsciously, your Secret Angelic Word will flower to full bloom, but only when you've completed early Platformation lessons.

"I can give you a few clues, but always remember, it's not important to find your Secret Angelic Word. Take your time. You need to learn other lessons, to share your LOve, and achieve your soul purpose, before your Secret Angelic Word can manifest. There's no hurry.

"In any event, of all the various secretive aspects of the lives of angels-on-earth, the most secretive is your Secret Angelic Word. Because your SAW is the true reason you are here.

"Think about this please. If you knew your Secret Angelic Word too soon, some of you might be too interested, too nosy, and use Free Will or Foolishness to go down paths to explore your Secret Angelic Word that are not appropriate for your

Path. So you should not know, and I cannot tell you, your Secret Angelic Word.

"Oh dear, I know angels. I've talked with you enough. Many of you so desire to find your Secret Angelic Word, as much as you desired to achieve any of your soul Platformations.

"I would much rather you focus on your love and LOve vocation, on your soul's calling, and let that one Secret Angelic Word develop unconsciously and beautifully within you.

"But to take away all those not-so-positive feelings of desperation to know your Secret Angelic Word that some of you will surely have, I can give you some clues. Is that OK with you?

"I'll give you four clues.

"First, there will be clues that you may gather from past lives, if you can remember enough of your past life situations and happenings.

"Second, I'll share clues, so that you might be able to find your Secret Angelic Word from events in this particular lifetime.

"Third, there are clues from genes, the inherited traits within your family line; traits that you or members of your family may exhibit, that could provide a path for your Secret Angelic Word.

"And fourth, there are clues you might be able to gain from a thesaurus.

"Alongside those four clues, it is recommended that you don't focus on the Secret Angelic Word you think you might find. Focus on sharing LOve.

"If you believe you have found it, it may help if you repeat the Word within you until it rebounds from atom to cell, and you become the Word.

"Your main focus though can always be on sharing LOve, and the ultimate attainment of your Destiny.

"Then your Secret Angelic Word will develop automatically, without you even consciously knowing."

The Secret Angelic Word Clue 1 – Past Lives

"The first clue is for those of you who remember your past lives. About 20% of you said you could do this, yes?

"If you remember quite a few past lives, here is the secret clue.

"Think about the threads that connect your past lives. What are the similarities between your various past life experiences?

"I'll talk about that more in a moment. But to emphasize, it's unimportant if you do not remember your past lives. 80% of people here cannot recall past lives, so it's OK if you don't. There are numerous other ways to achieve your Destiny. And three other methods to attempt to ascertain your Secret Angelic Word.

"Anyway, although this possibility is quite rare, maybe this is your first of many lifetimes, or perhaps you were already an angel, and came to Earth to fulfill a role just this once. Then you won't remember any lives from before this lifetime. But, you've done unusually brilliantly, and have learned enough to tread the Angelic Path, and to perhaps make this your final lifetime.

"Also, please, you do not have to go out there and suddenly start studying past lives. Although I teach Past Life Healing workshops, I teach that people should take past lives seriously as a healing, therapeutic subject. Past lives are not to be explored for entertainment. You should not just be nosy about what you were doing in the distant past. There are dangers attached to deliberately going back to past lives.

"Do not explore past lives just for lighthearted pleasure. You may find lives you wished you didn't recall. Maybe horrid past lives are supposed to be kept secret from you.

"You see, we've all done many things over many lifetimes. I know people who delved into past lives just for fun, or because they were curious about the type of lives they'd experienced. Would you like to know you'd been unLOving? Maybe you really don't want to know some things you've done.

"So this part of the Angel Story is only if you naturally remember the similarities and connecting threads which run through each of your lifetimes. If you do, consider these next thoughts.

"Past lives may offer clues on lessons to learn, clues to your highest Destiny, and clues to the band of angels you may join in your next angelic existence.

"Here's what to do, as a five-step process.

"First of all, think about every one of the past lives you can remember.

"Secondly, what were your experiences in each lifetime?

"Thirdly, assess what are the most common factors, and ask yourself this question. What is the strongest similarity that threads through each of your remembered lifetimes?

"Fourthly, consider, how does that strongest thread of common experience which affected your lifetimes make you feel now?

"Fifthly, calculate an answer to this question. What was your fundamental approach to life?

"You'll probably realize there's one positive, goodly, idealistic Secret Angelic Word to connect these lifetimes, one SAW only.

"It doesn't matter if you've often been a warrior; it's how you've been a warrior.

"It doesn't matter if you've often been a servant; it's how you've been a servant.

"It doesn't matter whatever you've often been or done in any lifetime. It's always how you did it.

"It's about how you created holy and divine harmony from ordinary situations.

"Let's suppose that you have inspected the connecting threads of your past lives. And you noticed that important events included your innate characteristics that demonstrated something in your communication abilities.

"Perhaps from that, you could maybe sensibly deduce that your singular Secret Angelic Word could be 'Communication'.

"So your eventual role, when you've learned enough, may be

an Angel of Communication?

"Oh dear, please do not think you'll become an Angel of Communication. I know from experience that if I suggest something, some word, some anything, some angels-on-earth will latch onto it and think it's their Secret Angelic Word or whatever. It's almost certainly **not**. Please, I am just giving examples.

"But, as almost impossible as it is, **if** you are due to be an Angel of Communication, as an example only, you have to become an expert of all possible angles about communication.

"You have to know, in-depth, every side of every coin about communication.

"For example, you may have to know about lack of communication, family or social communication, communication with every strata of society from beggars to royalty, or what it means to be dumb or deaf-mute. You might need to have a lifetime where you're furiously argumentative, another as a great orator, or a different life as a cathartic listener. Maybe you'll need to learn how to communicate in speech through video, in different genres of writing, via signs or body language, or through art or mathematical equations.

"There are so many unknowable facets of communication, probably too many for us mere mortals to contemplate.

"That's why it takes many lifetimes, that's the whole point and reason for all of your lifetimes. It's about how many lifetimes it will take to learn every side of every coin about communication.

"But please remember, communication was an example for demonstration purposes only, and communication is almost 100% certainly not relevant to you and your Secret Angelic Word.

"There are myriad different Angelic Words, because there are myriad different Angelic bands you could eventually join. Each Secret Angelic Word, each angelic band will need your deep understanding of the many sides of that one coin only.

"You will not need to know a broad selection of coins, of Angelic Words. You will need to know about your singular

Secret Angelic Word in depth, not width.

"It's about the purpose to be achieved with your LOve in your prospective final lifetime, and through your one and only true Secret Angelic Word. So that, when you pass on, your Angelic Service can be for greater good, and more Godly value."

The Secret Angelic Word Clue 2 – This Life

"If you can't recall past lives, other ways may suggest clues to finding your one Secret Angelic Word.

"The secret is, that your current life holds a similar clue to the connecting threads of your previous life.

"Consider events in your life that have often repeated. I do not mean personal events like birthdays or anniversaries, or annual events like religious or national festivities. I mean events that felt positive or negative.

"Positive events are favorable ones that created goodness. They are beneficial situations that you've regularly experienced. They may include repeated happy situations, positive attitudes, excellent relationships, or actions with good outcomes. If something positive was repeated often, this could be a clue to your Secret Angelic Word.

"Negative events are adverse situations you've experienced, and may include non-LOving relationships, or interactions, that repeated on many occasions.

"Now inspect the similarities of each repetition. No matter how the event feels, happy or sad, LOving or angry, or whatever, look logically at how you interacted.

"If you interacted negatively, you can still find your Secret Angelic Word. But you need to seek the opposite of your negative word, the antonym. You may not understand too deeply, so further suggestions will come later on how to use a thesaurus.

"If your positive clue is stronger, if you consistently interacted positively, in a specific way, within your fundamental positive nature can be the ultimate for your soul, your one, very special,

Secret Angelic Word.

"Some repetitive elements of life could lead to your Destiny. Maybe you can decode a repetition as a lesson to learn, or decipher if the repetition leads to your ultimate Secret Angelic Word.

"It's wonderful to become an angel of one Secret Angelic Word. It means you've become an ultra-expert in that one SAW. It means going beyond just sharing LOve.

"It might help some angels-on-earth to know their Secret Angelic Word, because introspection of your life in the context of your SAW may help heal your life, and have psychological benefits.

"Introspection doesn't depend on whether you've led a good life or not. Introspection focuses on the positive Secret Angelic Word, that could provide a logical Godly reasoning for any psychological interaction you've experienced.

"Introspection on your SAW can lift you above the challenges of life, while enhancing LOve perfection. It can create better balance and harmony within your body, and increased peace within your mind.

"But don't be concerned if you cannot discover your Secret Angelic Word. It's not important if you know your Secret Angelic Word now or late in this life, or not at all.

"It's not essential when the Secret Angelic Word comes, because one day it will come to you unconsciously, naturally, even after this life if necessary, and all will become wonder, joy, and bliss."

The Secret Angelic Word Clue 3 – Genes

"The third clue to check regarding your Secret Angelic Word is also about this lifetime. But it's not about life's events. It's about your genetic inheritance, your family line's traits.

"Some of you have explained, or perhaps confessed, you have traits in your families like fear, lack of confidence, anger, and so on.

"One lady has told many of you about her lifetime of anger, and how all of her family is angry too.

"I could appreciate the situations she might have experienced. One of my parents' genetic traits is anger. We all learn many lessons about anger in such a family.

(Laughter.)

"It is just how it is, just life.

"Somebody I spoke to recently said she felt furious because her husband was so angry with her, he deliberately left his clothes strewn all over the bedroom. Then her children got mad with her, for being mad with him for being mad at her.

(Laughter.)

"Genetically inherited anger is OK. Genetically inherited fear, sadness, lack of confidence, or anything is OK. It's OK for family members to have your particular genetic issue too. It is just a part of most angels-on-earth's learning to have a genetic inheritance that affects their loving, LOving, and angelic soul pathways.

"As discussed earlier, it's important to learn how to have peace and LOve for everyone and everything, everywhere, under every circumstance.

"On this highest Platformation things are different. You're at your mountaintop's peak, the end of your life path. You're trying to find your singular Secret Angelic Word.

"Here's the secret, the clue you need. The way is to seek the opposite word. This is the explanation.

"What's the opposite of anger?

(A few suggestions are called out.)

"No, it is not happiness, that's the opposite of sadness. And it is not love, which is the opposite of hate.

"The opposite of anger is probably peace.

"If you have anger, 'peace' might be your Secret Angelic Word. Your project in past lifetimes, your project in this life is, in a word, Peace. Maybe after you move on from this world, you'll be an Angel of Peace. That is your Secret Angelic Word, Peace under all circumstances.

"Similarly, if someone has genetically inherited fear from their family, what is the opposite word of fear? Most people say courage or bravery.

"Whatever might be the opposite of your genetic trait could be what your soul needs to learn. It may also be what you need to share with everyone and everything, everywhere, under all circumstances. That word can then perhaps, potentially, become your true Secret Angelic Word.

"And of course, some people have a positive genetic inheritance. They can view their family's positive traits, to find their Secret Angelic Word.

"Do you understand yet? Maybe this needs to be explained a bit more."

The Secret Angelic Word Clue 4 – Thesaurus

"This fourth clue about how to find your Secret Angelic Word overlaps with the previous three sections. You need to be like a dedicated detective attempting to uncover truth from repetitive aspects of past lives, this life, or genetic inheritances.

"To be honored to join an angelic band in one of the choirs, you probably slowly, unknowingly, developed a gift that is the exact opposite word of your repetitive past life, this life, or genetically inherited personality or character traits.

"You must be precise. You must find the exact opposite word of a repetitive feeling or action if you are intent on finding your SAW. Some people say love is the opposite of fear, anger, or many words. No! The opposite of love is hate.

"There's a handy book for angels nearing the top of their pathway wondering what their Secret Angelic Word is. It's called a dictionary.

(Lots of laughter.)

"It's actually a special dictionary. It's a thesaurus, a book of synonyms and antonyms. Whatever word you think of, you can look up its opposite. Your ultimate lesson is then the positive word.

"Please do not think I'm suggesting that anger, fear, sadness or trust is your Secret Angelic Word. There are innumerable other words that might become your SAW, not just something I happen to mention as examples. Examples are almost 100% not going to be your SAW.

"But a word of warning… Becoming the opposite of your past life, this life, or genetically inherited word may not be easy. It's not easy to be peaceful if you're angry, brave if you're fearful, happy if you're sad, or to have trust if you're distrusting. You might even need to write a thesis on your SAW. But it will be worth the struggle if you can make it.

"You all have positive traits too. Look at your positive qualities closely. I don't mean LOve, because all angels have LOve! I mean a genetically inherited positive aspect of your personality, or more likely, character. It's just as possible that you'll find your singular Secret Angelic Word for your band of angels in one of your positive attributes.

"Then you do not need a book on antonyms to discover the opposite of a negative word.

"Instead, you can use a book on synonyms for your naturally inherited positive trait.

"But whether your initial word is positive or negative, unconsciously the Secret Angelic Word becomes your life project.

"You share your SAW with your LOve and your soul purpose.

"You live your SAW.

"You are your SAW.

"And after you die, in the next life when you join a relevant band of angels, in that new beginning, there may be the fuller, more wonderful use of your Secret Angelic Word as your gift that can help the Hierarchy of Angels.

"You came, you SAW, you conquered."

Chapter 11

The Ends of a Path

The Prospective Final Lifetime

"Remember that others not yet on the Angelic Path still have a chance to be angels if they fulfill their Contracts, and learn enough about human love and Godly LOve. Otherwise, they will almost certainly have to return to Earth for another Contract and lifetime of lessons to overcome.

"But some of you who know you are angels-on-earth already realize this might potentially be your final lifetime. In other words, if you do well, if you fulfill your LOve Contract, if you can rise above all Platformations and truly achieve a life of LOve-Based Living, you might not need to return.

"Hands up if you've had this realization.

(Hands raised.)

"About half of you…

"Some people might find that half is a surprisingly high statistic, but it's common for people on the Angelic Path to have thoughts that you'll not have to come back again. It's one thing to have the thought though, and quite another to make the thought of not coming back a reality.

"Anyway, you may also have to prove to those above, probably without your conscious knowledge, that you are the epitome, the manifestation, of your Secret Angelic Word.

"Do try to get it right in this life.

"Try to climb through all your Platformations and experiential issues with the best possible loving and LOving manners.

"Try to go through all those lowly love barriers and out the other end to the higher LOve.

"Try to share your LOve with your highest soul purpose.

"Then, assuming you have learned your lessons, passed your

tests, and achieved well, you probably won't have to return to Earth again.

"That is, assuming you do not want to come back again.

"Or assuming that, when you move on, those above don't ask whether you'd like to return to be a special type of leader, or perhaps a creator, teacher, helper or innovator, for a new and better world to come.

"When you near the end of your path, the end of your reason for being, it's a beautiful, top-notch time. Keep it that way. Keep the bountiful beauty, harvest of happiness, sweets of success. It's a precious time.

"You see, you might be given the choice whether you should return to Earth, or not. I know angels who remember being given that type of choice when they made their latest Contract. Some of those angels remember thinking things like, 'I enjoyed it last time, I'll have another go,' or, 'I'll have an even better life next time, I'll have fun.'

"Then, when they arrived down here on Earth for another lifetime, although some are happy to serve humanity and do marvelous Angelic Service, boy oh boy, do some of them they wish they hadn't tried again!

(Laughter.)

"At least, they wish they hadn't had to go through their early Platformations again. This is because human love versus soul LOve lessons will be experienced again. And the life you experience the next time around may not even be as becoming as your current one.

"Always remember, if you achieve your Contract by doing your soul purpose properly, and you end up having an extraordinarily happy life, after this life you may be given the option not to return. Judging from the looks of you, some of you at the moment would prefer not to return?

(Sound of crying.)

"Yes, I recommend that you don't come back if you don't

have to.

"Let's hope these two days can help you evolve towards those gorgeous parts of life. No matter what you feel like now, you will almost certainly achieve exceptional wonder and beauty, and the people you help will make you feel delighted.

"Hearing this part of the story might bring tears of relief or happiness. There are still a few tissues left if anybody wants one.

"Remember too, you are in divine service, here to accomplish goodness on Earth. Aim to help, support, or relieve anything that can use your abilities. If you experience another life after this, you could earn extra rewards in the new age to come.

"Consider, though, that if much of what I've spoken about so far feels right for you, that's OK, it is just how it is. Then the next parts of the Angel Story may also be right for you, even if they are unexpected or mystifying, because you are not yet on that part of the path to fully understand. That is also OK, it is also just how it is.

"So let's talk about that now."

Clues Beyond a Soul Contract

"What happens if you've achieved your soul purpose, completed your soul purpose, and fulfilled your Contract?

"What happens when you've achieved all you were supposed to achieve in this lifetime?

"What happens when you've achieved your ultimate Platformation, and you overcame the peak of your path, and actualized your SAW?

"Maybe what you perceive to be the ultimate peak, isn't?

"Perhaps achieving a soul Contract is not much different to completing contracts of employment in a regular business.

"Maybe more Contracts could be made available for you to sign?

"For example, you could be allowed to stay on Earth with extensions or addendums to your original Contract, with no tasks to fulfill, just to retire gracefully and honorably.

"Or, when you've completed your Contract for this life, perhaps those in the angelic realms can offer you an option to help in the next part of existence. You will have gained respect from those above because you achieved so well. You've completed your earthly soul purpose in all respects, maybe with dispensations, but unquestionably with glory.

"So why would you choose, if given the choice, to stay alive as a human being?

"Certainly, it usually doesn't matter, in the scheme of universal needs, whether you have family or friends. For you to leave them behind is not too important in soul terms, no matter how close you are.

"Even your closest loved ones are simply souls on their paths learning their lessons. Whether you're there, physically in this world for them or not, no matter how you or they feel about it, it will not matter to their souls. Their souls will learn lessons in another way without you.

"You might die, move on, before your friends and family, or they may die before you. What if you put your loved ones' deaths in the context of all deaths that ever occurred throughout Earth's history? Does it truly matter?

"These comments may sound callous in strictly human terms. But death of the human body is inevitable. Every soul will pass to the next part of existence, in its specific way, on its personal journey, maybe unlike the path of anyone else. Purely in soul terms, death of the human body is not so terribly important.

"As much as you may not like to hear this, family and friends you love, and who love you, don't really need you. Someone else will play your role. Even if you were a carer, the person you are caring for will still learn the lessons their soul needs.

"On your personal soul level, it's definitely OK for you to pass away to another realm when you've achieved such an excellence for your soul, and helped enough others on the way.

"This is mainly to help you understand that, when you've achieved all your reasons for human existence, even if you have beloved children and grandchildren or other loved ones, it's OK to move on, it's safe.

"You might not agree, you might think your children or grandchildren need you, or you need them. But perhaps you don't really need each other, except on human terms, for human needs.

"Some persons who had a near-death experience were pronounced clinically dead by doctors. Unknown to the medics though, they agreed to return to life on Earth and fulfill another Contract. Maybe there's a dispensation to resolve broken family or friendship ties, support others' needs, share more LOve, inspire people into Godly service, or to achieve even more in the next part of this same life.

"There are other possibilities but you can move on to another Contract in this world or the next because you earned the right to progress your soul evolution.

"You might agree to reincarnate, and to enjoy your next reincarnation as a totally different human being, and overcome angelic Platformations in a more pioneering way, to make a greater difference.

Maybe you can climb the hierarchical angelic ladder in your next life, in your angelic band, higher up the angel realms, increasing your learning and helping, in wonderfully LOving and Godly ways. I will talk about that soon. Do not fear death, embrace it for the beauty of Angelic Service you can achieve.

Whatever path you choose next, most options will lead to you making a considerably constructive change for the better in any one of innumerable options that could be of your choosing. All options share LOve, improve something or someone, or plan a game-changing way forward in a niche area to create a new world order of beauty, peace, and love.

"Know that the sweetness of life can automatically be tasted within the fruits of success.

"When your next Destiny calls, achieve happiness through your Angelic Service."

Secrets of Levels in the Angelic Realms

"Do you recall discussing higher Platformations and bi-location, permeation, and other ways to create and share LOve? Such options are useful and needed for higher levels in the angelic realm, even if you think your soul purpose is unworthy and too small.

"To start with, you might not think your role is big, but for the angelic realms, that position might be huge.

"That is because there are myriad angels with distinct needs, and using distinctive gifts and SAWs within the angelic realms. As there are countless ways to help people on Earth, so there are innumerable ways to assist in resolving universal issues of LOving balance and harmony, and ultra-numerous ways to support your God.

"Do you recall that angelic realms need diverse help in similar ways to the personnel structure of corporations on Earth? As an analogy, angels might be needed as expert janitors, secretaries, messengers. You might be needed as a guard, manager, or cook, skills that are as needed as a competent chief executive or chairperson?

"As in an earthly corporation, in the angelic realms there may be higher, happier angelic Contracts waiting for you to enjoy and achieve.

"Within the massive angelic realms, inside your smaller but still-vast angelic band, there are numerous levels to which you could progress. A cleaner in a corporation has the potential, with dedication and ability, to rise to be a president.

"Of various philosophies about angelic Hierarchy, perhaps the most popular is that angels are organized like a corporation, into three groups, starting lowly and ending close to God.

"The three groups are sometimes called Hierarchies of Angels, or Spheres or Triads of Angels. Each Hierarchy contains three Orders, or Choirs. So there are numerous bands to join within each of the nine hierarchical levels.

"In the lowest Hierarchy, the Third Sphere, the levels from the bottom up are, Guardian Angel, Angel, Archangel, and Principality. Principality is also known as Ruler.

"In the middle Hierarchy, the Second Sphere, there are lower Powers that are also known as Authorities. Higher up are Virtues, that can also be known as Strongholds. At the highest peak of the Second Sphere, Dominions may also be called Lordships.

"In the highest Hierarchy, the First Sphere, angels are closest to God. There are Thrones, and above Thrones are Cherubim. At the peak closest to God, are Seraphim.

"There may be so many bands or choirs of angels to join on the nine levels of Hierarchy, it is near-impossible to discover exactly which band, within which level, and within which Sphere of angelic existence, you may join. So take the pressure off yourself. Relax. Put all your efforts into overcoming your Platformations, and achieving your current Contractual soul purpose.

"Maybe I should emphasize that, because I've met too many angels who can't wait. They thirst to know everything about their ultimate purposes on Earth and after. They feel it's all-important to know every aspect of their path, to be able to fulfill their Destiny, and achieve their purpose for existence. They desire total and complete knowledge of the path, now, immediately.

"So I will repeat. Please do not be concerned with what role you should play in the angelic realms. There are so many levels, and levels within those levels, and many functions within those levels within levels.

"It really is best to accept with gratitude that you are on an Angelic Path, and that you should tread the path to the utmost of your ability, and passively allow your role in the angelic realms to be revealed fully when you pass on.

"To try to determine the exact level of Hierarchy you will join may be futile, and lead you down an obsessive and inappropriate search, away from your real tasks. I'm sure you'd prefer to achieve your Contract, and not be led completely astray. Eventually, the Sphere level within the angelic Hierarchy you need to reach will be revealed, with joy, automatically.

"Canterbury Cathedral, the main cathedral of the Church of England, has organized staff into a sort of corporation or angelic Hierarchy. All workers have a name relevant to their post, even cleaners. Do you know the name of the cleaners in Canterbury Cathedral?

(Silence.)

"Shall I tell you? In the job descriptions in their contracts, the name of cleaners at the Cathedral is, 'Holy Dusters'.

(Laughter.)

"Gracious isn't it? It would look good on your resume.

(Laughter.)

"Holy Dusters... I really like that. Providing their cleaning is done LOvingly with perfection, enjoyment, and enthusiasm, the seemingly lowly act of cleaning becomes a Godly act.

"Maybe Holy Dusters are one of the lower forces to help in the hierarchical personnel that supports the Cathedral's good works? Certainly at the top is the Archbishop of Canterbury, who is the head, the leader of the Church of England. Between the Holy Dusters and the Archbishop are innumerable other helpers, paid and voluntary. They all do wonderfully to support the church's wider goals, plans, and objectives.

"So, don't think everyone has a huge soul purpose to achieve. Whatever you do may be an important cog in the wheel of the wider aims of the organization you're in, bigger Angelic Service than you realize.

"Don't think your position is lowly. It may not be what you do, but how you do it. I suppose that means, how Holy Dusters perform their duties may be a higher version of Angelic Service than how archbishops perform. A Holy Duster could be better than an archbishop.

(Laughter.)

"Yes, maybe that is just how it is. **How** a Holy Duster does the cleaning is the big deal. If they share their sweetest LOve with every movement of their duster and pour LOve into every part of the cathedral, the Holy Duster could, in the scheme of the Hierarchy within the angelic realms, be incredibly more worthwhile than the role of an archbishop who does not perform with the highest, divinely LOving ability and capability needed.

"After the death of your human form, when you move on, whatever gift you've mastered on Earth may be useful for a life you cannot currently dream is so exceptionally beautiful.

"Joining the Hierarchy of Angels could be the most positive, happiest, most fulfilling angelic purpose you could ever imagine."

Clues To Staying on for Another Contract

"When it is your turn to pass on you may be able to choose to stay on Earth, to humbly retire in the glory of your Contract success, or support friends or family.

"Or you might be offered a new Contract, an opportunity to attain a bigger, better and more effective project than your previous Contract to make a difference to humanity's existence in superbly effective ways.

"Maybe you can agree to stay on Earth to instigate or promote game-changing processes, or pioneering ideas, products, or services.

"Perhaps you could stay, just for a bit more fun.

"Or you could stay down to help one or more angels achieve and share LOve, and start projects for their Destiny. If even one angel is helped, and they progress the lives of countless others, your extra time on Earth would make a huge, beneficial difference.

"However, staying here on Earth when you've achieved everything needed for your soul's evolution into the Hierarchy of the angelic Choirs may sometimes be a waste of an opportunity to progress.

"The thing is, any of these new ways to help humanity may not be exactly part of your angelic progression. To stay and achieve further good works on Earth when you have already achieved everything in your Contract in full, and don't need to stay, might be more like moving sideways on your angelic pathway, not progressing upwards.

"Decide which of these options you'd prefer.

"Is it better to help a few loved ones, and perhaps additionally instigate or create a new project that may help hundreds, thousands, or even millions of people?

"Is it better to accept your Contract was fulfilled?

"Is it better to know that angels above will honor and respect you for everything you already achieved on Earth, and that they'll receive you with LOve?

"Is it better to appreciate that, if you have successfully attained every goal set for you, there would be no dishonor in the eyes of your Guardian Angel or God in dying and moving on?

"Is it better to know that something else of even greater value to an even greater number of people or something of even greater Destiny is waiting for you?

"All possibilities will almost certainly need another Contractual agreement. Knowingly accept and agree to exactly what you wish to achieve, and then consciously or unconsciously 'sign on the dotted line'.

"You can then be given a new lease of life, with a higher set of moral and ethical rules and karmic issues.

"At this point, a secret process of your wings will manifest, in an unexpected way. If you make another Contract, and if you are lucky enough to see your wings or know others who can see your wings, you may realize that your wings have changed to a different size, different color, different density, and different shape.

"It is similar to a member of an army who gains promotion to an elite battalion, and so wears a different colored uniform. When angels move up to a higher rank, they may 'wear' different colored wings.

"From personal experience, three times when doctors said they could do nothing to help, and death was inevitable, I vividly remember agreeing to stay on to offer additional, specified, help. Each time I agreed to stay down, soon afterward came an unexpected cure.

"My doctor is used to it. After every checkup his parting comment is always something like, 'Keep finding your ways to keep going, Allan.'

(Laughter.)

"When doctors said I would die, those above said I could move to realms where friends were waiting with greetings to honor achievements. They said I'd earned the right not to suffer on Earth anymore. But I decided to stay and help humanity, and physically signed another Contract.

"I've already warned you not to stay down if you don't have to. Sometimes I think it would have been better to move on when I had the chance. Maybe I should listen more to the advice I give.

(Laughter.)

"Many of you today have been cured with one of the healing and therapeutic techniques I've discovered from around the world, or personally developed. It's astonishing that so many countries have highly effective therapies, validated by peer-reviewed academic research, therapies that have success in curing a significant percentage of their citizens. But I'm equally astonished that those brilliantly successful therapies are not available in other countries.

"It's as if all countries don't try to find the very best therapies internationally, and just hobble along with therapies that are validated in their own country.

"One of the two missions I agreed to bring to Earth is to find a way to bring validated, game-changing, therapeutic techniques, methods and programs, out of just the one country where they are used to help and cure a minority, into the wider world to try to help and cure the majority.

"The other undertaking I agreed to is to guide, heal, and support as many angels-on-earth as possible. They can then rise through Platformations easier and quicker than they could themselves. The book of these two days may help angels-on-earth around the world.

"Maybe you can help? If everything here feels right to you, if this Angel Story seems to apply to you, could you please help, and start a "Secrets of Angels on Earth" Group? If it feels right, good and perfect, could you create a Facebook page to help evolving angelic souls?

"Would you like to belong to a Group of other angels-on-earth who know LOve like you? Would you like to help other angels-on-earth with their projects, and let them help you?

"If you answer yes to those two questions, starting a "Secrets of Angels on Earth" Group might be one of the most beneficial actions you ever take with your life. So, to help you, an appendix in the book may point your way.

"It could be wonderful, also, to have Groups to network with. Eventually you could create an army of angels-on-earth, with platoons of sweetly LOving angels around the world.

"Wouldn't that be satisfying, to help increase happiness, including yours, and support angels' spiritual and soul-healing evolution?

"Anyone who fulfills their Contract completely can agree to stay down here for another go. Yes, other non-angelic people might think your aims to help humanity are misguided. Yes, others may misunderstand, misjudge you.

"But when the time comes for fun in service to others, the pleasure you'll get will far outweigh anything.

"There's probably no rush. You might be allowed a waiting period to decide the best way forward. The waiting period will vary, but is often the waiting period that previously, regularly, manifested in your life.

"To check this out, think whether your life goes in cycles of a certain number of months or years. On a personal level, the main cycle is two years. I often feel a big shift, and move on to something else after about two years. You might enjoy space on your time cycle, to reflect on what you'd like to do next, whether to stay on Earth, what to achieve with a new Contract, whether to reincarnate, or when to move up to the Hierarchy of Angels.

"Whatever Free Will decision you take will be perfect, providing your choice was made with a motivation of LOve. Angels like you can achieve remarkable feats. At this moment in history, this planet needs your angelic LOve to raise its overall vibration and consciousness.

"And so your soul melts into oneness as the angel-on-earth flares beautiful wings to fullness, to show your absolute nature of LOve."

Chapter 12

Summaries

How My First Angel Party Began

"Many of you have said how astonished you are because almost every word of this Angel Story seemed spoken just to you, describing your energetic life.

"Some asked how I know all this information. Simply, I do direct channeling. Information comes through that I never dreamed of previously.

"To recap how this started, in the 1980s I knew zero about angels as souls on earth learning lessons.

"In the 1990s, as I taught a Spiritual Development class, information poured about people who did angelic works on Earth and who had souls of LOve. I had told the Angel Story for the first time, describing an angel-on-earth's life from pre-birth, to post-death.

"I didn't understand the words at that time, but allowed them to flow. Some students didn't understand the context of any words I'd said, and seemed confused. But surprisingly, many in the group cried.

"When I asked how the group felt about the story, those who cried made comments like they'd felt tears of joy that at last someone understood their LOve and their lives, and they felt at peace for the first time ever.

"How much the Angel Story empowered many of those present was astonishing.

"But it was also surprising because some said the story was irrelevant, or meant nothing to them whatsoever, seemed silly, or even that the story was made up, untrue.

"It was the dawning of comprehension that not everyone is an angel-on-earth, so not everyone would have the LOving angelic qualities needed to understand the story. I'd had an enlightenment, and realized that although everyone may become an angel one day, this is usually not until after many lifetimes; and that most people aren't destined to become angels until after this lifetime, unless they learn their lessons very well indeed.

"On the next spiritual development class, I told the same story. This time, more information came through, with similar results. Many students had joy and relief that someone understood them at last, while others thought the story a complete irrelevance, confusing, or stupid.

"Eventually, I realized that to understand the story, to become an angel in this lifetime, a person would answer 'Yes' to most of the specific set of Angelic Questions discussed earlier.

"I also realized that those who replied 'No' to the Angelic Questions, depending on the reasons for 'No', were almost 100% not angels-to-be. It did them no good service to listen to the story, because the Platformations I discussed were not relevant to their lives.

"I saw that most people had not experienced enough lessons. They still had much to do before reaching the type of Contract all of you here today made, the Contract of an angel-on-earth in the prospective final lifetime.

"If they could learn all relevant lessons in this life, they might be allowed to join the Angelic Path, but until then, the Angelic Path Platformations are not relevant to them. I saw that these people's other experiential life-lessons were more relevant, such as spiritual development to teach them how to know the LOve they don't yet have within.

"So I had little choice but eventually to decide to only tell the Angel Story to people who answered 'Yes' to the standard Angelic Questions or had mitigating reasons for certain 'No' replies.

"This is my first Angel Party, and I wanted only angels here. Perhaps I'll invite everyone, including non-angels, when I teach another. Maybe some non-angels need to know the Angel Story to understand their angelic partner!

(Laughter.)

"We now need to continue the Angel Story. May I share some information from an angel here today?

"Gary would like to speak about what happened to him after hearing the Angel Story. It will be a speech from someone who has been through most of the Platformations described so far.

"Afterwards, I may comment about his speech because it may seem to some of you that it's about his personalized human interactions.

"In the context of a beautiful angelic soul learning its lessons on its pathway back to God, whatever Gary's human drama is, he will have experienced Platformations that all of you angels-to-be will have been on in the past, and will almost certainly be on in the future.

"However Gary's human drama differs to yours, whatever type of human life he has experienced and endured, the angelic energy force propelling him forwards, the force of LOve emanating from his soul, is likely to be identical to yours.

"I may come in after to explain an angelic context. Although Gary has acted out his human drama, as far as the angelic soul is concerned he was just going through Platformations to progress a soul on its path. Is that OK?

"Good, and thank you.

"So may I introduce and have a round of applause for our angel speaker, Gary..."

Gary's Story

"Well, I don't know where Allan gets all this. I was going to tell you my life story, but of course, without knowing much about me, Allan has done that! Talking to you in the break-times, many of you feel the same. It's amazing how he knows so much of my life.

"I wondered how come I had never seen him following me around

on my path for 42 years examining my life and then standing up here and telling everyone about it.

(Laughter.)

"What I really want to say is, the first time I heard the story from Allan it was, well, a relief, and very touching. I knew there must be a purpose for all the horrors that had gone on in my life… And the pain! And, well, you know all that, because you all understand the story too.

"I thought nobody could go through that much stuff without there being a reason for it. Although I never knew what the purpose would be, I knew it would have to be something special. It just couldn't be a waste.

"I've found a kind of LOving Angelic Path that I work on now which is really, really good.

"And I think what Allan's story did was to release the stuff I had been through and give reasons why it happened. That gave me an understanding, almost an acceptance, of my life's problems and pains.

"Because certainly for me, I thought it was just me. I didn't know there were loads of other people, loads of other angels, kind of going down the same path.

"I just thought, 'Why do I have to suffer and go through so much stuff?' There must be learning in there somewhere, or something, you know.

"Some of you, like me, have been to perhaps the furthest and deepest of levels where we wouldn't want to go to again. At those stages, I guess there were choices one could make as to whether to go forward in this life, or go back and start another life.

"I'm just pleased we've all come forward to accept the learning we needed to become angels and to share our LOve with others.

"I want to thank Allan, because the first time I heard the story it completely changed me, it was like, 'Ah! Thank God.' It was such a relief.

"And then listening through it and hearing all of those words again today I was convinced he's just been following me around.

"So that's it, that's what I wanted to share with you.

"Thank you."

An Age Understanding, Not Ageist

"Thank you, Gary. You know, you've done well. You said you're 42. As I sometimes say, the understanding of this Angel Story is not ageist; it's an age thing.

"Teenagers almost certainly can't understand the story. You can tell it to teenagers, but they haven't had enough life experiences to understand details of the angelic soul issues. So teenage angels-on-earth almost certainly won't understand.

"Whereas those angels-on-earth who are in their 20s, yes, there would be a few by then who could have had adequate experiences to begin to understand their Angelic Path.

"Then in their 30s, there are a few more who understand in deeper ways. Further experiences will have opened some angels' eyes, and possibly their wings.

"In their 40s, now angels-to-be are really starting to get to grips with issues for their LOving souls. They begin to comprehend the reasons for past events in this life, and feel there could be a mission to achieve on Earth, to help others in need.

"In their 50s most angels-on-earth understand most paths, and they can facilitate a LOve project to achieve their goals to improve society.

"In their 60s almost 100% of angels understand, because understanding has progressed throughout life, and they are probably at or near the peak of their mountain.

"But now and again I tell this story to someone, and it hits them so deep in their soul, with such a feeling of enlightenment, they have a cataclysmic change like Gary did. He's in his 40s so he has more angelic understanding than some others of you here.

"Even though Gary has probably kept most parts of his story secret until now, it doesn't take much from the Angel Story to help him have a sudden release, and to enjoy an instantaneous understanding and acceptance of his path. This usually, as it did with Gary, instigates a near-complete and positive change.

"Like Gary, other angels-on-earth can change completely into the Godly soul stuff.

"It's very special when that happens. I hope this Party has helped some of you have such cataclysmic positive changes."

Honoring Angels

"It's fantastic to be in this Grand Hall teaching about your Angelic Path.

"Quite a few of you have said how much the story helped you. You see, it doesn't matter whether you're on this or that Platformation, even the toughest one. There's light at the end of it.

"That's part of the purpose of these lectures. To show you all will be well, and that those of you who are on higher Platformations have got there because you've learned the early lessons. So that was wonderful for those who have already achieved success, and it will be wonderful for those who will achieve success in the future.

"Also, I know quite a few of you are feeling the presence of angels, but do not necessarily see them. It was interesting when one of you asked, 'Can you feel anything up there in the corner?'

"I replied, 'I'll ask clairvoyants who can see these things, not just feel.' And I discovered that lots of you had seen the same huge angels in this room.

"Please raise your hands if you saw the angels that were here? (Hands raised.)

"That's about 10% of you. The angels here are rather different from the angels clairvoyants have seen on courses. Those of you who've seen angels on courses, and now during these two days, said these are much higher angels, with much bigger, denser, and brighter wings.

"Some of you said you've communicated with the angels and

that the higher angels have come to honor our first large angels-on-earth gathering.

"One lady came up to me and said her guides, masters, and angels had been here as well, and they wanted to say thank you because they have also had a wonderful day.

"You know, what you are doing here is so special, it's very different. This group is a very special group. If you were one of those angels above looking down on you, I think you would have the same positive type of feeling, a feeling of joy. You would want to give thanks to all here hoping that you can fulfill the pathways for your souls.

"Feel honored that such high beings have supported our Party and you. Perhaps all the high angels that have graced you here need occasional support, as all humans do. Please honor them.

"Please send your thanks, respect, and prayers as they have honored us with their presence."

Summary of Secrets and Clues on LOve Platformations

"Those high angels above us can see all of you here are angels. But the vast majority of human beings on Earth would never dream you could possibly be an angel.

"A butterfly might be able to understand a caterpillar that it once was, and all that a caterpillar experiences. But can a caterpillar understand a butterfly? That is unlikely.

"Most people are not destined to be fully-fledged angels after this life. They have much to resolve and evolve, so will not understand an angelic soul like yours. They couldn't possibly comprehend your inner conflicts between your diverse human loves and Godly LOves.

"The thing for you is that most people, non-angels and angels-on-Earth on early Platformations, will look at your faults, your idiosyncrasies, the things they're not like themselves. Then they may think you're strange, weird, or awfully imperfect. In some cases, they may consider you are in need of psychological support.

"Of course, you are imperfect and in need of help. Your human side needs help. But what these people do not see is your pretty, delicate, butterfly nature. They do not notice your gifts, inner warmth, or your near-secret knowing of LOve. Even though your LOve may shine from you throughout your life, and can sometimes be recognized for its beauty, most people cannot realize the deepest secretive beauty of your soul.

"This probably doesn't sit well with you.

"You want people to understand your LOve. You want them to appreciate you, to care for you, to LOve you in the same way that you want to appreciate and care for and LOve others.

"You want the whole world to recognize LOve and to be LOve because that would fit in nicely with your deepest inner knowing of God's all-embracing LOve.

"And that's how it is. LOve is what you are. LOve is what you desire. LOve is what you will share.

"LOve holds the secret keys to your life.

"LOve becomes the secret key to unlock knowledge for different issues of human love and Godly LOve on different Platformations of development.

"LOve is the secret key to loving yourself.

"LOve is the secret key when you try to love others.

"LOve is always the secret key that opens doors to marvelous days.

"It's just that, as you climb your life's mountain and rise through the Platformations, you'll find different ways to interact with LOve. Which LOve interaction is right for one Platformation may not be right for another.

"If I gave each of you personal advice now about how to interact with human love and Godly LOve, and then if I gave you personal advice on the same subject again in the future, probably I'll give each of you two different sets of advice.

"As you grow, you need changes to the advice on how to interact with love and LOve. You will one day leave the trapped, crawling caterpillar's earthy needs behind, and grow into a beauteous butterfly with the freedom to fly wherever your LOving heart is needed. One day you will enjoy happiness in Angelic Service.

"On the Angelic Path discernment is a secret because too few people attempt to discern openly. Most angelic souls' discernment on their LOving lives is kept close to themselves, with little discussion with friends or family. They discern inwardly, privately, secretly, trying to discern correct ways forward, yet discerning in the dark, unable to see the future Destiny.

"Accept that you won't always discern correctly. But do please try to discern how to LOvingly interact with yourself, other people, and this needy world. Discern at every LOving step on every Platformation, about what you should do with human love or Godly LOve.

"For when you experiment with discernment and discern a LOving way forward, that is when you gain the natural, automatic ability to move on to better things.

"In other words, when you know the tastes of the different and specific goodies of LOve available on your Platformation table, that is when you can move more happily toward a higher Platformation table with a tastier selection of foods of LOve.

"You'll have many needs along the path. A few examples are: a need to resolve issues as they arise, a need to persevere, a need to relax, a need to be passive, and a need to prepare for a long-haul journey of events that head toward the end of each Platformation.

"Procrastination never lent support to belief. What fairy-tale ending did procrastination ever produce? Never procrastinate, unless in the context of previous comments when you need to wait for signs on how to move along your path to the next stage of LOve learning.

"Experiencing LOve is wonderful. But in itself LOve experience is not enough. Your not-so-secret approach to life, an approach you can always seek, is something an angel is naturally good at; LOving action.

"Almost always try to hear your LOving sounds in action. For within your LOving action is loudness. It's a secret loudness of intention to act appropriately when needed to make something wondrously beautiful happen.

"Take action with motivations of LOve whenever you can. Try not to have too many or too long procrastinating periods during your life. Try not to just enjoy your special beautiful LOve. Try to have beautiful LOving thoughts, using LOve to help others. Action in LOve is critically all important.

"All of you, please remember to seek and offer LOve interaction on every Platformation, even though nothing will always satisfy your desire for LOve. Be aware of possible interactions needed, and aware of the many ways within each action, to achieve the ultimate acts of LOve in your soul purpose.

"And be aware that not all angels experience every Platformation. You might experience all, some, or a different order of Platformations. You might get stuck on one Platformation, and skim over another.

"Your Platformation story, your Angelic Path, is unique to you, with your human Free Will choices. It's why it's not easy for you to find other angels as friends or partners. How can you find other angel friends easily? Even if they are an angel, and the energy within their Platformation is similar to yours, the human story on the Platformation can seem so different.

"You also need awareness of your attention to details. What are your intentions on each Platformation? If you set your attention on your intention for LOve, relevant LOve action will soon follow. Then your Angelic Path can be the beauty you inwardly know it can be.

"Only then can you raise your LOve consciousness towards energetically supporting a new LOving way forward for humankind."

On Long-Term LOve Effects

"On the seekers' Platformation, you may notice that religions and spiritual organizations often suggest cycles of time for a soul's evolution. The Brahma Kumaris suggest a peak of spirituality every 5,000 years. And divine God-inspired philosophies have started since human time began, many of them about 500 years apart.

"About 5,000 years ago, yogic traditions began as a way to achieve harmony within, and enlightenment.

"Around 3,800 years ago, Judaism started with the covenant between God and Abraham.

"500 years later, 3,300 years ago, Moses related the Torah, Jewish law.

"About 2,500 years ago, Confucianism, Taoism, Jainism, Buddhism, and Zoroastrianism began.

"About 2,000 years ago Catholicism and Christianity started.

"Around 1,400 years ago, Islam began, at about the time St. Augustine brought Christianity to England.

"Around 1,000 years ago in Europe, both the Norman Conquest and the Crusades occurred.

"About 500 years ago, Sikhism began in India, at about the same time as the Church of England.

"In the past 100 years, numerous religions have begun, such as the soul-oriented Brahma Kumaris in 1936, Wicca or Pagan Witchcraft in 1954, Scientology in 1954, Satanism in 1966, and New Age in 1970s. The most recent religion, Kopimism, was recognized by the Swedish government as a religion in 2012.

"As you know from how I've discussed the Brahma Kumaris previously, I respect their human and angelic philosophies and teachings.

"But have you noticed something? The list I just mentioned includes most of the world's main religions. And mostly, they are approximately 500 years apart?

"Most of these religions had great leaders and admirably loving teachings. In each era, spiritual consciousness must have increased greatly.

"Oh, perhaps I should mention, I'm not saying there should be a religion called 'angels-on-earth'.

(Laughter.)

"A similar rising of spiritual consciousness is starting in this millennium. You are part of that rising wave, part of a stream of higher consciousness. You can spread LOve and create something worthwhile.

"It is like throwing a pebble into a pond, and knowing that, depending on the size of the pebble and the strength of the efforts of your throw, harmonious ripples will spread around to the farthest edges.

"See how long ago these religions started, and how, after all that time, they still provide support to segments of humanity now. Some provide guidance towards a life of LOve-Based Living.

"I am not trying to entice you to start a similar spiritual organization or religion yourself. Although looking at some of you, you never know!

(Laughter.)

"Certainly, what I am trying to help you focus on, is that every single person who helped start one of those religions was a human being. All had LOve that helped humanity in specific ways.

"But they are all human beings. Although we probably won't know much of their human stories, they will all have suffered. They will all have gone through issues, simply because they were human. They all had to suffer the consequences of others' words and actions.

"The thing is, they all passed their lessons adequately enough to have the strength of mind, will, and purpose, to not only help others. They also had the inspiration, and the motivation, to start something that could help others through the millennia.

"Do you see what I'm saying? This is an analogy for you, for your LOving pathway in this lifetime, for the hugely positive effect something could have, that might start just with a small idea.

"The simple fact is that one or some of you here, even though it might be unknown to you today, could make a gigantic splash in whatever gift you share to help others. That splash might last.

"The achievement of your soul purpose of LOve that you share to make a positive difference to humanity, or something, somewhere, that could last for generations to come.

"Think about this. What differences could you make to society if you harnessed your beautiful LOve and shared it in a project to boost health, hope, happiness, whatever?

"Then, even though you probably currently think you couldn't possibly be as good as the leader of a religion, as an analogy with those people who started religions, your LOving ripples could spread your version of LOve throughout this and the next millennium too.

"Whatever you can achieve in your life could spread after you pass on, in a far grander scale that may currently be in your wildest, most wonderful dreams.

"Wouldn't that be gorgeous? Wouldn't that be a fabulous reason for overcoming your trials and sharing your LOve?"

Final Comments, and the Angel Party

"So, that is it. Those secrets, clues, and Platformations are the major ones. When you move on to your next loving or LOving Platformation, you will find new experiences, new challenges, new ways of life to understand and make decisions about.

"You don't have to remember everything, but at least try to

memorize the Platformation you're on, and the lesson you need to learn about love or LOve before you move on to the next soul-learning level, and eventually reach LOve-Based Living.

"One day, when the book about this Angel Party is published, you can hold valuable comfort for your path in your hand. If you enjoyed this Angel Party, and found it relevant and useful for your life, the book may help you even more. After all, how much of a two-day lecture can you remember? The book will jog your memory, not once, but time and time again.

"Reading the book should provide a boost to more easily climb your route up your life's mountain. You'll reap great benefits from a conscious understanding of all parts of your life path, of every Platformation. Passages you read may provide necessary information to point you in a more appropriate direction. That might enable you to jump over hurdles on your Platformations quicker, calmer, and more peacefully.

"Parts of the book, describing each Platformation you could attain, will help you act more appropriately. As you reach higher levels on your soul path, you also decide how to think and act in ever stronger LOving ways, and what to say and do about human love and Godly LOve.

"So if you get a copy of the book about this Angel Party, do not give it away, even if you think a friend might need it. Keep it safe. Occasionally reread a section that seems relevant to the Platformation you reached. Then you will more likely receive, and be able to act on, the knowledge, guidance and support that you seek.

"I've already mentioned that "Secrets of Angels on Earth" Groups could support your life and LOve. If your Platformation's lessons pose too many challenges, gain support. Start a "Secrets of Angels on Earth" Group and Facebook page for your area. In this Angel Party, you've only been with angels. You've felt LOve. If you meet with a Group of LOving angels-on-earth regularly, you will not feel alone, separated, or detached anymore. Think of the beauty it will bring to all members to share LOve with others who truly understand.

"Or find a True Angelic Master, or an organization such as the Brahma Kumaris to help you overcome and move on from the Platformation you've reached.

"To prepare for the human fun part of the Angel Party later, let's split into little groups. Some of you asked me to do this. There's no big deal about being in one group or another. Don't feel embarrassed if you're not in the highest group. You are all on the Angelic Path. You were all on the lowest Platformations at one time.

"So please gather into groups according to which Platformation you are on.

"If you're on the suicidal Platformation, if you felt suicidal within the past year or so, please gather into a little group over here, on the left. We will try to help you.

"Regardless of your Platformation, try to help each other on whatever level you're on. And regardless of the fun Party later, if anyone still needs support, whatever that may mean to you, do ask. I'll help you. Is that OK?

"If you're on the Platformation of acceptance of humanity, let's gather in a group here on the right.

"If you're on the unconditional LOve Platformation, sharing your LOve, gather in front of the table here.

"I've stuck signs around the wall for these and other groups. Please gather by the sign that's most relevant to you now. If it's doing and sharing a soul purpose get into that group. If you've achieved your soul purpose, and know your Secret Angelic Word, make a group there.

"This is a way to help each other on the level you're on. You can meet others like you, on the Platformation you're on, share your experiences of the past, your approaches now, and your future dreams.

"After, we'll move on to the Angel Party's fun and games. I

asked you to bring something, if possible, for an act to entertain everyone. Did anyone bring a musical instrument? Or does anyone here have any natural talent, such as to tell a story, recite a poem, perform a dance, sing a song, or act an impromptu sketch?

"Some of you have stayed at my teaching center by the beach. We've done this many times. It's always worked out wonderfully. Do you have anything you'd like to share for the fun and games? It might be a spiritual or healing joke. Or maybe you know a joke about angels?

(Laughter.)

"Maybe you have something thought-provoking that might help people onto a spiritual path. Or you know a book, DVD, or website to help angels-on-earth grow.

"This is a chance to make friends and have fun. Please be brave to do something, a little sharing for everyone here. If you see me in the break, I'll arrange a little program for the final part of the weekend.

"The channeling before the start of the Party suggested the ending of these two days should be one of LOve. 'Let them experience LOve,' it said. 'Show them what to aim for permanently within their being.'

"During the Party, I'll teach an exercise for everyone here to experience total LOve. It's a foundation exercise for "Secrets of Angels on Earth" Groups. You'll love it, because you will feel LOve.

"Truly, as the two days went on, I enjoyed the Party more and more. As you know, it's my first large Angel Party, but I've enjoyed having you here.

"As I mentioned to a number of you before you came, there can be no finer thing than to achieve your soul path. What else you do in this world doesn't matter. It doesn't matter what career you choose. It doesn't matter what you know about the angels above us. There can be no finer force than learning about what you need to do to be positive and LOving. So I've enjoyed being here and helping that process.

"It's been a pleasure that many of you said being here at the lectures gave much relief by helping you understand numerous aspects of your lives.

"It's been splendid that lots of you say how happy you are to realize you're not alone. That is true. You're not alone anymore because you've found similar angelic friends, friends who understand the LOve that's inside you, your sincere desire to do a soul purpose, and your loving and LOving Platformations needed to get you there.

"Always try to make LOving angelic friends like you. Let's share names and addresses. Stay in touch with each other. Offer each other support. Let's share LOve.

"If you're on a higher Platformation, help your new angelic friends overcome early Platformations.

"If on an early Platformation, you can help angelic friends on higher Platformations achieve their Destinies.

"And remember you can join Angel Groups, and encourage other angels-on-earth to develop within a support network.

"Walk your path with confidence. Feel comfortable at tasks ahead. You don't need to do everything willfully and immediately. Evolve slowly and unconsciously if you wish. One step at a time is what angels need.

"This is also about what LOve action occurs next for you all. I pray that the main motivations for holding this Angel Party will, in the near future, come true.

"I pray that, based on the knowledge and wisdom taught in these two days, your Angelic Paths can unfold more happily.

"I pray that your Angelic Service will not take so long to understand, and that they'll manifest sooner than you expected to help countless people around the world find human love, Godly LOve, peace, and happiness.

"And I pray that you achieve all you are supposed to achieve in your LOving Contract so that, when you are ready to move on to the next part of existence as a fully-fledged angel, you can make a difference to our world in more skilled and pleasing angelic ways.

"Thank you for coming. May you all enjoy happy lives. May you fulfill the wonders of a LOving angelic soul. And may you always be inspired to achieve more LOving acts on your pathway toward LOve-Based Living.

"Bless you, all."

Appendices

Appendix 1. 14 Ways To Progress if You Feel This Book is Relevant To Your Life

It is OK to disagree with sections in the book, or think some sections are "not you". The point is, does the general feel of the book seem right for your life?

If yes, you may feel relief to understand the context of your life at last, or feel release from being misunderstood or being unable to share LOve fully. Or maybe you feel depressed or sad not to be fully with LOve, or elated or excited that there could be wonderful, positive reasons for life's trials. Or you could feel reassured that others are like you, so you are not alone anymore. Whatever, this book may offer a lifetime of aid for your human love and soul LOve Platformations. So how do you progress?

I agree with your numbering system in these appendices.

a) Apologies though, because even after many attempts I cannot find a way to change my numbering to yours. Please would you kindly change during your final edit, by accepting your numbering and deleting mine.

b) Similarly, I cannot 'accept' some of your edit suggestions within each 'clause'. Please note that I agree with your suggestions that are still in the appendices. Please 'accept' your own suggestions :-)

1. If you get stuck on a Platformation, seek clues from relevant sections of "*Secrets of Angels on Earth*", to progress more easily and effectively.
2. Seek support from an angel-on-earth you know, or new ones you meet.
3. Ask for help from within you, from your higher conscious mind, or your more unconscious angelic soul.
4. Ask for enlightenment from your angels above, your Guardian Angel, or the archangel in your band.

5. Study under a therapist who knows how to help you rise above the human issues holding you back.
6. Be careful who to approach about angelic subjects. You may be excited, but not everyone enjoys hearing about angels they don't believe in.
7. Attend courses of the Brahma Kumaris or another supportive organization. Stay with them if you can, to gain wise support and nurturing at each step.
8. Find a Master of soul development who can help you achieve your Destiny, your reason for existence.
9. Get updated info on angels-on-earth by logging on to www.angelsonearth.info.
10. Check the Facebook page, "Secrets of Angels on Earth"
11. Attend courses, download Apps, browse websites, whatever you need for your healing, spiritual, love, self-development, and LOve-Based Living journey.
12. It's a long life, with much to explore, develop, and progress. Tread your soul path happily to higher Platformations, and leave memorable footprints behind.
13. Reread the book as needed, to update how you are progressing and what you may need to do next.
14. Start a "Secrets of Angels on Earth Group in..." (your area), a Facebook page for angelic people near you. Benefits to you and others are potentially immense, so benefits and how to start a Group are outlined in the next appendices.

If you feel overwhelmed at the task ahead, remember, speed is not essential. Relax.

Don't pressure yourself to achieve the Platformations too quickly. Be at peace.

Don't pressure yourself to do a higher Platformation when you haven't finished an early one. Take it easy.

Allow yourself space to develop. Try to do your best, use your natural or learned gifts, and let it all flow naturally.

Appendix 2. How To Start a "Secrets of Angels on Earth in..." (Your Area) Group

If this book seems relevant to your life, you could benefit by starting a Group, "Secrets of Angels on Earth in..." (your area). You can make true angelic friends who, like you, experience LOve and love. When with other angels, you will not feel so alone, separated or detached. Angelic friends can support each other's journeys. Groups provide so many benefits for you and other angels-on-earth, there's another appendix just about the benefits!

It's easy to start a Group. For example, a small stand at a Mind, Body, Spirit exhibition will attract many angels. Or you can search online for local spiritual groups, and share your Group information, "Secrets of Angels on Earth in..." (your local area). Or you could search for "Meeting groups" such as Meetup, and post your "Secrets of Angels on Earth" Group in your locality. There are also free options.

Facebook though, makes it easy, so here's how to start a Facebook Group.

1. Use a name, "Secrets of Angels on Earth in... (your local area)". Probably it's best not to include your own name, to keep your privacy.
2. Keep the area you cover to less than 1 million population. With one angel in every 300-400 people, there are about 25 million angels spread around our planet. That's too many for one person to help. A local population of 250,000 could have about 750 angels, more than enough for a "Secrets of Angels on Earth" Group.
3. Search online for a picture, maybe "Free photos of angels", and choose something beautiful and radiant.
4. Go to your Facebook homepage. At present, you click on "Create".
5. Design your page.

6. Send to all your friends. If someone replies but you'd prefer them to not be in your Angel Group, simply reject them. It's acceptable and anonymous, so you're safe.
7. You could accept applicants as trial members for one meeting, to see if you mutually "like" each other.
8. Facebook ads are cheap. If you wish, choose a small budget, and target an area, sex, and age group. For example, you could target females in your town in their 30s and 40s. You'll soon find LOving angels like you.
9. There is an option to ask people who want to join a few questions. For example, you could ask:
"Have you felt alone, separated or detached most of your life? If yes, please describe briefly." If they answer no or inappropriately, do not accept them.
"If you have a feeling of love inside you, can you please briefly describe the feeling?" If they can't describe LOve as a potential angel might, decline them.
10. *"Do you feel you have a bigger job to do to help our world one day? If yes, please briefly describe."* If the answer is no, or is inappropriate, reject their application.

It is OK to reject someone, especially because you will be anonymous. They will not know who you are.

If answers are yes, or appropriate to all questions, they may be an angel-on-earth, and can join your Group.

The next page includes the benefits of starting your Group, "Secrets of Angels on Earth in…" (name of your area).

People in groups are human with human frailties, but you will all be on a journey to support each other. Life should be more enlightening, with more fun.

With best angelic wishes for an even happier future,

Allan

Appendix 3. Benefits of Starting a "Secrets of Angels on Earth in..." (Your Area) Group

Achieving angelic Destiny may be easier with help and guidance. But most angels cannot find an adequate group to support their growth. Your Group, "Secrets of Angels on Earth in..." (add your area), can help you and other angels lead a more comfortable and successful life, faster, and with greater happiness, than when alone.

Angels can help each other over human and soul Platformations, provide LOve care and support, share angel issues, and belong to international LOve networks.

Benefits of a "Secrets of Angels on Earth in..." Group in your area include:

1. Meet LOving angelic friends.
2. Easier human love and soul LOve development.
3. Learn more of spirituality, your soul, and Destiny.
4. No forcing of opinions or actions.
5. Support by LOving angels who understand you.
6. Help from angels to find life's solutions.
7. Achieve soul purpose and Destiny more easily.
8. Rise at a speed on Platformations right for you.
9. Progress more easily to achieve your soul role.
10. Safe, secure, confidential angelic conversation.

It's a worthwhile cause to help an angel. Just one angel can make a vast difference to society.

If you can help even one other angel-on-earth develop and achieve their soul purpose, and the angelic person then makes a beneficial change for our world, think of the immense positive change this will make. Perhaps for generations to come!

Appendix 4. Suggested Rules of a "Secrets of Angels on Earth in…" (Your Area) Group

To help members feel comfortable, Angel Groups need rules. Due to differences in international expectations, rules vary. The main rules suggested for a "Secrets of Angels on Earth in…" (your area) Group are:

1. Anyone who passes angelic tests is welcome.
2. Members come from any religion or part of society.
3. Members can suggest new angel-on-earth members. New members can be "interviewed" to see if suitable.
4. Start on time, so members arrive on time.
5. Conversations on personal subjects are confidential.
6. New members should have read their own copy of this book to enjoy Group discussions and support.
7. Study topics in this book relevant to members' needs.
8. LOve is the basis for all decisions on the angelic path.
9. Collect donations for costs, or a caring project.
10. Support members' human love and soul LOve paths.
11. Members have Free Will on beliefs, with LOve.
12. Progress lives. Promote health, wellness, and LOve.
13. Members may stay in the Group for life if they wish (it's their choice) to gain LOving angelic support.
14. Support each other's chosen LOve paths.
15. Members may change anything in their life with LOve.
16. Develop members' gifts to share with others.
17. Encourage members to earn money to help others.
18. Heal relationships, and faults in selves and others.
19. Help our planet and do good with harmlessness.
20. Make it a fun, harmonious, angelic journey!
21. These are suggested rules.
22. Choose rules that are LOving and right for your Group.

Appendix 5. Suggestions and Guidelines on How To Run Meetings of a "Secrets of Angels on Earth in..." (Your Area) Group

"Secrets of Angels on Earth in..." Groups' main aims to help angels-on-earth are: to overcome human challenges, increase happiness, share LOve, guide toward LOve-Based Living, fulfill soul callings and Destinies, make a bigger positive difference, be a good friend, and to care, help, and LOve. Aims may be helped by the following, and any positive way forward your Angel Group agrees.

1. Decide if nobody leads, or there's a leader, facilitator, or a small group like an informal committee leads.
2. Groups and agendas grow differently, according to members' abilities, human love, or soul LOve needs.
3. Donations may be accepted to cover any costs, or to raise funds to help a worthy cause.
4. Review a previous meet. Put questions to the Group.
5. Keep meeting sessions to 5-20 minutes, for interest.
6. A member researches a topic in this book, and presents findings at the next meeting.
7. Discuss a different Angelic Question at each meeting.
8. Change sessions' energies for interest. E.g., don't use two meditations or discussions back-to-back.
9. Open a page of this book at random. Discuss issues raised. Understand how it relates to each person.
10. Be flexible. Cater for sudden or changing member or Group needs.
11. New members write then discuss why they joined.
12. Every 3-6 months, members may write how the Angel Group helped them, and/or discuss outcomes and results.
13. Every 3-6 months, members write and discuss their or the Group's short-, medium- and long-term goals.
14. Set personal inner short-, medium- and long-term goals

for physical, emotional, mental, or spiritual issues. Or outer goals for family/friends, recreation/hobbies, money/income, or ideas/philosophies/LOve.

15. At set target dates, review if goals were met.
16. A member teaches how to help the Group's holistic health and wellness.
17. Discuss how members' soul missions can be helped.
18. Discuss how being an angel affects members' lives.
19. Share LOving acts or progress members achieve.
20. Discover which Platformation each member is on. Discuss how to resolve the issues and move on.
21. Repeat one meditation or exercise for every meeting, e.g. LOve, meet angels, or candle gazing.
22. Choose a local crime statistic. Members send LOve to the stat, with an intention that crime reduces. When the next stats are published, assess changes. Compare to other areas to validate any good results.
23. Use affirmations or prayers to help a member, their family or friends, or the world.
24. During the week, research a topic to support a member, and present at the next meeting.
25. Fund-raise for a good cause, or for a member's soul purpose. Start a charity for Group aims.
26. Post on your Facebook page, or ours, "Secrets of Angels on Earth".
27. Members bring snacks. Sharing food helps bonding.
28. Discuss reminders of confidentiality issues.
29. Suggest group hugs, if comfortable with members.
30. Ask what they might like to learn, change, or discuss.
31. Set next meeting time, date, place, agenda.
32. Close with summaries, thoughts, and thanks.

These are only suggestions and guidelines. You choose.

"Secrets of Angels on Earth in..." Groups grow according to

members' needs. Enjoy!

Appendix 6. The Golden Egg – a Creative Visualization for "Secrets of Angels on Earth in..." Meetings

The Golden Egg is a suggestion for a Group or individual meditation. It may create harmony and balance within, while it soothes, calms, and relaxes, revitalizes the aura and bio-fields, and expands feelings of LOve. Use any other meditation that you enjoy to bring LOve into your being.

If you wish, start meetings with The Golden Egg. Members can bring Light into their bodies, and gain LOving unity and peace.

1. Sit against the back of a chair, feet flat on the floor, one hand on each leg, back straight. If laying down, place pillow under knees, back, head if comfort is needed.
2. Breathe deeply in, and out, for 30 seconds. On each out breath, imagine you float down, just a little bit.
3. Imagine for 30 seconds in your stomach there is a spark of perfect LOve.
4. For 30 seconds, see the spark as a bright, pale, golden Light. See its brightness. (Or feel its warmth.)
5. For 30 seconds, see the bright, pale gold Light (or feel the warmth) double in size.
6. Repeat step 5 for 30 seconds, doubling the size again.
7. Repeat step 5 for 30 seconds double the size a third time.
8. Imagine the gold Light (or warmth) can fill you completely. It spreads until every pore and cell is full.
9. Imagine your aura is around you, shaped like an egg.
10. Breathe out the gold light or warmth to fill your aura.
11. Repeat until the aura is an egg of bright gold LOve.

This method helps development, it's not a goal. Regular and proper use enhances angelic LOve throughout your inner being and your external aura.

Appendix 7. Report from an Angel Group

This is a typical report from an Angelic Group. If you start a "Secrets of Angels on Earth" Group, choose any structure, meditation, healing, love or LOve session relevant to members. Experiment.

It is proving to be a very harmonious group, and a joy to facilitate! The three-hour sessions pass very quickly. We review how useful meetings are. All report looking forward to the meetings. Being connected to our group supports them between sessions. They like combining exercises and ways to LOve. Just to sit in the awareness of our angelic selves is bliss! The group is transcending. For some, changes are more apparent than others. Maybe their need was greater. They view themselves more positively, with an ability to look at others in a different light. We open with a meditation or contemplations to connect inwards. We used the exercise "I LOve You" from the Angel Party. Melina saw her own wings during this for the first time. She has always seen others' wings but not her own, so this was very special for her. We clarified "Platformation" levels, "goal-setting", and healing needs, linked to their angelic path. In the 4th session we looked at "What makes me happy?" on all levels: physical, mental, emotional, spiritual, and we linked this to how we can raise our vibration more consistently through personal goals. There is momentum building. We are guided to find themes each session for the whole group. Questions in members' minds seem answered in a synchronistic way. Meetings help improve my skills, confidence and intuition. I feel blessed to have such a wonderful group!

Angel Group Facilitator

Appendix 8. Holding Expos To Help Angelic Souls and Your "Secrets of Angels on Earth in..." Group

This 2006 article is about how my Angels on Earth stand and lectures at the Mind, Body, Spirit Exposition in Mexico City's World Trade Centre were amazing. They showed the reality that angels exist. Can you join a small expo or festival near you, and help other angels too?

"Angels flew high at our first angel-on-earth expo stand and lectures. We invited angelic people to Groups, to help their lives and destinies. Hundreds felt peace, joy, and bliss. At last someone understood their lives.

"Most stands were for therapies, reiki, and yoga. Only our stand offered help for angels.

"Our stand was decorated simply with lilac crepe paper walls, angel pictures, and posters describing an angel's life. Hundreds of angelic people left their details.

"Patients sat as our angel healers channeled blissful angelic energy. Many felt the ecstasy of angelic experience, touched by the presence of angels. Others saw angels helping them, or cried happily to feel their own wings fluttering. To experience reality, is to believe!

"A common question was, 'How can you know I'm an angel?' Our helpers knew some were angels because they saw them flex their back to flutter their wings, or saw angel guides of those who were angels too. Also, answers to the Angelic Questions showed who were angels. Many cried. They already knew they were angels. Tears of happiness or relief were common. Like a dance teacher who burst out crying, saying, 'Of course I'm an angel.'

"Many came to the expo just for this lecture. Of about 400 in the audience, maybe 200 knew they had wings, and cried as they recognized that if the Angel Story could explain their life from pre-birth to where they are now, messages for their future may also be true.

"Smiling people said at last they understood their lives. It took an hour to sign autographs, and share love hugs. Friends and family wanted to hear the Angel Story too. So we gave non-programmed lectures on the next two days in a corner of the expo. 50 seats were not enough. There was standing room only for both lectures.

"Angels shared experiences. Three women said a helper on the stand had helped them in dreams. Many saw that another helper had bright gold wings with a pale blue center. A lady who hugged him was

shocked to feel the wings' solid shape. Some saw his halo, and a child drew his wings. It was lovely. To show himself as an angel helps others to understand.

"Many felt empowered to discuss their own wings. Sadly they could not tell friends for fear of negative comments.

"One day angels will openly discuss their wings and soul purpose, and achieve bigger soul jobs, faster. Our world will then become a happier place."

To start or expand a "Secrets of Angels on Earth in..." Group, search for small Mind, Body, Spirit Expos or similar near you. Then:

1. Exhibit at a stand with a trusted friend.
2. Existing Group members may help.
3. Find angels via your own Facebook page, or our Facebook Page, "Secrets of Angels on Earth"
4. Form or expand a "Secrets of Angels on Earth in (your area)" Group.

Appendix 9. If This Book Seems Not Right for Your Present Life

This book was written for the one in every 300 or 400 people with angelic souls. After fully reading angelic concepts, if it doesn't feel right for you, maybe it isn't.

Perhaps you were attracted by the words in the title, "Secrets", and "Clues". If you then reject the subjects as outlandish or not relevant, I apologize.

Maybe, though, the angelic title attracted you? Is there potential that, deep within you, inspired LOve might be trying to explore its path of service? You may have chosen the book for reasons you can only know in the future, or even after you pass on.

As you plod your path and learn about this world, even if

you think angelic ways are not for you, perhaps positive ideas on love and LOve can help you or others.

Even to absorb a morsel of one LOve idea, and apply it to improve your or others' lives, that's a win-win.

Life is a network of webs of pleasing and non-pleasing incredible complexities. That's simply how it is. No network of any web applies to everyone.

But if you feel you need guidance on where to go now, here are seven thoughts on how to progress.

1. Forget all you read. Not even one idea of this world applies to everyone. If it unwittingly does apply to you, one day the issues may rear up in other ways. Then decide again, is the Angelic Path for you?
2. Do not use suggestions you think are unsuitable or amiss. That is OK too. Just move on with life. Perhaps someone one day will explain in a way that's ripe for your understanding then.
3. If you prefer your current ways of life, that's OK. Stay on your path for the rest of your life, or tread two paths at once, or go through phases, switching from path to path, until you find what is right for your Destiny.
4. Respect your doubts. Move on with your life. But keep the book handy. Maybe an angelic LOve path will one day automatically develop within you.
5. Stay aware of love fallibility as a human, and potential for LOve perfection. Why not share love in any small way, to make a positive difference, and improve a need?
6. Watch for clues. If universal forces need to plot you a new path, they might conspire in positive ways to help you seek and find better LOving soul options. They may then lead to your most gorgeous dreams.
7. Explore spirituality, that may lead you down the right LOve path. Read spiritual books, attend courses. At the end of

an adequate period of exploration, decide whether or not the LOve pathway of your soul is how you would like to proceed.

Always remember, you only need to share tiny amounts of spiritual LOve seeds, for some to grow into acres, hectares, or regions of LOve.

Even if you are not an angel-on-earth, isn't it a wonderfully positive ideal that you can learn to be even more LOving and spiritual, and increase happiness somewhere? That can make a constructive change for the better to our world?

Appendix 10. Please Help Us To Help Others

Thank you for buying this book. I sincerely hope it will help you throughout your life, like my lectures have aided the evolution of numerous angels. Your comments would be appreciated, and may help us to help others like you. Please return this form via enquiries@angelsonearth.info.

Name: ______________________________

Country: ______________________________

Was/did the book…?

A. Help you understand your life

Least 1 2 3 4 5 6 7 8 9 10 Most

Describe in words how this felt ____________________

____

____

B. Give you feelings of peace or reassurance
Least 1 2 3 4 5 6 7 8 9 10 Most
Describe in words how this felt ______________________

____

____

C. Eye-opening
Least 1 2 3 4 5 6 7 8 9 10 Most
Describe in words how this felt ______________________

____

____

D. Make you want to know more
Least 1 2 3 4 5 6 7 8 9 10 Most
Describe in words how this felt ______________________

____

____

E. Make you cry (state feeling with the tears)
Least 1 2 3 4 5 6 7 8 9 10 Most
Describe in words how this felt ______________________

____

____

F. Give you a positive or negative feeling (state what)
Least 1 2 3 4 5 6 7 8 9 10 Most
Describe in words how this felt ______________________________

____

____

G. Did this book show or confirm you are an angel?
Yes _____ No _____
If yes, please describe how you knew __________________________

____

____

H. Might you start a Group to help other angels?
Yes _____ No _____
Please add any additional comments

____

____

____

____

Comments may be used as testimonials.
Apologies that it might not be possible to reply to all letters.
Thank you for your LOve,
Allan J. Sweeney

Appendix 11. International Language of "Angel"

Regardless of whether you believe in angels, or belong to a particular society or religion, stories about angels exist in almost every country, throughout history.

Most languages have a word for "angel", including languages from Europe, the Middle East, Africa, Southeast Asia, and the Far East including China and Japan. The beauty is, angels are here for everyone, everywhere.

Hopefully this book, the website "www.secretsofangelsonearth.com", and the Facebook page "Secrets of Angels on Earth" will help start a network of angelic help and support across the world, in every society, in every language.

هيبرعلا (Arabic) (مسالا) ملاك
Nederlands (Dutch) Engel
English (English) Angel
Français (French) Ange
Deutsch (German) Engel
Ελληνική (Greek) (θρησκ), άγγελος, άνθρωπος, αγγελούδι, (μυστικός), χρηματοδότης (θεάματος), χορηγός
תירבע (Hebrew) ךאלמ
Italiano (Italian) Angelo
Português (Portuguese) Anjo
Русский (Russian) ангел
Español (Spanish) ángel
Svenska (Swedish) ängel

Appendix 12. Brief Chronology

It may be helpful to some readers to see a shortened chronological list of events that may occur during the life of an angel-on-earth. Remember these main points…

1. Not every child or adulthood is identical. Platformations for angels-on-earth's lives, though, may be similar.

2. Some Platformations may be missed, or experienced in chaotic order, or lessons are learned fast, slowly, or easier. No golden rules show what occurs, if at all, or when it will.
3. Here are a few of the Platformations angels might sense or experience, in ways that impact their soul's Destiny. Other Platformations are in the book. Enjoy the lessons.
The next Realm
The Angelic Word
Destiny and LOve-Based Living
The Soul purpose
The practice run of LOve
Money as goodness
Free Will and four forces
Signposts
Acceptance
Partner type
Grief process
Karma
Human imbalances
Teens and 20s
Childhood after seven
Childhood before seven
Two-year incarnation
Birth
Conception
Contract
Pre-birth

Appendix 13. Illustration Credit

A glorious thank you to an angel, Julliett McCann from Sydney, Australia, from whom I bought her original painting of an angel-on-earth. It seemed ideal for this book's cover.

The head is bowed in angelic humility.

On the left of the original picture, darker colors surround the human being, representing humanity's imperfect nature.

On the right of the original picture, brighter colors surround the angel's wings, representing the Light an angel brings.

Non-gender hair and body contours represent an angel's cohesive bond and unification.

The wings are larger than the human being, depicting the wider ability and importance of an angel.

Thank you, Angel Julliett.

LOve

Allan

Appendix 14. Previous Publications

Sweeney, A., 1995, *Reiki 1st Degree Manual*

Sweeney, A., 1995, *Reiki 2nd Degree Manual*

Sweeney, A., 1996, *Reiki 3 Healing Mastership Manual*

Sweeney, A., 1996, *Reiki 4 Manual, Teaching Mastership*

Sweeney, A., 1996, Danish Manuals for Reiki 1st Degree

Sweeney, A., 1997-2005, 32-page magazine, *Healing News*

Sweeney, A., 1998, *Reiki Healing Symbols in Sound* Music Therapy CD

Sweeney, A., 1999, Danish Manuals for Reiki 2nd Degree

Sweeney, A., 2000, *Stress Management For Your Whole Being* CD

Sweeney, A., 2001, *Screen Therapy* – emotional cures CD

Sweeney, A., 2002, *The Reiki 1 Manual* – 504 pages

Sweeney, A., 2003, SPARK Guidelines: Standard Procedures for Accredited Reiki Knowledge

Sweeney, A., 2004, PURE: Universal Reiki Ethics

Sweeney, A., 2004, "SEED: Study into the Effectiveness of Energy on Deafness", Case study research on healing for deafness, *International Journal of Healing and Caring On-Line*, September 2006, Volume 6, Number 3, pp. 1-24

Sweeney, A., Goble, M., 2005, "SHADES: Study of Hyperactivity and Attention Deficit using Energy Systems", *International Journal of Healing and Caring On-Line*, May 2006, Volume 6, Number 2,

pp. 1-21
Sweeney, A., 2005-6, SPARK Level 1, 2 and 3 Syllabi
Sweeney, A., 2007, *Tri-Dynamics* – preventative exercise
Sweeney, A., 2008, *Get Rich Happily: Become a Spiritual and Financial Millionaire*
Sweeney, A. and Shortt F., 2011, *Usui's Teacher*

Appendix 15. Author Bio

Website: www.secretsofangelsonearth.com
Facebook: Secrets of Angels on Earth
Twitter: Secrets of Angels on Earth @secretsofangel1

Allan J. Sweeney was born with a serious immune deficiency. Doctors said he would not live to be a teenager. As an adult, he was often hospitalized, about twice a year. The UK health service registered him as 80% disabled. One day a lady placed her hands on him for ten minutes. He was substantially cured.

Seeing no therapy including orthodox medicine can cure everything, he was inspired to travel the world to seek therapies accepted in one country but not in others. He found effective, cost-effective, permanent, safe ways to cure, prevent or alleviate specific ailments that were evidenced in one country but not available elsewhere. Consequently, from 1996 he practiced and taught Complementary and Alternative Medicine (CAM), and spiritual and soul subjects, full-time.

He became the British Psychological Society's CAM faculty research officer, a therapy trainer for UK prisons, and a member of the UK government's CAM health committee via the Doctor Healer Network. He published the 32-page Reiki *Healing News* magazine, began Reiki's 1st Codes of Conduct/Practice/Disciplinary procedures/insurance policy, had a prestigious Harley Street clinic, was Honorary President of Japan's Reiki Oneness World Network, and Honorary Teacher of Hiroshi Doi's Gendai Reiki in Japan. He has conducted international seminars on energy healing, angelic, and mystical mastership, appeared on TV/radio, his own TV show, ran a 22-bed residential therapy/ teaching/retreat center, and has authored books, manuals, videos, and CDs. Allan J. Sweeney is available for lectures, workshops, and TV and radio appearances globally.

BOOKS

SPIRITUALITY

O is a symbol of the world, of oneness and unity; this eye represents knowledge and insight. We publish titles on general spirituality and living a spiritual life. We aim to inform and help you on your own journey in this life.

If you have enjoyed this book, why not tell other readers by posting a review on your preferred book site?

Recent bestsellers from O-Books are:

Heart of Tantric Sex

Diana Richardson

Revealing Eastern secrets of deep love and intimacy to Western couples.

Paperback: 978-1-90381-637-0 ebook: 978-1-84694-637-0

Crystal Prescriptions

The A-Z guide to over 1,200 symptoms and their healing crystals

Judy Hall

The first in the popular series of six books, this handy little guide is packed as tight as a pill-bottle with crystal remedies for ailments.

Paperback: 978-1-90504-740-6 ebook: 978-1-84694-629-5

Take Me To Truth

Undoing the Ego

Nouk Sanchez, Tomas Vieira

The best-selling step-by-step book on shedding the Ego, using the teachings of *A Course In Miracles*.

Paperback: 978-1-84694-050-7 ebook: 978-1-84694-654-7

The 7 Myths about Love...Actually!

The Journey from your HEAD to the HEART of your SOUL

Mike George

Smashes all the myths about LOVE.

Paperback: 978-1-84694-288-4 ebook: 978-1-84694-682-0

The Holy Spirit's Interpretation of the New Testament
A Course in Understanding and Acceptance
Regina Dawn Akers
Following on from the strength of *A Course In Miracles*, NTI teaches us how to experience the love and oneness of God.
Paperback: 978-1-84694-085-9 ebook: 978-1-78099-083-5

The Message of A Course In Miracles
A translation of the Text in plain language
Elizabeth A. Cronkhite
A translation of *A Course in Miracles* into plain, everyday language for anyone seeking inner peace. The companion volume, *Practicing A Course In Miracles*, offers practical lessons and mentoring.
Paperback: 978-1-84694-319-5 ebook: 978-1-84694-642-4

Your Simple Path
Find Happiness in every step
Ian Tucker
A guide to helping us reconnect with what is really important in our lives.
Paperback: 978-1-78279-349-6 ebook: 978-1-78279-348-9

365 Days of Wisdom
Daily Messages To Inspire You Through The Year
Dadi Janki
Daily messages which cool the mind, warm the heart and guide you along your journey.
Paperback: 978-1-84694-863-3 ebook: 978-1-84694-864-0

Body of Wisdom

Women's Spiritual Power and How it Serves

Hilary Hart

Bringing together the dreams and experiences of women across the world with today's most visionary spiritual teachers.

Paperback: 978-1-78099-696-7 ebook: 978-1-78099-695-0

Dying to Be Free

From Enforced Secrecy to Near Death to True Transformation

Hannah Robinson

After an unexpected accident and near-death experience, Hannah Robinson found herself radically transforming her life, while a remarkable new insight altered her relationship with her father, a practising Catholic priest.

Paperback: 978-1-78535-254-6 ebook: 978-1-78535-255-3

The Ecology of the Soul

A Manual of Peace, Power and Personal Growth for Real People in the Real World

Aidan Walker

Balance your own inner Ecology of the Soul to regain your natural state of peace, power and wellbeing.

Paperback: 978-1-78279-850-7 ebook: 978-1-78279-849-1

Not I, Not other than I

The Life and Teachings of Russel Williams

Steve Taylor, Russel Williams

The miraculous life and inspiring teachings of one of the World's greatest living Sages.

Paperback: 978-1-78279-729-6 ebook: 978-1-78279-728-9

On the Other Side of Love
A woman's unconventional journey towards wisdom
Muriel Maufroy
When life has lost all meaning, what do you do?
Paperback: 978-1-78535-281-2 ebook: 978-1-78535-282-9

Practicing A Course In Miracles
A translation of the Workbook in plain language, with mentor's notes
Elizabeth A. Cronkhite
The practical second and third volumes of The Plain-Language *A Course In Miracles*.
Paperback: 978-1-84694-403-1 ebook: 978-1-78099-072-9

Quantum Bliss
The Quantum Mechanics of Happiness, Abundance, and Health
George S. Mentz
Quantum Bliss is the breakthrough summary of success and spirituality secrets that customers have been waiting for.
Paperback: 978-1-78535-203-4 ebook: 978-1-78535-204-1

The Upside Down Mountain
Mags MacKean
A must-read for anyone weary of chasing success and happiness – one woman's inspirational journey swapping the uphill slog for the downhill slope.
Paperback: 978-1-78535-171-6 ebook: 978-1-78535-172-3

Your Personal Tuning Fork

The Endocrine System

Deborah Bates

Discover your body's health secret, the endocrine system, and 'twang' your way to sustainable health!

Paperback: 978-1-84694-503-8 ebook: 978-1-78099-697-4